Success on the Tenure Track

Success on the Tenure Track

Five Keys to Faculty Job Satisfaction

Cathy Ann Trower

The Johns Hopkins University Press
Baltimore

The Johns Hopkins University Press
2715 North Charles Street
Baltimore, Maryland 21218-4363
www.press.jhu.edu

Library of Congress Cataloging-in-Publication Data

Trower, Cathy A. (Cathy Ann)
Success on the tenure track : five keys to faculty job satisfaction /
Cathy Ann Trower.
p. cm.
Includes bibliographical references and index.
ISBN 978-1-4214-0597-1 (hdbk. : alk. paper)
ISBN 978-1-4214-0649-7 (electronic)
ISBN 1-4214-0597-0 (hdbk. : alk. paper)
ISBN 1-4214-0649-7 (electronic)
1. College teachers—Tenure—United States. 2. Universities
and colleges—United States—Faculty. I. Title.
LB2335.7.T76 2012
378.1'20973—dc23   2011047324

A catalog record for this book is available from the British Library.

*Special discounts are available for bulk purchases of this book. For
more information, please contact Special Sales at 410-516-6936 or
specialsales@press.jhu.edu.*

The Johns Hopkins University Press uses environmentally
friendly book materials, including recycled text paper that is
composed of at least 30 percent post-consumer waste, whenever
possible.

To Richard Chait

Whose generosity inspires
Whose teaching transforms
Whose mentorship made all the difference
And whose friendship is priceless

and

In memory of Mara Wasburn

Contents

Acknowledgments

I wish to thank all the faculty members and administrators at the seven exemplary institutions listed below who were interviewed for this book. I am most grateful for their time and commitment to improving the quality of life of early career faculty.

Institutions
Auburn University
North Carolina State University
Ohio State University
University of Illinois at Urbana-Champaign
University of Iowa
University of Kansas
University of North Carolina at Pembroke

I also wish to thank the COACHE team members who were vital to this project.

Interviewers
Anne Gallagher (former COACHE assistant director)
Kiernan Mathews (COACHE director)

Data Analysis
Todd Benson (COACHE assistant research director)
Brendan Russell (graduate research assistant)

Literature Review Writers
Gregory Esposito (graduate research assistant)
Megan Mitrovich (graduate research assistant)
Brendan Russell (graduate research assistant)

Author's Note

The views expressed in this book are mine alone.

Seven public universities are featured in this volume as "exemplary," in that their mean results on certain Collaborative on Academic Careers in Higher Education (COACHE) survey benchmarks exceeded those of all other public university participants (32 in total) in 2005–6. It should be noted, however, that many other institutions of different types—small colleges and large universities, private and public—also participated in COACHE surveys in that academic year. In the years since those data were gathered, more than 200 institutions have administered COACHE surveys, many of them more than once. In various respects, several of these schools, too, are models for faculty support and success.

Information on past and current COACHE survey exemplars is available on the project's website at www.coache.org. In addition, announcements about these results are typically published in popular higher education media outlets.

Success on the Tenure Track

Introduction

Purpose

This book describes the elements of the workplace that pre-tenure faculty say are most critical to their satisfaction and success (discussed in chapters 3–6), provides quantitative data about faculty satisfaction and dissatisfaction with those factors, and showcases the policies and practices at seven public research universities that are exemplary in one or more category.

The Collaborative on Academic Careers in Higher Education (COACHE) has collected data on the job satisfaction of over 15,000 pre-tenure faculty members at more than 200 four-year colleges and universities in the United States and Canada. The COACHE staff, of which I am a member, interviewed faculty members and administrators at seven "exemplary" COACHE public institutions, detailed in chapter 2. We were most interested in learning what makes these institutions great places to work by uncovering the policies and practices to which they attribute their success. What specific policies and practices are in place at these exemplary public research universities? What is the faculty experience like at these great places to work? What explains high levels of faculty satisfaction? What norms or activities help ensure faculty satisfaction? How might other institutions use this information to attract and retain early career faculty?

Armed with quantitative and qualitative data, we now have a deeper understanding of institutional culture and campus climate as they relate to the recruitment, development, and retention of tenure-track faculty. We can substantiate a connection between action (policy and practice) and COACHE survey results; thus, we can recommend effective policies and practices to help institutions recruit, retain, and develop top early career academics,

manage generational differences, and ultimately maintain a satisfied and productive faculty workforce.

The book is organized around the themes most important to the satisfaction and success of probationary faculty. For each theme, I define what junior
faculty want, provide quantitative data about the experiences of pre-tenure
faculty, and showcase exceptional practices through vignettes about specific
universities.

What Is Covered in This Book, What Is Not Covered, and Why

Full-time, tenure-track faculty at four-year universities in the United States
in 2007 included approximately 106,000 men and women. When conceptu-
alizing this book, I initially considered writing separate chapters on women[1]
and faculty of color,[2] or one that encompassed women and minority faculty,[3] but decided against it because I wanted to keep the focus on all the
ways that pre-tenure faculty are alike rather than how they are different.
Our research has shown that what is good for women is good for men, and
what is good for faculty of color is good for white faculty. This is not to say
that programs targeting, for example, women in science[4] or African Americans at Historically White Institutions are not important; it is simply not my
focus here. The exemplary universities we visited received high marks in one
or more of the categories that COACHE measures (e.g., tenure clarity, support for teaching and research, work-life balance, and climate) and were not
exemplary *only* for women or men or *only* whites or faculty of color; they
were exemplary for all.

This book is not about the growing population of part-time and non-
tenure-track faculty[5] (data provided later in this chapter)—again, not because
they are not important but, in this case, because those faculty have not yet
been studied by COACHE.

In chapter 2, I discuss the methodology behind the COACHE survey of
pre-tenure faculty satisfaction, which yields rich data about the academic
workplace and life on the tenure track. We know which institutions are rated
the highest in key areas by the faculty who work there. The public universities showcased in this book include Auburn University; North Carolina
State University; Ohio State University; the University of Illinois at Urbana-

Champaign; University of Iowa; University of Kansas; and University of North Carolina at Pembroke. We interviewed a total of 104 faculty and administrators about why they think their institution scored well and learned what makes each institution a great place for junior faculty to work.

In chapter 3, I address one of the most critical components of faculty work life: tenure. When it comes to tenure, junior faculty are most interested in clarity of standards, process, and criteria; in transparency, consistency, and equity; and in reasonable expectations for achieving it. This is a lot to ask for, especially as tradition has allowed the tenure process to be largely shrouded in secrecy. After presenting the data from pre-tenure faculty on the COACHE survey, as well as quotes from interviews with pre-tenure faculty and administrators about tenure issues, this chapter showcases exemplary tenure practice and policies from universities with high COACHE scores in this category.

One of the most troublesome issues for early career faculty is having a balanced and meaningful life, as many struggle to integrate work and home life in a reasonable fashion. Chapters 4 through 6 follow the format of chapter 3 in presenting survey data, quotes from interviews with pre-tenure faculty and administrators, and showcasing exemplary tenure practice and policies from universities with high COACHE scores in the relevant category. The focus of chapter 4 is work-life integration: balance; support for families; stop-the-clock/extension; child and elder care; dual-career hiring; parental/personal leaves; benefits; and flexible academic career paths (tenure window, part-time tenure). The nature of work is the subject of chapter 5, specifically support for research and teaching. Such support includes protection from service and a heavy teaching load, research leave, travel funds, start-up package, grant support (pre- and post-award), workshops (grant-writing 101, getting your lab started), support for teaching (peer reviews, centers for teaching and learning), and other support services, including facilities and administrative support. Mentoring and fostering supportive, collegial workplace cultures are challenges for most department administrators. Chapter 6 addresses culture and climate, mentoring, networking, and relationship-building.

Creating and sustaining a culture of support and excellence for tenure-track faculty at all levels of the institution involves the president, provosts, deans, department chairs, and senior faculty. After highlighting some of the most important aspects of leading for culture change, chapter 7 showcases the most practical tips for university leaders.

I speculate about the future of the faculty workplace in chapter 8, where I envision two possible but very different academic worlds twenty years from now. One is the path of least resistance—maintaining the status quo. If we do not re-imagine the academic workplace and change the supporting culture, practices, and policies accordingly, the academic workplace of the future will look much like it does today, but with still fewer tenured and tenure-track faculty. The other path will require remaking rules that reflect the twenty-first-century global, social, demographic, economic, and technological realities, as well as the values of new faculty members and doctoral students. This will necessitate rethinking basic, core assumptions underlying faculty life and the academic workplace, including employment practices, which I do in this concluding chapter.

Faculty Employment Data

If American higher education is to retain its global competitiveness, it must have a vital, engaged faculty. However, the "faculty" is not what it used to be. This book considers a shrinking group of faculty in the United States—full-time, tenure-track at four-year colleges and universities. The downward trends in traditional (tenured and tenure-track) faculty at U.S. four-year colleges and universities has been well documented (American Federation of Teachers 2009; Snyder et al. 2009) and reported (Jaschik 2009c; June 2009; Finder 2007). Because I have found it difficult to find comparative data in one place, this chapter opens with just that—a look at the faculty employment pictures for 1997 and 2007.

Full-Time and Part-Time Faculty Overview

Excluding faculty at two-year colleges, private liberal arts colleges, and medical schools, in 1997 U.S. university faculty included 677,800 instructional staff, with 67 percent (457,111) full-time. By 2007, instructional staff had risen to 899,171, but only 63 percent (569,730) were full-time. Over the course of just ten years, these institutions experienced a 13 percent increase in part-time faculty and a 6 percent decrease in full-time faculty (fig. 1.1).[6]

Gender of Full-Time and Part-Time Faculty

Of all instructional faculty in 1997, women represented 37 percent, as compared with 43 percent in 2007—a 16 percent increase. Of full-time faculty, women represented 33 percent in 1997 and 40 percent in 2007—a 21 percent increase (fig. 1.2). Of part-time faculty, women made up 45 percent in 1997 and 50 percent in 2007—an 11 percent increase (fig. 1.3). A look at the distribution of all instructional faculty (fig. 1.4) reveals that men held 13 percent fewer full-time positions and 6 percent more part-time positions in 2007 than they did in 1997; for women, both percentages increased—they

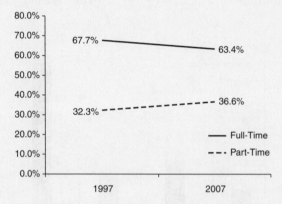

Figure 1.1. Percentage of Full-Time and Part-Time Faculty, 1997 and 2007

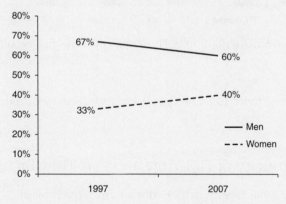

Figure 1.2. Percentage of Men and Women Full-Time Faculty, 1997 and 2007

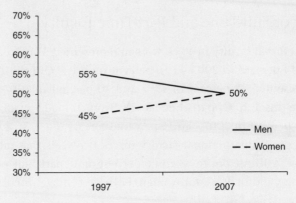

Figure 1.3. Percentage of Men and Women Part-Time Faculty, 1997 and 2007

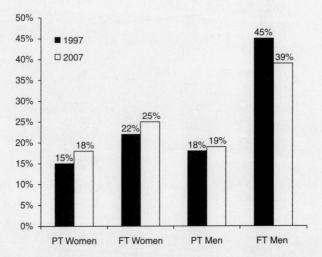

Figure 1.4. Gender Distribution of Full-Time and Part-Time Faculty, 1997 and 2007

held 14 percent more full-time positions and 20 percent more part-time positions.

Race/Ethnicity of Full-Time and Part-Time Faculty

Of all instructional faculty in 1997 (for whom race/ethnicity is known), 87 percent were white, compared with 83 percent in 2007—a 5 percent decrease. Faculty of color represented 14 percent of full-time faculty in 1997 and 19 percent in 2007—a 36 percent increase (fig. 1.5). Of part-time faculty, faculty of color represented 12 percent in 1997 and 15 percent in 2007—a 25 percent increase (fig. 1.6).

As for the distribution of white and faculty of color among all instructional faculty from 1997 to 2007 (fig. 1.7), full-time white faculty decreased by 10 percent, part-time white faculty increased by 11 percent; faculty of color saw both percentages increase—full time by 20 percent and part time by 25 percent.

The actual distribution by race/ethnicity reveals that Asian / Pacific Islanders composed the largest percentage of faculty of color in the full-time ranks

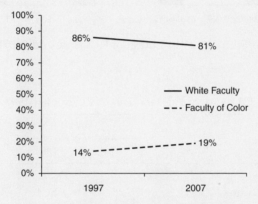

Figure 1.5. Percentage of Full-Time White Faculty and Faculty of Color, 1997 and 2007

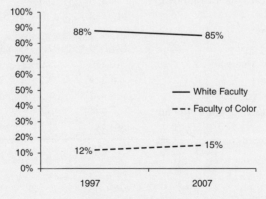

Figure 1.6. Percentage of Part-Time White Faculty and Faculty of Color, 1997 and 2007

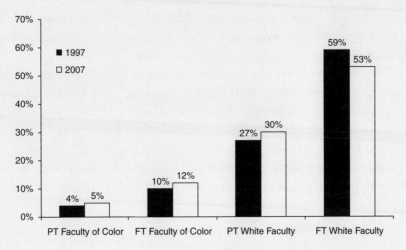

Figure 1.7. Race/Ethnicity Distribution of Full-Time and Part-Time Faculty, 1997 and 2007

Table 1.1. Race/Ethnicity of Full- and Part-Time Faculty, 1997 and 2007

Race/Ethnicity	1997		2007	
	No.	%	No.	%
Full-Time Faculty				
White/Non-Hispanic	381,456	86.1	431,943	81.7
Black/African American	21,053	4.8	27,930	5.3
Hispanic	10,845	2.4	18,225	3.4
Asian/Pacific Islander	27,862	6.3	48,615	9.2
Native American/American Indian	1,566	0.3	2,303	0.4
Total	442,782		529,016	
Part-Time Faculty				
White/Non-Hispanic	176,200	87.3	246,231	84.8
Black/African American	10,100	5.0	17,694	6.1
Hispanic	6,229	3.1	11,705	4.0
Asian/Pacific Islander	8,471	4.2	13,150	4.5
Native American/American Indian	741	0.4	1,599	0.5
Total	201,741		290,379	

in both 1997 and 2007, while Black/African Americans did so for the part-time ranks in both years. Native American/American Indians represented the lowest percentage in both categories in both years (table 1.1).

Gender and Race/Ethnicity of Full-Time and Part-Time Faculty

In 1997, of total instructional staff for whom race/ethnicity was known, women of color represented 5 percent, men of color 8 percent, white women 32 percent, and white men 55 percent. In 2007, those percentages were 8, 10, 35, and 47, respectively. See figure 1.8. The distribution of full-time faculty by gender and race in 1997 was 5 percent women of color, 9 percent men of color, 28 percent white women, and 58 percent white men. In 2007, those percentages had shifted to 8, 11, 32, and 49, respectively—increases of 60 percent for women of color, 22 percent for men of color, and 14 percent for white women; the corresponding percentage decrease for white men was 16 percent. See figure 1.9. The distribution of part-time faculty by gender and race in 1997 was 6 percent women of color, 7 percent men of color, 39 percent white women, and 48 percent white men. In 2007, those

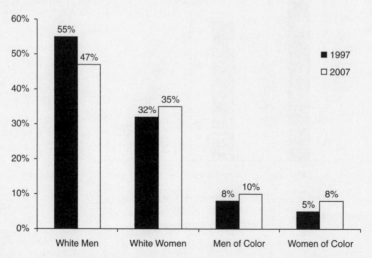

Figure 1.8. Gender and Race/Ethnicity Distribution of all Faculty, 1997 and 2007

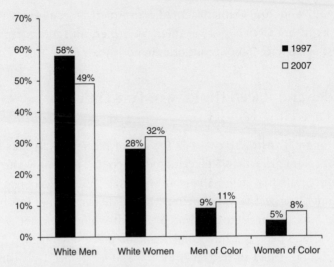

Figure 1.9. Gender and Race/Ethnicity Distribution of Full-Time Faculty, 1997 and 2007

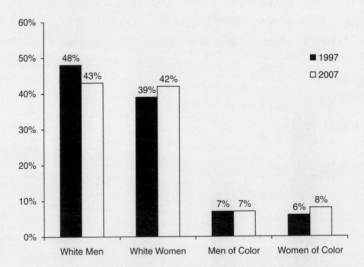

Figure 1.10. Gender and Race/Ethnicity Distribution of Part-Time Faculty, 1997 and 2007

percentages were 8, 7, 42, and 43, respectively. Thus, the percentage of women of color in part-time positions rose 33 percent, while that for white women went up nearly 8 percent. The percentage for men of color in part-time faculty was unchanged, while that for white men decreased by 10 percent. See figure 1.10.

As shown in figures 1.8, 1.9, and 1.10, despite some growth, women of color remain but a small percentage of the faculty at four-year U.S. academic institutions.

Underrepresented Minorities

Tables 1.2 and 1.3 show that Native American/American Indians, men and women, full and part time, remained but a fraction of the faculty in the United States, with little change over the years under study. Among full-time faculty, the percentage of Black/African American women shows little change, whereas among part-timers it increased 26 percent. For Black/African American men, the ten-year period saw a 13 percent increase in full-time faculty and a 17 percent increase in part-timers. Hispanic men saw increases of 45 percent in full-time faculty and 34 percent among part-timers. Hispanic women saw their

Table 1.2. Gender and Race/Ethnicity of Full- and Part-Time Faculty, 1997

Race/Ethnicity	Men		Women	
	No.	%	No.	%
Full-Time Faculty				
White/Non-Hispanic	255,575	87.0	125,881	85.0
Black/African American	11,158	3.8	9,895	6.7
Hispanic	6,615	2.2	4,230	2.8
Asian/Pacific Islander	20,339	6.9	7,523	5.1
Native American/American Indian	924	0.3	642	0.4
Total	294,611		148,171	
Part-Time Faculty				
White/Non-Hispanic	96,910	87.6	79,290	86.9
Black/African American	5,151	4.6	4,949	5.4
Hispanic	3,239	2.9	2,990	3.3
Asian/Pacific Islander	4,913	4.4	3,558	3.9
Native American/American Indian	370	0.3	371	0.4
Total	110,583		91,158	

Table 1.3. Gender and Race/Ethnicity of Full- and Part-Time Faculty, 2007

Race/Ethnicity	Men		Women	
	No.	%	No.	%
Full-Time Faculty				
White/Non-Hispanic	263,487	82.3	168,456	80.6
Black/African American	13,686	4.3	14,244	6.8
Hispanic	10,206	3.2	8,019	3.8
Asian/Pacific Islander	31,600	9.8	17,015	8.1
Native American/American Indian	1,175	0.4	1,128	0.5
Total	320,154		208,862	
Part-Time Faculty				
White/Non-Hispanic	125,578	85.5	120,653	84.0
Black/African American	7,962	5.4	9.732	6.8
Hispanic	5,852	3.9	5,852	4.1
Asian/Pacific Islander	6,575	4.5	6,575	4.6
Native American/American Indian	800	0.5	800	0.5
Total	146,767		143,612	

Table 1.4. Gender and Race/Ethnicity of Full- and Part-Time Faculty, 2007

Gender and Race/Ethnicity	Full Time (%)	Part Time (%)
White men	49.8	43.2
White women	31.8	41.5
Asian/Pacific Islander men	5.9	2.3
Asian/Pacific Islander women	3.2	2.3
Black/African American men	2.6	2.7
Black/African American women	2.7	3.4
Hispanic men	1.9	2.0
Hispanic women	1.5	2.0
Native American/American Indian men	0.2	0.3
Native American/American Indian women	0.2	0.3

numbers increase by 36 percent among full-time faculty and 24 percent among part-timers.

Asian/Pacific Islanders

The greatest growth in full-time faculty occurred among Asian/Pacific Islander faculty, with men seeing a 42 percent increase and women a 59 percent rise. In part-time positions, Asian/Pacific Islander men experienced very little growth (only 2 percent), while the percentage of Asian/Pacific Islander women in such positions grew by 18 percent.

Whites

The decade 1997 to 2007 brought a corresponding decrease in the percentages of white men and white women in both full- and part-time faculty positions; however, these groups continued to be represented in much larger numbers than any other gender–racial/ethnic groups. The percentage decrease for white male full-time faculty was 5, and for part-timers it was 2; the percentage decrease for white women full-time faculty was also 5, while for part-timers it was 3.

Table 1.4 shows the distribution of full-time and part-time faculty by race and gender in 2007.

Employment Status of Full-Time Faculty

An examination of the data by tenure status for 1997 and 2007 shows there were fewer tenured faculty as a percentage of the total in 2007, a decrease of 14 percent; only slightly more tenure-track faculty, an increase of nearly 5 percent; and a much higher percentage of non-tenure-track faculty, an increase of 26 percent (fig. 1.11).[7]

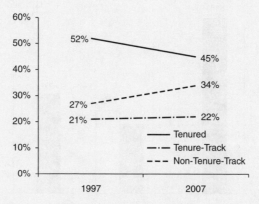

Figure 1.11. Employment Status of Full-Time Faculty, 1997 and 2007

Gender and Employment Status of Full-Time Faculty

In addition to composing the highest percentage of full-time faculty, men were also better represented than women among those with tenure; 75 percent in 1997 and 70 percent in 2007. Fifty-eight percent of those on the tenure track in 1997 were men, the percentage decreasing to 56 in 2007. Among

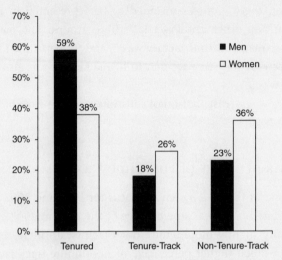

Figure 1.12. Employment Status of Male and Female Full-Time Faculty, 1997

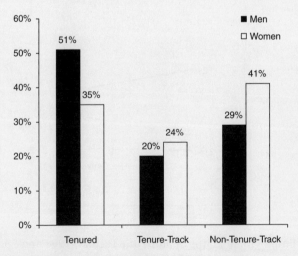

Figure 1.13. Employment Status of Male and Female Full-Time Faculty, 2007

those with full-time, non-tenure-track appointments, the percentage of men fell from 57 in 1997 to 52 in 2007.

Figures 1.12 and 1.13 show that men held a much larger percentage of the tenured positions than women in both 1997 and 2007; however, the percentage of men and women with such posts dropped during the same period (see fig. 1.11). Women were much more likely than men to be employed outside of the tenure system, holding neither tenured nor tenure-track posts.

Race/Ethnicity and Employment Status of Full-Time Faculty

In 1997, 55 percent of white faculty were tenured (fig. 1.14); in 2007, 49 percent were tenured (fig. 1.15)—the highest percentages for any racial/ethnic group. However, in both 1997 and 2007, only 19 percent of white faculty were tenure track—the lowest percentages among the racial/ethnic groups.

While the percentage of faculty in non-tenure-track positions increased for all racial/ethnic groups during the period under consideration, Asian/Pacific Islander faculty alone saw a percentage increase among tenure-track faculty.

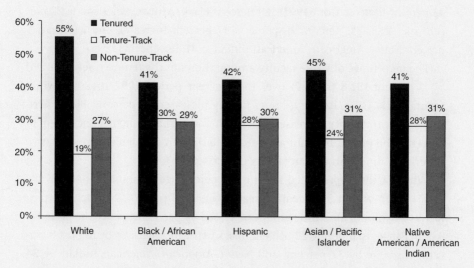

Figure 1.14. Employment Status of Full-Time White Faculty and Faculty of Color, 1997

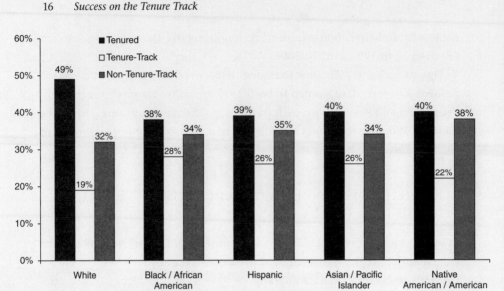

Figure 1.15. Employment Status of Full-Time White Faculty and Faculty of Color, 2007

Of tenured faculty in 1997, 89 percent were white; in 2007, that percentage was 84.7—a percentage decrease of 4.5 (table 1.5). In 2007, the distribution of faculty of color among the tenured was 7.6 percent Asian/Pacific Islander (a 43 percent increase from 1997), 4.4 percent Black/African American (a 22 percent increase), 2.8 percent Hispanic (a 47 percent increase), and less than 1 percent Native American/American Indian (a 41 percent increase).

The percentage of white faculty among those on the tenure track declined by 6 percent (81.8 to 76.9) over the ten-year period 1997 to 2007, while tenure-track Asian/Pacific Islander faculty increased 50 percent, Black/African American faculty increased 4 percent, and Hispanic faculty increased 30 percent. The period brought a 4 percent decline in the percentage of Native American/American Indian faculty on the tenure track.

White faculty represented the highest percentage of non-tenure-track faculty, though with a 3 percent decrease from 1997 to 2007. Non-tenure-track faculty of color of all ethnic groups increased by percentage over the period— Asian/Pacific Islander by 22 percent, Black/African American by almost 8 percent, Hispanic by 32 percent, and Native American/American Indian by 24 percent.

Table 1.5. Employment Status and Race/Ethnicity of Full-Time Faculty, 1997 and 2007

| Race/Ethnicity | Employment Status | | | | | |
| | Tenured | | Tenure-Track | | Non-Tenure-Track | |
	No.	%	No.	%	No.	%
1997						
White/Non-Hispanic	208,898	89.0	74,042	81.8	98,417	84.1
Black/African American	8,581	3.6	6,330	6.9	6,140	5.2
Hispanic	4,566	1.9	3,000	3.3	3,284	2.8
Asian/Pacific Islander	12,472	5.3	6,727	7.4	8.661	7.4
Native American/ American Indian	648	0.27	435	0.48	482	0.41
Total	235,165		90,534		116,984	
2007						
White/Non-Hispanic	203,631	84.7	80,947	76.9	134,331	81.2
Black/African American	10,496	4.4	7,551	7.2	9,274	5.6
Hispanic	6,812	2.8	4,485	4.3	6,125	3.7
Asian/Pacific Islander	18,252	7.6	11,682	11.1	14,927	9.0
Native American/ American Indian	909	0.38	490	0.46	851	0.51
Total	240,199		105,155		165,503	

Gender and Race/Ethnicity and Employment Status of Full-Time Faculty

In 2007, white men still held the majority of tenured faculty positions, though their total percentage had decreased 12 percent from 1997. The percentage of white women in tenured positions increased by 18 percent during the period; for men of color, the increase was 25 percent, and for women of color it was 67 percent; nonetheless, women of color made up only 5 percent of total tenured faculty in 2007 (fig. 1.16).

White men, in 2007, composed 41 percent of the tenure-track faculty—down almost 11 percent from 1997—while white women composed 35 percent of the total, unchanged over the ten-year period. Men of color on the tenure track increased by 18 percent; for women of color, the increase was 38 percent (fig. 1.17).

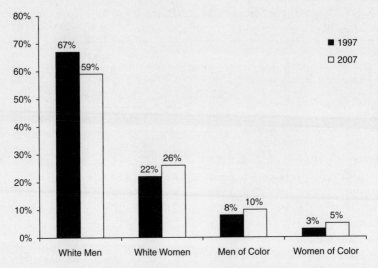

Figure 1.16. Gender and Race/Ethnicity of Tenured Faculty, 1997 and 2007

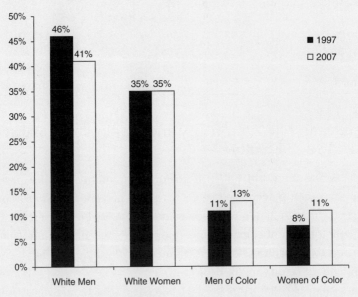

Figure 1.17. Gender and Race/Ethnicity of Tenure-Track Faculty, 1997 and 2007

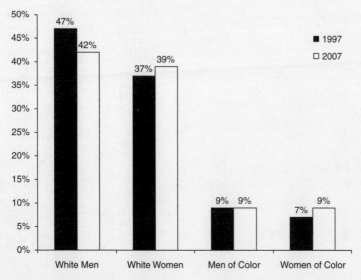

Figure 1.18. Gender and Race/Ethnicity of Non-Tenure-Track Faculty, 1997 and 2007

White men composed 42 percent of non-tenure-track faculty in 2007, down almost 11 percent from 1997; while the percentage of white women increased 5 percent. The percentage of faculty of color men in non-tenure-track positions was unchanged from 1997 to 2007, while the percentage of faculty of color women increased by almost 29 percent (fig. 1.18).

Underrepresented Minorities

Tables 1.6 through 1.8 show that Native American/American Indians, men and women, tenured, tenure-track, and non-tenure-track, were a small fraction of each employment category and that the percentage increased slightly for men and women, both tenured and non-tenure-track, from 1997 to 2007 but decreased among tenure-track faculty. Among tenured faculty, the percentage of Black/African American women was unchanged but the percentage of Black/African American men went up 28 percent. The ten-year period saw no change in the percentage of tenure-track faculty positions held by Black/African American men, and only a slight increase of 2 percent in those held by Black/African American women. Black/African Americans in non-tenure-track positions saw an increase of 4 percent for men and 8 percent

Table 1.6. Gender and Race/Ethnicity of Tenured Faculty, 1997 and 2007

Race/Ethnicity	Men		Women	
	No.	%	No.	%
1997				
White/Non-Hispanic	158,106	89.0	50,792	87.8
Black/African American	5,148	2.9	3,433	5.9
Hispanic	3,210	1.8	1,356	2.3
Asian/Pacific Islander	10,440	5.9	2,032	3.5
Native American/American Indian	463	0.26	185	0.32
Total	177, 367		57,798	
2007				
White/Non-Hispanic	140,986	84.9	62,645	84.5
Black/African American	6,075	3.7	4,421	5.9
Hispanic	4,364	2.6	2,448	3.3
Asian/Pacific Islander	14,034	8.5	4,217	5.7
Native American/American Indian	542	0.32	367	0.49
Total	166,001		74,098	

Table 1.7. Gender and Race/Ethnicity of Tenure-Track Faculty, 1997 and 2007

Race/Ethnicity	Men		Women	
	No.	%	No.	%
1997				
White/Non-Hispanic	42,076	81.4	31,966	82.3
Black/African American	3,084	5.9	3,246	8.3
Hispanic	1,691	3.3	1,310	3.4
Asian/Pacific Islander	4,606	8.9	2,121	5.4
Native American/American Indian	203	0.39	232	0.59
Total	51,660		38,875	
2007				
White/Non-Hispanic	44,986	76.8	36,666	76.5
Black/African American	3,462	5.9	4,089	8.5
Hispanic	2,406	4.1	2,079	4.3
Asian/Pacific Islander	7,465	12.8	4,777	9.9
Native American/American Indian	209	0.35	281	0.58
Total	58,528		47,892	

Table 1.8. Gender and Race/Ethnicity of Non-Tenure-Track Faculty,
1997 and 2007

Race/Ethnicity	Men		Women	
	No.	%	No.	%
1997				
White/Non-Hispanic	54,827	84.0	43,590	84.0
Black/African American	2,983	4.5	3,157	6.1
Hispanic	1,765	2.7	1,519	2.9
Asian/Pacific Islander	5,425	8.3	3,236	6.2
Native American/American Indian	256	0.39	226	0.44
Total	65,256		51,728	
2007				
White/Non-Hispanic	69,220	81.5	65,111	80.8
Black/African American	3,969	4.7	5,305	6.6
Hispanic	2,971	3.5	3,154	3.9
Asian/Pacific Islander	8,361	9.8	6,566	8.2
Native American/American Indian	393	0.46	458	0.57
Total	84,914		80,594	

for women. Hispanic men saw their number increase in all employment categories—44 percent for tenured, 24 percent for tenure-track, and 30 percent for non-tenure-track. For Hispanic women, the percentage increases were 43, 26, and 34, respectively.

Asian/Pacific Islanders

The period under study saw growth in Asian/Pacific Islander tenured faculty, a 44 percent increase for men and a 63 percent increase for women. For tenure-track Asian/Pacific Islander men, growth occurred at the rate of 44 percent, while the percentage of tenure-track Asian/Pacific Islander women grew 83 percent. Among non-tenure-track faculty, the decade saw 18 percent and 31 percent increases in Asian/Pacific Islander men and women, respectively.

Whites

From 1997 to 2007, white men and white women saw corresponding decreases in the percentage of tenured, tenure-track, and non-tenure-track faculty positions held. The percentage decreases for white men were 5 among

Table 1.9. Gender and Race/Ethnicity of Tenured, Tenure-Track, and Non-Tenure-Track Faculty, 2007

	Employment Status		
Gender and Race/Ethnicity	Tenured (%)	Tenure-Track (%)	Non-Tenure-Track (%)
White men	59.0	42.0	42.0
White women	26.0	35.0	39.0
Asian/Pacific Islander men	5.8	7.1	5.0
Asian/Pacific Islander women	1.7	4.5	3.9
Black/African American men	2.5	3.3	2.4
Black/African American women	1.8	3.9	3.2
Hispanic men	1.8	2.3	1.9
Hispanic women	1.0	1.9	1.8
Native American/American Indian men	0.22	0.19	0.27
Native American/American Indian women	0.26	0.27	0.24

the tenured, 6 among the tenure-track, and 3 among the non-tenure-track. The percentage decreases for white women were 4 percent among the tenured, 7 percent among the tenure-track, and 4 percent among the non-tenure-track.

Table 1.9 shows the distribution of tenured, tenure-track, and non-tenure-track faculty by race and gender in 2007.

Faculty Age and Generation

According to an American Council on Education Issue Brief (King 2008), using NSOPF[8] data from 2003–4, only 3 percent of faculty at four-year institutions in tenured or tenure-track positions were individuals aged 34 or younger; when tenured or tenure-track faculty aged 35 to 44 are considered, the percentage increases to 15 percent (p. 1).

Using COACHE data and generational age demarcations,[9] the tenure-track faculty at the universities considered for this book includes 75 percent Generation X faculty (born 1965–1981) and 25 percent baby boomer faculty (born 1946–1964). While we have begun to examine the COACHE data comparing job satisfaction of baby boomers and Gen Xers and published some findings (Quinn and Trower 2009; Trower and Quinn 2009), this work is still in its nascent stages.

It is important to note here that the five themes of this book about what's important to pre-tenure faculty—clear and reasonable tenure requirements, support for effective teaching and scholarship, work-life integration, a sense of community and colleagueship, and effective university leadership—are not new and are not specific to Gen Xers; rather, these themes have been at the heart of the academic enterprise for decades. However, a lot has changed for those working on tenure-track lines at research universities (Trower 2008a) since 1940 when the American Association of University Professors codified tenure and academic freedom (AAUP 2001a).

What's different today? To name just a few majors factors—knowledge production and dissemination (there are new methods, technologies, and venues for publication); funding (state and system-wide budget cuts); increased competition for grant-funding and different funding sources; longer lead times for getting published (in top-tier journals in many disciplines and by university presses); increased pressures for transparency and accountability; and a ratcheting up of expectations for all faculty, including teaching, research, service, and outreach. On the personal side, there is increasingly a 24/7 expectation for faculty work and accessibility to students; and the new norm for faculty with partners is dual career, with few able to stay at home to raise children. The demographics and learning needs of students have changed dramatically. In fact, just about everything is different today *except* the tenure system.

As mentioned, the vast majority of faculty members teaching at U.S. institutions now work outside of the tenure system, but this book is about those who are on the tenure track and hoping to achieve it. While they may want the same things as their predecessors, younger boomers and Gen X faculty live and work in a very different world than that of older boomers and those before them. Because of this, Gen X faculty in particular have been vocal about wanting increased flexibility, greater integration (some say balance) of their work and home lives, more transparency of processes, a more welcoming and supportive workplace/department, and more frequent and helpful feedback about progress.

CHAPTER TWO

Study Background and Methodology

COACHE Background

COACHE began as the Study of New Scholars (SNS), a research project funded by the Ford Foundation and Atlantic Philanthropies with two primary goals: (1) to make the academy a more equitable and appealing place for new faculty to work in order to ensure that academic institutions attract the best and brightest scholars and teachers, and (2) to increase the recruitment, retention, status, satisfaction, and success of all faculty, and particularly women and faculty of color.

This section describes the steps members of the study team used to develop a survey instrument and action plan to meet the needs of academic administrators while also remaining relevant to the special issues faced by today's early career faculty.

Focus Groups

Six focus groups were conducted with a total of 57 full-time tenure-track faculty (including 24 faculty of color and 34 women) to learn how they viewed specific institutional policies and practices, structural and cultural barriers, work climate, the ability to balance their professional and personal lives, and current job satisfaction.

Literature Reviews

Our early work included extensive literature reviews about tenure-track faculty in general, women and faculty of color in particular, the faculty socialization process, and the primary determinants of faculty job satisfaction, morale, and productivity.

Pilot Survey

Drawing from the focus groups and prior surveys of satisfaction among academics and other professionals, as well as from conversations with Harvard University experts, we developed a survey instrument for full-time, tenure-track (pre-tenure) faculty to rate the relative attractiveness of the terms and conditions of employment at their institutions, and their level of satisfaction and fulfillment. The web-based, 30-minute survey was completed by 1,188 junior faculty members at a dozen pilot institutions: Brown, Carleton, Duke, Morehouse, Mount Holyoke, Oberlin, Sarah Lawrence, Smith, the University of Arizona, UC Berkeley, the University of Illinois at Urbana-Champaign, and the University of Washington.

Pilot Site Reports

The president and provost of each pilot site received a report that provided a compilation of all quantitative findings from the pilot sites. Each report was over a hundred pages, with question-by-question summaries that highlighted major findings relative to peer pilot sites. Statistically significant differences by race and gender were also highlighted.

Faculty Interviews

We conducted sixty-six follow-up interviews with full-time pre-tenure faculty who completed the survey at four of the pilot research universities (including 12 faculty of color and 35 women). Those interviews provided a more nuanced and detailed picture of the work life of pre-tenure faculty as well as the factors that contribute to a great academic workplace.

Academic Leaders Meetings

SNS staff members met with academic leaders from ten of the twelve pilot sites in October 2003 for the purposes of (1) learning what was happening on campuses as a result of the study, (2) discussing data dissemination, and (3) seeking input about how to roll out the survey nationally in what would become COACHE. These discussions have become the basis for COACHE's user workshops and conference-based events.

Project Reports

SNS staff members produced statistical reports on survey results by gender, race, and institutional type. Related research appeared in *Trusteeship, The Academic Workplace, Connection, Harvard Magazine*, and many other outlets.

As a direct result of the SNS project, pilot sites became actively involved in producing changes on campus by

- sharing the results with boards of trustees and targeting areas for improvement;
- stimulating discussions among academic leaders who, in some cases, compete directly for faculty to discover what each campus does well in order to better understand best practices;
- using disconfirming data to account for the disparities between the perception of administrators and the realities experienced by faculty;
- using data to confirm good practice among policies effectively implemented and producing desired outcomes;
- analyzing and publicizing exemplary departments, while addressing less successful areas for improvements; and
- closely examining gender- and race-based differences among faculty.

Many campus leaders were surprised to learn that issues of transparency and equity had still not been satisfactorily addressed despite past efforts.

With a debt of gratitude to the academic leaders who made the project a success, the Study of New Scholars ultimately provided the proof of concept for a widespread dissemination of a pre-tenure faculty survey instrument and of the best practices that emerged. This core instrument of COACHE was developed, tested, validated, and is continually improved with assistance from participating institutions. Our survey assesses early career faculty experiences in several areas deemed critical to their success, including

- clarity and reasonableness of tenure processes and review;
- workload and support for teaching and research;
- integration and balance of work and home responsibilities;
- climate, culture, and collegiality on campus;
- compensation and benefits; and
- global satisfaction.

Today, the COACHE Survey of Tenure-Track Faculty Job Satisfaction is the only peer-based, diagnostic tool designed specifically for management to aid in recruiting and retaining the best faculty possible. Underlying the comparative data is the collaborative spirit of our partners at COACHE institutions.

As explained in chapter 1, we identified seven public university exemplars, described in the next section and summarized in table 2.1.[1] To be considered exemplary, an institution needed to have several, but not all, scores within a category in the 80th or higher percentile compared to other COACHE public universities and, in most cases, also have an overall mean score for the category above the pooled mean for all public universities.

Site Descriptions
Auburn University

Founded in 1856, Auburn is located in Auburn, Alabama. Its Carnegie Classification is "Research University/High Research Activity" (RU/HRA). It is further classified as "large 4-year, primarily non-residential" and is "more selective." Its undergraduate instructional program is classified as "professions plus arts and sciences, with high graduate coexistence," and its graduate instructional program is "comprehensive doctoral with medical/veterinary."

In 2009, Auburn had 24,530 students (20,037 undergraduates) in a dozen schools, including Agriculture, Architecture-Design-Construction, Business, Education, Engineering, Forestry and Wildlife Science, Human Sciences, Liberal Arts, Nursing, Pharmacy, Sciences and Mathematics, and Veterinary Medicine. It offers bachelor's, master's, doctoral, and first professional degrees as well as post-master's certificates.

The university had 798 tenured and 274 tenure-track faculty members.

University of Kansas

The University of Kansas, informally known as KU, was founded in 1891 and is located in Lawrence. It is classified as a "Research University/Very High Research Activity" (RU/VHRA), as "large 4-year, primarily non-residential," and is "selective." Its undergraduate instructional program is classified as "balanced arts and sciences/professions with high graduate coexistence," and its graduate instructional program is "comprehensive doctoral (no medical/veterinary)."

KU had approximately 27,000 students (20,811 undergraduates), not including students at the medical center, in 14 schools, including Allied Health,

Table 2.1. Institutional Data, 2008–9

	AU	KU	NCSU	OSU	UIUC	UI	UNCP
Carnegie Class	RU/HRA	RU/VHRA	RU/VHRA	RU/VHRA	RU/VHRA	RU/VHRA	MA/MP
Number of Tenure-Track and Tenured Faculty	1,072	1,154	1,373	2,167	1,993	1,226	214
Number of Schools/Colleges	12	14	10	17	15	11	4
Selectivity	More selective	Selective	More selective	More selective	More selective	More selective	Inclusive
Number of Students	24,530	27,000	32,872	53,715	41,496	30,561	6,303

Note: AU = Auburn University; KU = University of Kansas; NCSU = North Carolina State University; OSU = Ohio State University; UIUC = University of Illinois at Urbana-Champaign; UI = University of Iowa; UNCP = University of North Carolina at Pembroke; RU/HRA = Research University/High Research Activity; RU/VHRA = Research University/Very High Research Activity; MA/MP = Master's College/Medium Programs.

Architecture-Design-Planning, Business, Liberal Arts and Science, Continuing Education, Education, Engineering, Journalism and Mass Communication, Law, Medicine, Music, Nursing, Pharmacy, and Social Welfare. KU offers bachelor's, master's, doctoral, and first professional degrees as well as post-baccalaureate, post-master's, and first professional certificates.

Excluding the medical center, KU had 868 tenured and 286 tenure-track faculty members.

North Carolina State University

North Carolina State University (NCSU) was founded in 1887 as a land grant university, in Raleigh, and its Carnegie Classification is "Research University/Very High Research Activity" (RU/VHRA). It is further classified as "large, 4-year, primarily non-residential" and "more selective." Its undergraduate instructional program is classified as "balanced arts and sciences/professions with high graduate coexistence," and its graduate instructional program is "doctoral, STEM dominant."

NCSU had 32,872 students (24,741 undergraduates) in 10 colleges, including Agriculture and Life Sciences, Design, Education, Engineering, Natural Resources, Humanities and Social Sciences, Management, Physical and Mathematical Sciences, Textiles, and Veterinary Medicine. NSCU offers associate's, bachelor's, master's, doctoral, and first professional degrees as well as post-baccalaureate and post-master's certificates.

The university had 1,026 tenured and 347 tenure-track faculty members.

Ohio State University

Founded in 1870 as a land grant university, Ohio State University (OSU) is located in Columbus. Its Carnegie Classification is "Research University/Very High Research Activity" (RU/VHRA). It is further classified as "large, 4-year, primarily residential" and "more selective." Its undergraduate instructional program is classified as "balanced arts and sciences/professions with high graduate coexistence," and its graduate instructional program is "comprehensive doctoral with medical/veterinary."

OSU had 53,715 students (40,412 undergraduates) in 17 colleges, including Arts, Biological Sciences, Business, Dentistry, Education and Human Ecology, Engineering, Food-Agricultural-and Environmental Sciences, Humanities, Mathematics and Physical Sciences, Medicine, Nursing, Pharmacy, Public Affairs, Public Health, Social and Behavioral Sciences, Social Work, and Veterinary Medicine. OSU offers associate's, bachelor's, master's, and doctoral (research/scholarship and professional practice) degrees as well as post-baccalaureate and post-master's certificates.

The university had 1,626 tenured and 541 tenure-track faculty members.

University of Illinois at Urbana-Champaign

Located in the Champaign-Urbana metropolitan area, the University of Illinois at Urbana-Champaign (UIUC) was founded in 1867. Its Carnegie Classification is "Research University/Very High Research Activity" (RU/VHRA). It is further classified as "large 4-year, primarily residential" and "more selective." Its undergraduate instructional program is classified as "balanced arts and sciences/professions with high graduate coexistence," and its graduate instructional program is "comprehensive doctoral with medical/veterinary."

UIUC had 41,496 students (31,174 undergraduates) in 15 schools, including Agriculture-Consumer-Environmental Sciences, Applied Health Sciences, Institute of Aviation, Business, Education, Engineering, Fine and Applied Arts, Labor and Employment Relations, Law, Liberal Arts and Sciences, Graduate School of Library and Information Science, Media, Medicine, Social Work, and Veterinary Medicine. It offers bachelor's, master's, doctoral, and first professional degrees as well as "2- but less than 4-year" and post-master's certificates.

UIUC had 1,469 tenured and 524 tenure-track faculty members.

University of Iowa

Founded in 1847 and located in Iowa City, the University of Iowa (UI) is classified as a "Research University/Very High Research Activity" (RU/VHRA). It is considered "large 4-year primarily residential" and "more selective." Its undergraduate instructional program is classified as "balanced arts and sciences/professions with high graduate coexistence," and its graduate instructional program is "comprehensive doctoral with medical/veterinary."

UI had 30,561 students (20,823 undergraduate) in 11 colleges, including Business, Dentistry, Education, Engineering, Law, Liberal Arts and Sciences, Medicine, Nursing, Pharmacy, Public Health, and the Graduate College. UI offers bachelor's, master's, doctoral, and first professional degrees as well as "2- but less than 4-year" post-baccalaureate, post-master's, and first professional certificates.

The university had 918 tenured and 308 tenure-track faculty members.

University of North Carolina at Pembroke

Founded in 1887 as a school for American Indians, the University of North Carolina at Pembroke (UNCP) is an outlier from the other institutions in this study in several ways—one being its rural location in Pembroke. In the Carnegie Classification system UNCP is a Master's College (Medium Programs) (MA/MP), "medium 4-year primarily residential," and "inclusive." Its undergraduate instructional program is classified as "balanced arts and sciences/professions with some graduate coexistence," and its graduate instructional program is "post-baccalaureate professional education dominant."

UNCP had 6,303 students (5,578 undergraduates) in four colleges, or schools, including Arts and Sciences, Business, Education, and Graduate Studies in Public Administration and Social Services. It offers bachelor's and master's degrees.

The university had 103 tenured and 111 tenure-track faculty members.

Methodology

Interviews

At the seven exemplary public universities we visited (table 2.2), we conducted 104 (table 2.3) in-depth interviews (see appendix A for interview guide) during the period December 2008 through April 2009.

The sample for interviews was selected by each institution after they were instructed to choose those "who would know something about the administration of the COACHE Survey and its results" and "would be able to hypothesize about campus COACHE results." In all cases we asked to interview the provost or the provost's designee, a cross section of deans, department chairs or heads, and some senior and junior faculty.

The premise behind in-depth interviews is that the "perspective of others is meaningful, knowable, and able to be made explicit. We interview to find out what's in or on someone else's mind, to gather their stories" (Patton 2002, p. 341). We used a mixed methods approach utilizing a general interview guide that included some standardized open-ended questions that we asked of everyone (appendix A).

At each site, we conducted the first several interviews in pairs, in the morning, and then split up to enable the completion of a greater number of interviews in a short time frame. The interviewing pair met during lunch to

Table 2.2. Exemplary Categories by Site

Institution	Climate	Nature of Work	Tenure	Work-Life
Auburn University	X	X	X	X
University of Illinois at Urbana-Champaign		X		X
University of Iowa	X		X	X
University of Kansas	X	X	X	
North Carolina State University			X	
Ohio State University	X	X	X	X
University of North Carolina at Pembroke			X	X

Note: The categories Policy Effectiveness and Global Satisfaction are not examined specifically in this book. However, it is worth noting that Auburn, Iowa, Kansas, and Ohio State scored well in Policy Effectiveness, Iowa scored well in Global Satisfaction, and Illinois scored well in both categories.

Table 2.3. Post–COACHE Survey Interviews, December 2008–April 2009

Interviewees	AU	KU	NCSU	OSU	UIUC	UI	UNCP	Total
Admin (Provosts, Deans)	6	5	5	7	7	5	5	40
Chair/Department Heads	3	3	2	2	4	3	2	19
Full Professors*	2	2	0	4	0	1	4	13
Associate Professors*	0	3	1	3	1	0	0	8
Assistant Professors	4	4	4	0	4	4	4	24
Total	15	17	12	16	16	13	15	104

Note: AU = Auburn University; KU = University of Kansas; NCSU = North Carolina State University; OSU = Ohio State University; UIUC = University of Illinois at Urbana-Champaign; UI = University of Iowa; UNCP = University of North Carolina at Pembroke.

* Does not include chairs or deans

discuss themes and ideas for additional probing in the afternoon interviews and those the next day.

Interviews were audio-recorded, with permission and guarantee of anonymity per the Harvard University Institutional Review Board, Use of Human Subjects requirements. Interview recordings were then transcribed.

Coding

The software program ATLAS.ti (version 5.2) was used to organize and code the raw qualitative data collected for this study. This software is specifically designed for social scientists working with large amounts of qualitative data. Due to the number of interviews conducted for this study, ATLAS.ti provided an efficient and effective tool for identifying common themes and patterns. All transcribed interviews were uploaded into ATLAS.ti and coded appropriately. Once the coding was complete, the software's query function enabled quick data sorting and retrieval. This function is particularly useful because it allows the researcher to pull coded data from multiple sources simultaneously while staying within designated parameters. The output generated by the queries in this study helped to organize and illuminate broader findings.

We began by reading all transcripts. Based on that initial reading, we generated a list of forty-four categories of interest (see appendix B) that we would later filter into subsets. Those subsets are as follows:

Climate
- Creating/sustaining a culture of support: Deans
- Creating/sustaining a culture of support: Department Heads/Chairs
- Creating/sustaining a culture of support: Faculty governance
- Creating/sustaining a culture of support: President, Provost, Vice Provosts/Presidents
- Culture/climate
- Diversity: gender and racial/ethnic equity
- Interaction among junior faculty
- Interaction between senior and junior faculty
- Interdisciplinary research/collaboration across disciplines
- Mentoring, networks, and relationship-building

Nature of Work: Overall
- Facilities
- Grant support
- Protection from teaching/service overload
- Research leave
- Research support

- Research/travel funds
- Teaching support/Center for Teaching and Learning
- Workshops/orientation/seminars

Nature of Work: Research
- Facilities
- Grant support
- Protection from teaching/service overload
- Research leave
- Research support
- Research/travel funds
- Teaching support/Center for Teaching and Learning
- Workshops/orientation/seminars

Tenure
- Clarity of standards, process, criteria
- Evaluation, feedback, reviews
- Reasonableness of expectations
- Transparency, consistency, equity
- Window/flexibility

Work-Life Balance, Flexibility, and Family-Friendly Policies
- Child and elder care
- Dual-career hiring
- Flexible academic career paths (e.g., windows, part-time tenure, modified duties)
- Parental/personal leave
- Salary/benefits
- Stop-the-clock/tenure extension
- Support for families
- Tenure: Window/flexibility

Readers will note that there is some category overlap between subsets; for example, both the tenure and work-life categories include subsets for tenure "Window/flexibility"; flexible academic career paths encompass several aspects of tenure.

Survey Response Rates for Each Site

In the following chapters, I will discuss each theme, present overall COACHE data, and then present what we discerned about exemplary practices at each site. Since these sites were singled out as exemplary, it is important to know the COACHE survey response rates for the universities featured here. See tables 2.4, 2.5, and 2.6. In all cases but one (the University of Iowa–administered AY 2006–7), the COACHE survey was administered during the 2005–6 academic year.

For each institution, a weighting scale was developed to adjust for the under- or overrepresentation in the data set of subgroups defined by race and gender (e.g., white males, Asian females, etc.). Applying these weights to the data thus allows the relative proportions of subgroups in the data set for each institution to more accurately reflect the proportions in that institution's actual population of pre-tenure faculty.

In the next chapter, I consider the category of tenure by laying out recent issues, presenting the quantitative COACHE data, and then exploring the six sites with exemplary tenure scores.

Table 2.4. COACHE Survey Response Rates, Overall

Institution	Total Population	Number of Responders	Response Rate (%)
Auburn University	176	118	67
University of Illinois at Urbana-Champaign	402	181	45
University of Iowa	297	184	62
University of Kansas	189	128	68
North Carolina State University	238	150	63
Ohio State University	349	168	48
University of North Carolina at Pembroke	62	44	71

Note: The COACHE survey was administered during the 2005–6 academic year at all the universities shown here except the University of Iowa, where it was administered during the 2006–7 academic year.

Table 2.5. COACHE Survey Response Rates, by Gender

Institution	Men			Women		
	Population	Number of Responders	Response Rate (%)	Population	Number of Responders	Response Rate (%)
Auburn University	113	73	65	63	45	71
University of Illinois at Urbana-Champaign	249	104	42	153	77	50
University of Iowa	193	115	60	104	69	66
University of Kansas	94	56	60	95	72	76
North Carolina State University	148	90	61	90	60	67
Ohio State University	206	89	43	143	79	55
University of North Carolina at Pembroke	33	22	67	29	22	76

Table 2.6. COACHE Survey Response Rates, by White Faculty and Faculty of Color

Institution	White Faculty			Faculty of Color		
	Population	Number of Responders	Response Rate (%)	Population	Number of Responders	Response Rate (%)
Auburn University	115	80	70	61	38	62
University of Illinois at Urbana-Champaign	269	134	50	133	47	35
University of Iowa	209	139	67	88	45	51
University of Kansas	154	104	68	35	24	69
North Carolina State University	173	108	62	65	42	65
Ohio State University	248	129	52	101	39	39
University of North Carolina at Pembroke	53	38	72	9	6	67

CHAPTER THREE

Tenure

The Tenure Debate

It seems some things never change, and one of those is that there has always been a debate[1] around tenure—a debate that, simplistically stated, has pitted academic freedom and the attraction of talent to the professoriate against institutional flexibility and the prevention of complacency. What *has* changed is the nature of the discourse as new realities are affecting academe in many ways unanticipated by the American Association of University Professors in its 1915 *Declaration of Principles on Academic Freedom and Academic Tenure* and further codified in its 1940 *Statement of Principles on Academic Freedom and Tenure* (AAUP 2001a and 2001b). The twenty-first century has brought sweeping advances in technology and corresponding pressures on university presses, increased demand for collaboration and interdisciplinary research, and changing faculty demographics (e.g., more women and racial/ethnic minorities—addressed in chapter 1; and more dual-career faculty members— addressed in chapter 5). At the same time, the percentage of tenured and tenure-track faculty has dropped precipitously (see chapter 1), in part because of pressures on university finances.

Publish or Perish

The old adage about publishing or perishing still rings all too true for junior faculty despite the fact that publishing the all-important monograph, especially in the humanities, has become increasingly difficult. "The academic monograph is widely and only half-jokingly referred to as the 'holy grail' or the gold standard of the tenure process. Most tenure-track assistant professors have to publish one in order to gain promotion and job security. The competition to publish a book is thus just as intense as the competition to get a tenure-track job. Indeed, the two competitions increasingly bleed into one another, as many take to heart the rule of thumb that it takes a book just to get a job" (Donoghue 2008, p. 42). In 2004, in response to "widespread anxiety in the profession about ever-rising demand for research productivity and shrinking humanities lists by academic publishers, worries that forms of scholarship other than single-authored books were not being recognized, and fears that a generation of junior scholars would have a significantly reduced chance of being tenured" (MLA Report 2006, p. 3), the Executive Council of the Modern Language Association (MLA) created a task force to look into trends in publication requirements for tenure and promotion in U.S. English and foreign language departments.

Primary relevant findings from the MLA study include the following.

• The demands placed on candidates for tenure, especially demands for publication, have been expanding in kind and increasing in quantity. Over 62 percent of all departments report that publication has increased in importance in tenure decisions over the last 10 years. The percentage of departments ranking scholarship of primary importance (over teaching) has more than doubled since the last comparable survey, conducted by Thomas Wilcox in 1968: from 35.4 percent to 75.7 percent (p. 4).

• Junior faculty members are meeting these ever-growing demands even though this is a time when universities have lowered or eliminated subsidies for scholarly presses and libraries have dramatically reduced their purchases of books in the humanities. And despite a worsening climate for book publication, the monograph has become increasingly important in comparison with other forms of publication. Indeed, 88.9 percent of departments in Carnegie doctorate-granting, 44.4 percent in Carnegie master's, and 48 percent in Carnegie baccalaureate institutions now rank publication of a monograph "very important" or "important" for tenure. The status of the monograph as a gold standard is confirmed by the expectation in almost one-third of all departments surveyed (32.9 percent) of progress toward completion of a second book for tenure. This expectation is even higher in doctorate-granting institutions, where 49.8 percent of departments now demand progress toward a second book (p. 4).

• While publication expectations for tenure and promotion have increased, the value that departments place on scholarly activity outside monograph publication remains within a fairly restricted range. Refereed journal articles continue to be valued in tenure evaluations; only 1.6 percent of responding departments rated refereed journal articles "not important" in tenure and promotion decisions. Other activities were more widely devalued. Translations were rated "not important" by 30.4 percent of departments (including 31.3 percent of foreign language departments), as were textbooks by 28.9 percent of departments, bibliographic scholarship by 28.8 percent of departments, scholarly editions by 20 percent of departments, and editing a scholarly journal by 20.7 percent of departments (p. 5).

• Even more troubling is the state of evaluation for digital scholarship, now an extensively used resource for scholars across the humanities: 40.8 percent of departments in doctorate-granting institutions report no experience evaluating refereed articles in electronic format, and 65.7 percent report no experience evaluating monographs in electronic format (p. 5).

The growing importance of publishing in the tenure process has bumped up against pressures and technological advances in publishing to squeeze tenure-track faculty into a system where their most urgent goals are increasingly more difficult to obtain. An increase in publishing costs has raised the bar for publishing, while new platforms for publishing are opening up new options for faculty to present their work.

Furthermore, cuts in university library budgets are robbing university presses of their best customers, leading to smaller print runs (Donoghue 2008). "Several university press directors recall that not long ago during their careers, they could count on selling 1,000 or more copies of any title they published to the libraries of colleges and universities across the country. Now they can count on only 200 or so purchases from these strained institutions. This means that the sales of a typical academic book, which could once have been relied on at least to pay for the cost of its own production, now does not stand a chance of doing so" (p. 41).

The growing demand for digital journals has devoured book-purchasing budgets at university libraries, flip-flopping the percentage of acquisition budgets spent on books and journals from 80 to 20 percent in favor of books a generation ago to 80 to 20 percent in favor of journals today (Donoghue 2008). Electronic publication does not relieve the bulk of the costs associated with publishing, such as marketing and soliciting peer review, and it presents new up-front technological costs for wide-scale electronic distribution. Still, some university presses are looking to technology as a way to hold down costs in the long run (Donoghue 2008).

University of Michigan officials explained their decision in 2009 to make the university press primarily digital as a way to allow for scholarly work to be published without the constraint of profitability questions: "Michigan officials said that they don't plan to cut the budget of the press—but to devote resources to peer review and other costs of publishing that won't change with the new model. Significantly, they said, the press would no longer have to reject books deemed worthy from a scholarly perspective, but viewed as unable to sell" (Jaschik 2009b).

But while faculty members are engaged in digital scholarship, as mentioned previously, departments appear unable or unwilling to evaluate it. This creates a Catch-22 situation where further junior faculty participation in digital publishing is dependent in part on institutional recognition of the work and institutional recognition of the work may be influenced by how widespread the practice becomes.

The Rise of Interdisciplinary Research

The widespread growth in research collaboration (within universities, between universities, and with partners outside universities) and the inability or resistance of universities to adapt tenure policies to reward such work is another developing theme in the tenure debate. Not all of the trends, changes, and problems are contained within the humanities; while interdisciplinary research has become increasingly popular across many fields, it is the predominant model in the sciences.

With its vast proliferation of university research centers, the recent "period in U.S. science and technology policy could credibly be deemed the era of inter-institutional research collaboration" (Boardman and Bozeman 2007, p. 430). These university-based research organizations focus on research topics rather than disciplines, and they are often funded by federal monies and support scientists from industry as well as from other universities (Boardman and Bozeman 2007).

A major consequence of the shift to multidisciplinary research centers working on problems and issues that span traditional disciplinary lines is that "university scientists, now more than ever, are subject to multiple and competing demands" (Boardman and Ponomariov 2007, p. 51). The research and other behaviors those centers expect of university scientists "generally do not align with the traditional university reward system" (p. 52). Specifically, what is required in the center is often part of a multidisciplinary and inter-institutional effort that is applied, rather than basic, in nature and where success is often measured in terms of technology transfer from university to industry. Boardman and Ponomariov (2007) point out that this misalignment between the work expected and the reward structure is a problem not just for university faculty in the hard sciences but also for those in the social sciences, medicine, business, and management (p. 52).

Industry-sponsored work, done in these centers, can be especially problematic for probationary faculty because when the primary reward is tenure, the typical work required is to conduct basic research in a discipline and then publish refereed academic journals articles, book chapters, and academic monographs (Boyer 1990; Lattuca 2001). "Many informants across institutions shared the opinion that junior faculty should concentrate on disciplinary research and teaching before tenure; only after tenure was it safe . . . to make interdisciplinary research and teaching a major scholarly focus" (Lattuca 201, p. 177).

Furthermore, academic peer review is better suited to well-defined fields than to interdisciplinary work, and for assessing new knowledge for its own sake rather than measuring its usefulness or applicability (Brooks 1978). In addition, researchers have shown that traditional tenure and promotion policies favor single-discipline and basic research over interdisciplinary and applied or commercially relevant projects. "The vast majority of interviewees noted that promotion and tenure decisions are based exclusively on publications and federal research grants, with no weight placed on patents and industry partnerships" (Siegel et al. 2003, p. 121).

Numerous scholars have suggested policy changes in order to broaden the scope of outcomes that count in tenure and promotion decisions, advocating new criteria such as "publicness, amenability to peer review, replicability, documentability, impact, and innovativeness of an activity—be it publishing, basic or applied research, teaching, collaborating with industry, developing prototypes, or mentoring graduate students" (Boardman and Ponomariov 2007, p. 65). The authors reflect on this list and note, importantly, that it is no surprise why the "traditional university reward system has persisted, more or less unchanged, for so long"; some of these criteria are "simply difficult to conceptualize due to vagueness (publicness, impact, innovativeness), while others are most easily conceptualized as a result of publishing" (p. 65). They concluded that, despite the obvious challenges of changing the reward system, it must nonetheless "be altered if we are to get university scientists to focus on the wide variety of tasks we as a society deem equally important as, if not more important than, the publication of basic research" (p. 65).

Pressures on University Finances

With state appropriations to higher education stagnant or shrinking and university endowments suffering setbacks from the recession, cost shifting appears to be one motivating factor for the move away from tenured faculty. Donoghue (2008) argued that the shifting financial model that has led to the growing importance of grant funding hurts especially the humanities and those who seek tenured careers as professors in the social sciences. In an interview, he said that "tenure is disappearing largely for financial reasons" (Jaschik 2008); further, he explained that the movement away from the liberal arts does not bode well for the fate of tenure.

> The tenure-track professoriate will never be restored. Two factors seal its fate. First, the hiring of adjuncts continues to outpace the hiring of tenure-track professors by a rate of three to one. . . . Second, the demographics of American higher education don't help us either. For 40 years, students have been moving away from the humanities toward vocationalism. This trend has been accompanied by an equally pronounced shift in enrollments from four-year schools (with English and History majors) to community colleges, where the humanities have never had a strong presence. Tenure-track professors don't have a place in this new higher education universe. (Jaschik 2008)

Pressures on universities to hold down the costs of instruction have also played a role in increased hiring of non-tenure-track faculty. Full-time tenured/tenure-track faculty earned an average salary of $59,000 from their institutions in 1998, as compared to $41,500 for full-time non-tenure-track faculty (Anderson 2002). The cost incentives for universities to hire non-tenure-track faculty extend beyond salary. Only 36 percent of institutions provided medical insurance or care to part-time faculty, as compared to 99 percent for full-time faculty. The percentage of faculty receiving institutional support for professional/association fees decreased by group from 41 percent of full-time tenured/tenure-track faculty, to 33 percent of full-time non-tenure-track faculty, to 8 percent of part-timers (Anderson 2002).

There is evidence that these measures are helping colleges save on the bottom line. Instructional support—defined by the 2009 Delta Cost Project "Trends in College Spending" report to include faculty salaries and benefits as well as office supplies, academic administration, and support for departmental research and public service—has decreased as a percentage of the "education and related expenses" budget across all institution types. From 1995 to 2006, instructional support decreased from 64.4 to 63 percent of educational and related expenses at public research universities; from 53.9 to 50.8 at public master's universities; from 52.8 to 50.2 at public community colleges; from 62.3 to 57.9 at private research universities; from 45 to 43 at private master's institutions; and from 40.7 to 38.9 at private bachelor's colleges (Delta Cost Project, pp. 22–23). With increasing pressures to offset recent declines in state support and endowment values and growth in administrative and energy costs, the pressure on institutions to hire more non-tenure-track faculty is likely to increase.

COACHE Tenure Data

Despite the ongoing and ever-present tenure debate, there are still more than 100,000 faculty members on the tenure track who are hoping to earn it. During our focus group research, around which we designed the COACHE survey, pre-tenure faculty stressed the desire for clarity (Trower and Gallagher 2008a, 2008b) of tenure process, criteria, standards, the body of evidence required, and the specific expectations for research, teaching, and service. Tables 3.1 and 3.2 show the average clarity ratings by survey items.

Table 3.1. COACHE Survey Average Ratings about Tenure Process, Criteria, Body of Evidence, and Standards Clarity

Please rate the clarity of the following aspects of earning tenure in your department.	Average Rating
I find the tenure *process* in my department to be . . .	3.71
I find the tenure *criteria* (what things are evaluated) in my department to be . . .	3.61
I find the *body of evidence* that will be considered in making my tenure decision to be . . .	3.52
I find the tenure *standards* (the performance threshold) in my department to be . . .	3.26

Scale: 5 = Very clear; 4 = Fairly clear; 3 = Neither clear nor unclear; 2 = Fairly unclear; and 1 = Very unclear

Table 3.2. COACHE Survey Average Ratings about the Clarity of Tenure Expectations

Is what's expected in order to earn tenure clear to you regarding your performance as . . .	Average Rating
a scholar (e.g., research and creative work)?	3.73
a teacher?	3.73
a colleague in your department?	3.24
an advisor to students?	3.21
a campus citizen?	3.11
a member of the broader community?	2.89

Scale: 5 = Very clear; 4 = Fairly clear; 3 = Neither clear nor unclear; 2 = Fairly unclear; and 1 = Very unclear

Pre-tenure faculty were most clear about the tenure process (what they need to submit, when, to whom/which office) and least clear about tenure standards (the performance threshold—how good is good enough?). The need for increased clarity about tenure standards was a resounding theme among the pre-tenure faculty we interviewed; they wanted to know "where the tenure bar is" and worry that it has risen or will shift before they reach the tenure decision. In addition, while faculty handbooks typically say the expectation is "excellence" in research and teaching, they too often do not describe what excellence is. Tenure-track faculty desires for explicit statements about tenure standards are often countered by administrators who may be hesitant to spell out the specific requirements for tenure. It is often accepted as de rigueur that pre-tenure faculty members should *not* receive concrete definitions of what excellence in teaching, scholarship, and service means (Trower and Gallagher 2008b). Said a dean, "The faculty policy manual states what the expectations are—excellence in scholarship, excellence in teaching, and excellence in service. It's the scholarship part that people would like to see more contractual . . . junior faculty say that it isn't transparent. . . . What they're looking for isn't just quantification but also information about where to publish. 'If I write five articles, and if I put two in top-tier journals and three in mid-tier journals, will I get tenure?' They would like a contract with all of this written out, and while I completely understand the impetus for that, it just isn't possible."

Perhaps not surprisingly, pre-tenure faculty were most clear about the performance expectations for scholarship and teaching and least clear about what's expected from them as a member of the broader community (table 3.2). Assistant professors reportedly understand the research and teaching requirements, but they are also expected to be good colleagues and many are not quite sure what that means. And while they are typically expected to perform a modicum of service, no one says, "Serve on this committee but not that one." One assistant professor mused, "What is good campus citizenship anyway, and does it factor into my tenure bid?" Another stated, "We're expected to get outside letters of support, so we need to also be known in our academic discipline—the broader community . . . but how to do it and what's considered good enough is completely unclear."

Campuses with High Tenure Clarity Scores

The six public universities that scored especially well on the tenure clarity dimensions were Auburn, Ohio State, North Carolina State, the University of Iowa, University of Kansas, and University of North Carolina at Pembroke. Each is showcased here with respect to tenure clarity. The next sections describe the elements of good tenure practice and showcase some of the policies and provisions at these campuses.

Effective Practice 1: Be Explicit at the Outset about Institutional Mission, Context, and How That Affects Faculty Work and the Promotion and Tenure Process

Our site visits revealed important contextual dimensions of each campus, described briefly here, that are reflected in each institution's tenure policies and practices.

At the time of our visit, Auburn was striving to improve (e.g., adding graduate programs, bringing in grants, supporting the sciences) and move from its current "High Research Activity" Carnegie designation to "Very High." In addition, as a land-grant institution, Auburn includes outreach as a criterion for tenure along with teaching, research, and service. Auburn is unique in that its tenure policy includes a fifth criterion—professional collegiality. The full clause may be found on the provost's page, faculty development tab, faculty handbook personnel policies and procedures. The clause reminds departments that a "successful candidate for tenure will assume what may be an appointment of 30 years or more" and that "collegiality should not be confused with sociability or likeability." Rather, collegiality is a "professional, not personal" issue relating to the performance of one's faculty duties including establishing relationships compatible with departmental mission and goals, a demonstrated willingness to take on administrative tasks, and the ability to maintain high standards of professional integrity.

Those we interviewed at Auburn were, by and large, comfortable with the clause and understood its intent. One assistant professor admitted that he had never read the statement but remembered being asked in an interview, "Do you know how to be collegial and what does being collegial mean to you?" He explained that he felt it was "not a matter of being likeable," rather, it was "being able to work with people, and being able to overcome whatever differences you may have with others professionally . . . being able to get along with others." He got the job and hasn't looked back. Said another pre-tenure faculty member, "Collegiality is just something we constantly hear about here. It's expected and we're fine with that."

Like Auburn, NC State is a land-grant institution. It is also part of the University of North Carolina system, whose *Policies, Regulations and Rules* are applied in all institutions within the system. The policy manual may be found at the system website, "Board of Governor's" tab, under "Code/Policy Manual, Section 400.3, Guidelines on Tenure and Teaching in The University of North Carolina." Regarding its land-grant mission, one senior administrator said, "NC State is driven to be useful to the State of North Carolina; it's in our DNA. This means partnerships and collaborations outside the confines of campus; we are located in all hundred counties. Outreach is extremely important here." In fact, this person noted that NC State's "partnership orientation" and "collaborative spirit" provide the "axis of differentiation here. When we hire faculty, it's our expectation that they will get tenure and be our colleagues for the next thirty years." The pre-tenure faculty with whom we spoke agreed that part of their attraction to the institution was its location, its connection to community, and its mission; they also felt a "nurturing" spirit of collaboration and clarity about expectations—the opposite of what many of their peers' experience at places where tenure is said to be "shrouded in secrecy" and "nearly impossible to achieve."

Like Auburn and NC State, Ohio State is a land-grant institution, but it has slightly different stated goals, or at least frames outreach more broadly, referring to "public service" instead. The stated mission of OSU is "the attainment of international distinction in education, scholarship, and public service" and to move from "excellence to eminence." For purposes of faculty performance reviews under these rules, "public service" is broadly defined to include administrative service to the university, professional service to the faculty member's discipline, and the provision of professional expertise to public and private entities beyond the university; it is referred to simply as "service" in the faculty handbook. For purposes of faculty performance reviews, "scholarship" is broadly defined to include "research, scholarly, and creative work." To be promoted to the rank of associate professor and earn tenure at OSU, the faculty member must achieve "excellence" as a teacher and scholar, and must provide "effective" service. For more information, see OSU's website, "Governance" tab, "Board of Trustees link," "University Rules Chapter Six."

In part, because the University of Iowa is not a land-grant institution, its tenure policies reflect teaching, research, and "to a lesser extent" service (and not outreach) as expectations, with an emphasis on teaching and research. As noted in Iowa's *Procedures for Tenure and Promotion Decision Making* document (which maybe be found on the provost's website, "For Faculty & Departments" tab, "Faculty Handbook, Policies and Procedures"), all colleges must have written policies regarding the requirements for tenure, and all candidates for tenure must be treated with consistency.

Like Iowa, KU is not a land-grant institution. The KU *Faculty Senate Rules and Regulations* state, "Teaching is a primary function of the University" and, for tenure, one's record must reflect "effective teaching." Further, "Scholarship is an essential component of the University's mission . . . and the award of tenure . . . must be based on a record of accomplishment reflecting a substantial program of scholarly activity." Service is described as "an important responsibility of all faculty members," and, for tenure, the record "must demonstrate a pattern of service" within the department, college, or school, as well as to the discipline, and/or to the broader community (local, state, national, or international). For more information, see the provost's webpage, "KU Policy Library tab, Faculty Senate Rules & Regulations, Article VI," on "Promotion & Tenure."

UNCP is different from the other universities featured in many ways, perhaps most importantly for this chapter in that it is a master's college where teaching is the university's central mission. The teaching load, therefore, is heavy by comparison to that at the other institutions featured in this chapter—four per semester—but that is considered "reasonable" for the faculty who take jobs there. Said a senior administrator, "This is where learning is personal. It's a calling; it's the mission. We don't bring anyone in for an interview who doesn't want to teach and engage the needs of this rural community."

Effective Practice 2: Set Weights or Priorities for Faculty Work

Auburn's expectations for achieving tenure are discussed with candidates up front, during the interview process. Section 2 of the Auburn *Faculty Handbook* states that in some colleges or schools the percentages of time and effort to be devoted to each assigned area (teaching, research, and outreach are required, as is "modest" service) are determined by funding sources and in others the percentages are agreed upon by the department head and the faculty member. An administrator said, "We tell each new faculty member that, for example, 'You are being hired 50 percent in teaching, 40 percent research, and 10 percent outreach,' so they know how to spend their time." The percentages for each area are part of the employment contract.

UNCP's *Faculty Handbook* states that "teaching is the single most important responsibility of regular full-time faculty members," and therefore it is given the most weight in faculty evaluations, typically between 50 percent and 70 percent. Scholarship and service receive weights of 10 percent to 40 percent. Because of the importance of classroom teaching, effectiveness is evaluated along six dimensions delineated in the handbook, including imparting general knowledge, imparting specific knowledge, developing skills, motivating students, setting requirements and evaluating performance, and success with effective teaching practices. (For more information, see the UNCP website, "Faculty Resources" tab, "Faculty Handbook," Section 4A-2.2.) Said a full professor, "The expectations are simple—do an excellent job teaching and with students—teaching comes first, period. We like scholarship and service, but job one is teaching."

At KU, when tenure-track faculty members first arrive on campus, they receive a copy of the "Blue Form" (something that dates back to paper copies of policies and documentation that were printed). The Blue Form is the tenure dossier; it includes materials that will be required for promotion and tenure. In addition to providing new faculty members with easy links to various evaluation documents, the percentage of effort expected for the basic categories of duties are determined and documented, which becomes part of the "progress toward tenure" review. Said an associate professor, "Faculty know their allocation of effort at the outset; for many in our department, it is

40-40-20, but junior faculty might be more like 50-40-10, or even 60-30-10. While teaching is important, research usually gets the most weight." All plans are approved by the dean of the appropriate school and department chairs encourage tenure-track faculty to download the form right away and complete it as they accumulate experience.

NC State was described by several people we interviewed as "very process and rules-oriented," which some like and some do not. One thing is clear, though—pre-tenure faculty know what is expected to achieve tenure. Said one senior administrator, "Specificity is a trade-off . . . a balancing act. Too much specificity can lock someone into something rigid and inflexible, which is something NC State does not want to do. On the other hand, tenure-track faculty don't want vague guidelines." The solution at NC State is what is known as the Statement of Mutual Expectations (SME)—"a written description of the appropriate mix of the faculty member's realms of responsibilities and the mutually-agreed-upon expectations from both the faculty member and the department during the faculty member's appointment."[2] Detailed in the SME are the specific areas of work on which the faculty member is supposed to concentrate, which is dependent, in part, on the faculty member's discipline/department. These include (1) teaching, advising, and mentoring of students; (2) scholarship; (3) creative artistry and literature; (4) technological and managerial innovation; (5) extension and engagement; and (6) service.[3] Interviews revealed that administrators and faculty alike enjoy the clarity provided by the tenure and promotion guidelines and SME. Said an administrator, "I've been at several other institutions and our P&T process is the most transparent I've ever seen. It's a great recruiting tool because the junior faculty love it." Said an assistant professor, "The SME is very clear about what the chair and I agreed that I would do. I know what percentage is expected in each area; we discussed quality and quantity as well, but that's not written down; I wouldn't expect it to be, but it was discussed."

The approaches at Ohio State and Iowa are slightly different but have the same appealing end result of ensuring that pre-tenure faculty members understand what's expected of them to achieve tenure. All units/colleges at Ohio State must have a written document called a "Pattern of Administration" that specifies the unit's (1) mission; (2) types of faculty and governance or decision-making structure; (3) committee structure and responsibilities; (4) dean, unit, and department head and faculty responsibilities; (5) faculty review structure and criteria for promotion and tenure; and (6) policies governing resource allocation, including faculty grievance and appeals processes. Thus, by policy dictate, OSU has explicitly stated criteria for tenure. Said one chair, "When I bring a candidate to campus, I give them a copy of our department's tenure criteria and say, 'This is the expectation for teaching, research, and service.' There is no gray here. It is all very clearly stated," a view echoed by assistant professors. A full professor said, "Every department has a very clear promotion and tenure document. Sometimes there are complaints that it's a little too formulated, but it is very clear."

At Iowa, each department has criteria for rank that must be approved by each college. The College of Liberal Arts and Sciences, for example, has a website that provides links to specific tenure criteria. The specificity of the documents for each department varies widely; the Chemistry Department's documents are exemplary in that they provide not only criteria but also standards for review.[4] For example, the following are listed as factors for consideration for research and scholarship:

- successful funding of multiyear grant applications to external agencies, such as NIH, NSF, ACS-PRF, EPA, DOD and ONR;
- publications in appropriate media, such as peer-reviewed journals, invited chapters in monographs and symposium volumes, and invited articles or reviews;
- production of disseminated software packages and other teaching materials, such as laboratory manuals, textbooks, and the like;
- presentations at professional meetings and workshops, including poster presentations, podium presentations, and invited seminars; and
- indications of national and/or international recognition, such as invitations to speak at universities, colleges, industries, and at national or international meetings.

In addition to these factors, policy documents provide still more guidance in terms of standards, including listing appropriate peer-reviewed journals for publication, conferences for speaking, and agencies from which grants may be sought. Another noteworthy college at Iowa is the College of Public Health (CPH), which provides not only criteria and standards but also samples and checklists for ease of use; the site has twenty-six links to such items as a third-year renewal review checklist, a peer evaluation of teaching form, department-specific performance expectations for specific ranks, professional productivity defined, teaching defined, and a sample letter from the departmental executive officer to an external reviewer. Said a senior administrator, "The CPH has five departments and all have very detailed sets of expectations . . . two- or three-page documents that spell out exactly the range of papers . . . everything they want people to have."

Effective Practice 3: If Factors Beyond Excellence in Research and Teaching Matter for Tenure, Define the Concept and Say How They Will Count and Be Measured.

At Auburn, because of the importance of outreach at a land-grant university, outreach is the third criteria (rather than service) of the tenure requirements and carries an actual percentage expectation (along with research and teaching). Not only do tenure candidates understand the expectation weight, they also have access to clearly stated criteria for outreach, and examples of outreach portfolios may be found in the Auburn *Faculty Handbook*. The Auburn policy manual addresses the documentation of appropriate outreach for tenure and is divided into two parts: a five-page personal commentary that describes the outreach program undertaken, how it fits with the unit's mission, the scholarly aspects of the program, and its impacts; and a list and description of activities and products generated through the program. A senior administrator explained the outreach policy: "We have added a piece to the handbook that says if you're doing outreach scholarship what it means and what it looks like, because this can be tricky. It's not enough to say that you worked with some community group. We want to see some demonstration of the outcomes and the scholarly piece associated with that. We hold forums for faculty about how to document outreach. It can't just be outreach for outreach sake . . . there has to be a scholarly contribution associated with it."

As mentioned previously, NC State considers six factors when evaluating faculty for tenure; one of them is outreach. The policy manual defines both outreach and extension and notes that for outreach to count as scholarship, it must be "planned and evaluated in a systematic and objective manner." Faculty file annual reports of outreach activities by describing the program, its relevance, and any associated publications, honors, or awards; in addition, faculty are expected to provide evidence of excellence as well as get letters from peers and clientele in support of their outreach efforts.

At UNCP, beyond teaching, engagement in the community is important and it is rewarded. Said a senior administrator, "Engagement is not something that's placed on your back; it's included in the promotion and tenure criteria because of our broad definition of what constitutes scholarship." According to the UNCP *Faculty Handbook*, service is divided into three categories: service to the university, professional service, and external and community service. The handbook provides descriptions of all three, how each should be documented, and criteria for how each will be evaluated. "The expectation faculty have is that there is recognition and reward for teaching and service here. If you are a good teacher and a responsible citizen of this community, you'll likely achieve tenure," said an administrator. "We encourage all faculty to serve on committees and a lot of junior faculty volunteer for this work because they know it counts—it's not just one more thing added onto their full plates. There's a lot of camaraderie here."

Effective Practice 4: Provide Relevant Written Information about How to Achieve Tenure, Mentorship, and Guidance

One of the most comprehensive examples of providing relevant information to faculty may be found on the provost's website at NC State (www.provost .ncsu.edu/promotion-tenure/). The site informs readers of everything they need to know about the promotion and tenure process by providing links to all relevant policy language, rules, and regulations. The site includes links for first-term assistant professors applying for a second term or for tenure (e.g., academic tenure policy, tenure process description, college and department rules, timeline, required dossier and instructions, external evaluation letters, and frequently asked questions); associates seeking appointment to full; departmental voting faculty; department heads (to remind them of all rules and regulations that apply, their responsibilities to provide guidance to tenure-track faculty in preparing their dossiers and to obtain external evaluations, and how to provide documentation for the written assessment and departmental recommendation); college reappointment, promotion, and tenure (RPT) committee members; department or college coordinators; and deans, providing overviews of what each type of individual needs to know. The site also includes links to policies that explain academic tenure, tenure process, the statement of mutual expectations (along with a sample), dossier instructions and related regulations, qualifications for rank, college and departmental RPT rules, scheduling mandatory reviews, and extending the tenure clock.

Another excellent example is KU's provost's website, which provides a link to resources for new faculty, where faculty can learn more about (1) the Center for Teaching Excellence; (2) Instructional Development and Support; (3) the New Faculty General Research Fund (providing up to $3,000 for research support and up to $8,000 in seed funding for major external research); and (4) the *Faculty Handbook* (www.provost.ku.edu/areas/faculty/newfaculty .shtml). A section called "Faculty Evaluation" provides links to the annual evaluation process, progress toward tenure review, and promotion and tenure policies and procedures.

Effective Practice 5: Provide New Faculty Orientation and Workshops on Tenure and Promotion

NC State offers numerous workshops for junior faculty, beginning with new faculty orientation. The provost's office holds two meetings per year during which pre-tenure faculty can ask whatever questions they have about getting tenure and what goes into a dossier, so that the tenure expectations and body of evidence are clear from day one. Said an administrator, "We have high expectations, but we also provide the support to help faculty achieve tenure. We have numerous support mechanisms for teaching, professional development, grant-writing."

Pre-tenure faculty told us about various workshops conducted as part of the Assistant Professors' Learning Community (an informal discussion group open to all faculty, with a special emphasis on issues of importance to assistant professors, that meets three times each semester) about grant writing, preparing a dossier, and a P&T workshop on "how to get tenure if you do outreach and the scholarship of engagement" (which includes a walk-through of the provost's website on tenure). One junior faculty member described her very first faculty meeting: "My first meeting here was a reappointment, promotion, and tenure meeting (RPT) and it was great to be able to see exactly what it's like, especially knowing that I would be going through this process in two years. It makes it very transparent when you know what people are discussing in meetings. Assistant professors get an advisory vote on reappointments and we're there for all the discussions." When asked if it was a little awkward to actually be there for discussions of other pre-tenure faculty members, this assistant professor said, "Well, yes, a little . . . but it's just so personally relevant. This is the point at which there is still time to change something that you might recognize as a weakness in your own record."

Iowa offers a two-day new faculty orientation program that includes faculty panels on strategies for success on a clinical or tenure track, conducting research, teaching effectiveness (in large lecture hall and clinical settings), and establishing effective habits of writing productivity. A "New Faculty Resources Series" that includes a paper called "Getting Off to a Good Start" addresses teaching, research, service, work-life balance, and career development, complete with checklists for the early stages of the faculty career.

The associate dean of the College of Liberal Arts and Sciences conducts workshops on CV preparation and promotion and tenure. Assistant professors bring their CVs, and strengths and weaknesses are highlighted during the workshop. The dean prepares junior faculty in how to present their credentials to the collegiate consulting group (the senior faculty who judge each tenure case). Said the associate dean: "I consider myself some sort of coach . . . knowing how these senior faculty and the collegiate consulting group work . . . the kind of things they look at. I tell junior faculty that they must be prepared to answer all possible questions that may arise: If you have a year without publications, can you explain that? If an external reviewer is critical of a publication, why? Some absences from classes are noticed, what explains? We don't push anything under the rug; it all must be examined . . . transparency at all times is critical."

Iowa also offers numerous faculty development workshops throughout the year; in 2009, topics included "Tenure and Time Management," "Creating a Faculty Writing Group," "Writing, Procrastination, and Resistance," "Negotiating Workshop for Women Faculty," "Symposium on Promotion and Tenure," and dozens more on teaching and other topics of interest.

Because of the importance of teaching at UNCP, the university's Teaching and Learning Center conducts numerous workshops throughout the year, including a four-hour session called "Tenure and Promotion at Pembroke," in which, according to a senior administrator, the director "goes over the faculty handbook and tells new faculty the expectations for tenure and encourages them to start working on those tenure documents right away." Another session is about "Faculty Evaluation." Considerable time during both sessions is spent on teaching, including the creation of a teaching portfolio and how to document excellence in teaching. An assistant professor noted, "The Teaching and Learning Center here is so amazing, and the director is a great resource. She is very honest and candid in her advice; when I've been unclear about the handbook, I go and ask her and she helps me understand."

Ohio State has workshops at the departmental and college level during which "people share best practices about completing the core dossier—how they did it; and this has demystified the tenure process."

Effective Practice 6: Host Q&A Sessions and Provide Other Venues for Tenure-Track Faculty to Safely Ask Questions and Get Answers from People Who Know

Noteworthy at KU are public forums and seminars for junior faculty to ask questions and get answers about tenure policies and practices. A seminar is held for incoming faculty "to give them insight into what's going to happen at the university level," said a senior administrator. All junior faculty are encouraged to attend the meeting, with their mentors, to listen to a panel of experts discuss what the expectations are, followed by a Q&A session at the end. Said an administrator, "The idea is to help people understand the tenure process, how they need to think about it as they begin their careers at KU, what they need to do so that they can effectively present a case about their contributions as a scholar, as a teacher, and in terms of service to the university and to the profession. I think it helps to get people engaged early about what is most important . . . it sets the tone at the top."

New Iowa faculty can email newfaculty@uiowa.edu with questions that will be answered individually and confidentially by a staff members in the provost's office; says the website, "No question is too mundane and none too challenging." In addition, Iowa publishes a new faculty newsletter full of information about who to see about what, frequently asked questions and answers, and resources.

An associate professor at Ohio State said that "the college has workshops for junior faculty where they walk them through a fourth-year review for tenure . . . expectations, process, procedures . . . which have been enormously helpful and supplement what's going on in the departments." Pre-tenure faculty feel comfortable asking their questions because the people evaluating them aren't in the room.

Effective Practice 7: Provide Plenty of Feedback Along the Way—Annually, and More Thoroughly Still, in a Third- or Fourth-Year Review

Auburn provides extensive annual reviews of all tenure-track faculty, so extensive that some (but not all) departments have done away with conducting the most comprehensive review in the third year. Said an assistant professor, "The annual review process in my department is very thorough; each year, I sit with the department chair and we look at everything I've done in the year and also at how close I am to meeting tenure standards, what are the expectations, and what I still need to do. There are no surprises and you don't have to wait until the third year to know where you stand."

At NC State, annual reviews provide written feedback to junior faculty about their work and progress toward tenure. Said a department head, "I am a big fan of our system; it is very clear. The process forces departments to meet with pre-tenure faculty every year and they have to work on their dossiers. The dossier shows where they are, how far they've come, and we let them know if they're on track or not and where there needs to be improvement." Assistant professors echoed this sentiment. Said one tenure-track faculty member, "The review process is very clear and consistent. I would be stunned to ever hear of anyone who was surprised in this process. There's just no way to be blindsided; it's all transparent."

Like Auburn and NC State, OSU has instituted a very thorough, well-documented, written annual review process for all faculty (see chapter 3—"Annual Review"—of the OSU *Faculty Handbook,* oaa.osu.edu/OAAP_PHand book.php). Nearly everyone we spoke with at OSU mentioned the annual review process as being very helpful from administrator and faculty points of view. In some departments, the chair does all of the annual reviews, in others they are done by committees. What is not negotiable is that annual reviews for all faculty will be conducted and written summaries provided to the faculty member and placed in the personnel file. The provost's office investigates any concerns about the conduct and completeness of annual reviews. Said an administrator, "I talk with all my assistant professors each year to go over the criteria upon which they're being evaluated. I actually use an evaluation sheet that has been developed as an Excel spreadsheet, so they can see what is counting in their evaluation for teaching, service, research dollars, publications, and their work with graduate students; it's strict, but clear." Said a senior administrator, "When we recruit new faculty they get a copy of our college promotion and tenure documents and we discuss it in the interview process. For annual reviews faculty must submit what we call a Faculty Activity Statement, which lists everything they've done in the past year including peer and student evaluations of teaching, publications, grant activity, and service."

In addition to written annual reviews at Ohio State, there is an extensive fourth-year review of all tenure-track faculty members. It is in the fourth-year review that faculty receive a really clear indication about their prospects for tenure. "Some faculty are counseled out at this time, but I've never heard anyone say that the process wasn't fair. That, in part, has to do with the messages they get every single year," explained an associate professor who received tenure at OSU. An administrator said, "In the last ten years we really tightened up on the promotion and tenure guidelines . . . insisting that there be annual reviews and the importance of the fourth-year review, and also the sixth—making sure people know what is expected from day one."

The review process at Iowa is very thorough and well documented on various websites; the College of Liberal Arts and Sciences site specifies what happens in each yearly review (see appendix C). Said a senior administrator, "Junior faculty cannot escape knowing whether they're on track or not. Even if they're deluding themselves in the first year or two, the third-year review really lays it out; they know what they should be doing and how they stack up." A department chair noted: "Every year a junior faculty member is evaluated by his or her colleagues and the evaluation is very formal. Teaching is observed, students are interviewed, the senior faculty review the service record and research productivity. We then meet as a group to discuss each person. We spend a long time going over their dossiers . . . the strengths and weaknesses; then I draft a letter for dean comment."

Iowa also does a lot to equip department heads with the tools they need to assist junior faculty. Because annual review feedback to pre-tenure faculty members is written, not just verbal, Iowa provides those who write the reviews with a website link to best practices for being comprehensive (see provost.uiowa.edu/faculty/facappt/evaluation/bestpractices.htm) and to help recipients understand how they can improve and what campus resources are available for them to do so. In addition, there is a link to "Common Problems" with annual reviews, which include consistent reports of peer observations of teaching; poor timing of comments; lack of feedback from the faculty of the secondary appointment (in cases of joint appointments); no description of the evaluation process; inadequate reappointment review; vague exhortations to "more" or "better" work (along with poor and better language for writing reviews); pure evaluation without description providing the evidentiary basis (including examples of poor and better language to use); and pure description without evaluative feedback (including

examples). (See provost.uiowa.edu/faculty/facappt/evaluation/commonprob
lems.htm.)

Those responsible for conducting annual and third-year reviews found the
website suggestions quite helpful, and junior faculty are the direct beneficiaries. An assistant professor said, "We have annual reviews that spell out where
we stand and each review culminates in a written evaluation of your teaching in a very clear, organized fashion. The same is true for scholarship. In my
department, I have to write a book and the chair was very clear each year regarding my progress. You get plenty of verbal feedback along the way, but I
like the 'on the record' part of the annual reviews that makes everything especially transparent and clear." Said another, "Every year you receive a letter
and feedback from the department consulting group (the committee that's
helping to decide on tenure for all probationary faculty in the department).
I met with the dean who gave me a notebook that basically is to help me
collect all the information I'll need for the third-year review, which is quite
similar to the tenure review I will eventually go through. My annual reviews
are all part of this process of documentation."

In addition, Iowa has a spreadsheet called "DEO Strategies for Supporting
Early Career Faculty" (as part of the provost's DEO Resources Series) that
includes sections on teaching, research/productivity, service, work-life balance, career development, and leadership at critical junctures including:
before arrival, two weeks before classes start, in the first month, in the first
year, and in the first three years. (See provost.uiowa.edu/faculty/docs/DEO-
EarlyCareerSupport.pdf.)

KU has annual reviews (see appendix D) of all assistant professors as well
as a "mini" tenure review about halfway through the tenure track. The annual reviews are used to determine merit salary increases and, for junior faculty, to document progress toward tenure. Regarding annual reviews a department chair said, "We have two different forms of annual review. We have
an annual performance review in our department that is done by the chair
and the associate chair, so junior faculty get feedback on how they're doing
relative to tenure. You've got to be a three or better in teaching and research
to be on track for tenure. In addition, another body looks at the annual review and determines if it's meritorious for a raise."

By KU *Faculty Senate Rules and Regulations*, each department must provide
all faculty members with written criteria for promotion and tenure and use a
system that specifies ratings from "excellent" to "poor" for teaching, research,

and service.[5] A senior-level administrator explained, "The university requires that each unit have explicit guidelines about the tenure and promotion process and their standards which are submitted for periodic review to the college or school and then go to the Provost's Office. Every two to three years, the guidelines come up for discussion and are reviewed by the unit to ensure that all is in order and that changes aren't required. There is a sense of explicit centralized coordination."

An assistant professor described the process in his department:

> There were meetings about what qualifies as average performance and what it would take to excel. This has evolved over time. But it has all been spelled out by the chair. I was told, "We expect you to get external funding, attend meetings to present your research, two papers per year in top journals, do invited talks, teach one course per semester" . . . and I had one semester off from teaching to get my lab started. There was some debate about service; some are very opposed to junior faculty doing any service, but my previous chair encourages it, so I do some. And I have to get a 4 (very good) or 5 (excellent) in teaching and research.

The "progress toward tenure," or third-year review, is thorough and appreciated by junior faculty and administrators alike. Tenure-track faculty are told, in writing, how they're progressing toward tenure so that adjustments can be made well before the tenure decision year. An assistant professor noted, "If you're publishing a couple of articles, in good journals, and you have a grant, you're on track for tenure . . . they understand that you're a productive scientist . . . and they inform you of what to work on harder to help ensure tenure. There are, of course, no guarantees, but the third-year review gives you a good indication of where you stand."

All faculty at UNCP undergo annual reviews, with the first one being especially thorough. At that time, faculty are either awarded a two-year contract, if all is going well, or a one-year terminal contract, if not. For new faculty, the first-year review includes an extensive self-evaluation, a student evaluation report, a peer evaluation, and a chair's report. Said an assistant professor,

> They were very clear in terms of what would happen and when and how the process works. My chair at the time was very clear in terms of saying I would be reviewed in my first year and then would receive a two-year contract if all was well; if not, I'd have a year to find another job. I knew who would be on my

committee and how that would work. No one ever said precisely what my evaluations from students would need to look like or how many publications I'd need, but I'm not advocating for that. I like having some flexibility as long as it's fair, and it seems to be.

Effective Practice 8: Provide Sample Dossiers to Pre-Tenure Faculty and Sample Feedback Letters to Those Responsible for Writing Them

In addition to being clear about expectations at the outset, North Carolina State scores so well in tenure clarity because it provides detailed descriptions and templates for the tenure dossier, and junior faculty are encouraged by the provost to start their dossiers "the minute they leave new faculty orientation."

NC State even has a senior vice provost whose job it is, in part, to look at all dossiers to ensure that all the essential elements are included; "Our office personnel are described as the 'Dossier Nazis' and in some ways we are! We read all the dossiers for content, format, length . . . everything. It's our job to make sure that nothing is missing and that the dossier is as good as it can be. What we provide ensures fairness and consistency." An assistant professor said, "There are designated people at the various schools who help us get everything together for our reviews; they do a content analysis of your student evaluations and a citation analysis and all that stuff, so I didn't have to spend the time to do all that. It was very smooth. I was amazed."

In addition to clearly stated tenure criteria, OSU's policy statements include a section (4.1.3.3), Core Dossier Outline (see appendix E), that lists all materials for teaching, research, and service that all pre-tenure faculty should include as documentation of their work in their tenure dossier.

As at Ohio State, the components of the dossier at Iowa are clearly delineated (see appendix F). "I was told about the dossier at the outset and my department chair suggested that I begin work on it almost immediately . . . to not let it slide, but to keep up with it . . . so I did, and that was a big help in not only being prepared for the annual reviews, but for always knowing where I stood," said an associate professor who had recently received tenure. An assistant professor said, "All expectations for tenure were explained to me at the outset, during the interview, actually. And at the moment we're hired, the tenure process is very transparent. The dossier documentation specifies all the key areas." Said a full professor, "This dossier outline is literally a template complete with roman numerals that says what you need to go forward for tenure." There is also a software program called OSU Pro into which faculty can enter everything needed for the core dossier.

Policy and Practice Implications

To summarize, looking across the six sites with high tenure-clarity scores, we can make several recommendations for administrators based on established models of success:

1. Tell tenure-track faculty what to expect at the outset—during the interview stage—and then reinforce that prior to their arrival on campus and again upon arrival.
2. If possible, set weights or priorities (e.g., Auburn's percentages; UNCP's weights; KU's allocation of effort; NC State's SME) with tenure-track faculty members so that they know what counts most and can focus their work in those areas. If all areas are equally important, that should also be made clear to tenure-track faculty. (OSU specifies criteria for tenure by department through patterns of administration, as does Iowa by tenure-initiating unit.)
3. If concepts such as collegiality (Auburn), outreach (Auburn; NC State), and service (UNCP) count in the tenure process, be sure to define the concept and say how it counts and how it will be measured.
4. Provide relevant written information (e.g., KU's Resources for New Faculty; NC State's provost website) and mentors/guidance. Pre-tenure faculty members should be informed about where to find all the information they need to get started and feel comfortable on campus and also about how to get tenure. They appreciate clear websites with easy links to relevant policies and people. Mentors serve to help explain not only the written policies but also the unwritten rules of the game (see chapter 6).
5. Provide new faculty orientation (Iowa, KU, NC State) as well as workshops (Iowa, OSU, NC State, UNCP) to support effective teaching and research throughout the pre-tenure years.
6. Host Q&A sessions (KU's and NC State's public meetings) or provide other venues (Iowa's confidential website; Ohio State's fourth-year

review forum) where pre-tenure faculty can safely ask difficult
questions and have them answered by those who know.

7. Provide plenty of feedback all along the way—annually and more
thoroughly still in a third- or fourth-year review. Very few new
faculty members want less feedback; in fact, I've never heard one say,
"Too much; no more!" when it comes to performance feedback and
advice. Annual reviews, in writing, are very helpful and midpoint
reviews with specific guidance are crucial to pre-tenure faculty
clarity, satisfaction, and success. All six sites with high tenure-clarity
scores recognized the critical importance of providing thorough
reviews of pre-tenure faculty performance.

8. Provide sample dossiers (Iowa, NC State, OSU) to pre-tenure faculty
and sample feedback letters (Iowa) to those responsible for writing
them.

9. Provide education sessions, as needed, for new chairs to learn how to
deliver clear performance feedback to pre-tenure faculty annually
and more comprehensively at mid-point.

10. Hire tenure-track faculty with the expectation that they will achieve
tenure, as at NC State. This may sound obvious, but it isn't always,
and it should be explicit. After all, hiring on the tenure track is an
expensive proposition and, if all goes well, the faculty member may
stay for her/his entire career.

11. Ensure open doors to the chair and senior faculty members. The
most clear and satisfied junior faculty have access to the chair and
other senior colleagues, not only for questions about tenure but also
for feedback, opportunities to collaborate, and colleagueship (see
chapter 6).

CHAPTER FOUR

Work-Life Integration

Work-Life Integration Challenges

In any conversation with faculty, it does not take long before the issue of work-life balance, or lack thereof, arises. Many pre-tenure faculty members find themselves wrestling with the constraints imposed by the traditional tenure-track model. Academic careers are increasingly considered a mismatch for men and women facing family demands, especially those unaddressed by existing university policies. While the focus of this book is not on gender, the issue cannot be avoided in this chapter—when it comes to integrating work and home life and trying to find a sense of balance, female faculty face greater barriers than male faculty.[1]

The Balancing Act Gender Gap

Because the tenure track was originally designed to accommodate a male trajectory (Grant et al. 2000), females, whose pre-tenure experience typically coincides with their prime childbearing years, face much greater odds (Armenti 2004a). In their study of over 800 postdoctoral fellows at UC Berkeley, Mason and Goulden (2002) found that 59 percent of married women with children were considering leaving academia.

> Married women with children were far more likely than others to cite children as one of the reasons they changed their career goals away from academia, and they were the most likely to indicate that balancing career and family was a source of high stress for them. Such women worked significantly fewer hours per week in the laboratory (averaging a little over forty hours per week in comparison to more than fifty hours a week for the other groups) and presented research findings at far fewer national conferences (45 percent of married women

with children did not present findings at national conferences in the last year in comparison to only 24 percent of other groups). With these performance indicators you can imagine that their mentors, professors, and others would be less likely to recommend them for research university positions. (Mason and Goulden 2002, pp. 25–26)

According to Sorcinelli and Billings (1993), pre-tenure female academics experience far greater difficulty than males in balancing work with family commitments. Women reported significant work overload, dedicating more time to domestic tasks and child care and less to academic research and teaching (Mason and Goulden 2004b). It is likely for this reason that many abandon their tenure pursuits in favor of job opportunities that allow for improved work flexibility (Mason et al. 2009b).

For those females who do stay the course and obtain tenure, personal sacrifices must be made. Women who achieved tenure were more than twice as likely as their male counterparts to be single twelve years after earning the Ph.D. (37 percent versus 15 percent) and were more likely to be single and childless than were male academics (26 percent versus 11 percent) (Mason and Goulden 2004a). While the majority of male academics were married with children, nearly half of their female counterparts remained childless, regardless of marital status, 51 versus 63 percent (Perna 2001). Yet this is in direct conflict with the desire of most Americans to marry and have children (Thornton and Young-DeMarco 2001).

The Pipeline

According to the National Science Foundation (2009), in 2008 the number of doctorates awarded to men rose by 95 (to 26,271) over the previous year, while those awarded to women rose by 612 (to 22,496). Women's share of all doctorates earned in 2008 was 46 percent, similar to that in 2007; 2008 was the thirteenth consecutive year in which the representation of female doctorate recipients has surpassed 40 percent. The percentage of all doctorate recipients who are women has increased from 27 percent in 1978, to 42 percent in 1998, to 45 percent in 2003.

In addition, the proportion of doctorates earned by women has grown consistently within all broad fields of study. In 2008, women constituted 67 percent of all education doctorates and the majority in social sciences (58 percent), life sciences (53 percent), and humanities (52 percent). The representation of women among doctorate recipients in physical sciences and engineering was 28 percent and 22 percent respectively, up from 10 percent and 2 percent in 1978. Women earned 41 percent of the science and engineering doctorates and 58 percent in non–science and engineering fields.

While not all who earn doctorates intend to pursue academic careers, many do. Yet, as revealed in chapter 1, women represent a lower percentage of the tenure track (44 percent) and tenured faculty (30 percent). The deficit of women faculty is especially pronounced in the sciences. For example, women constituted only 8.7 percent of tenured math and science professors (Winkler 2000). Women who couple tenure-track careers with family responsibilities experienced greater stress (Civian 2009), which can, in part, be attributed to the long acknowledged "greedy" nature of careers in science and engineering disciplines, requiring full, unwavering commitment. Such an investment leaves little room for work-life balance, prompting many women to exit academia (Grant et al. 2000). Mason et al. (2009b) found that when starting their doctoral programs 45 percent of males and 39 percent of females wanted to pursue a professorship with a research focus. However, at follow-up (one to seven years later) only 36 percent of men and 27 percent of women maintained this career goal.

In fact, research has shown that marriage and having young children have strong negative effects on the probability of women *entering* tenure-track positions (Mason et al. 2006).

> Married men with children under 6 are 50 percent more likely than married women with children under 6 to join the ranks of tenure-track faculty in the first year out from the Ph.D.; this increased likelihood holds steady for all years after Ph.D. receipt. Because single women without children under 6 do as well as married men with children under 6, family formation completely explains why women are less likely than men to enter tenure-track positions. The message is clear: for women, babies and marriage, particularly in combination, dramatically decrease their likelihood of entering a tenure-track faculty position.

Marriage

Upon marriage, women have traditionally fulfilled the role of caregiver to the home, looking after both house and husband. In turn, woman's tenure outcomes have been negatively affected. While a single female has greater odds of obtaining tenure than a male, the opposite is true for a married woman (Wolfinger et al. 2008).

Historically speaking, male academics have played the role of bread-winner, while their wives have claimed responsibility for household chores. This is largely true in academia, as 89 percent of female academics are married to full-time working professionals as opposed to only 56 percent of men (Mason et al. 2009b); the propagation of this gender-role expectation adversely affects female academics' productivity in relation to that of their male colleagues. Relative to their spouses, women spend significantly more time on household tasks; for example, although percentages vary by activity, 59 percent of tenure-track women claim to perform all household cleaning (O'Laughlin and Bischoff 2005).

Somewhat surprisingly, single women publish slightly less than their married counterparts (Davis and Astin 1990). For those who marry academics within their discipline, publication rates increased by an astounding 40 percent (Winkler 2000). Because access to male-dominated academic networks has proven to be the biggest research barrier for female academics, it has been suggested that intradisciplinary marital partnerships may provide opportunities for collaboration (Sonnert and Holton 1995; Winkler 2000) and networking with other male academics (Grant et al. 2000).

Dual Academic Careers and Accompanying Spouses

It appears as though the benefits of dual-career marriages between academics are limited; such marriages tend to solely benefit females who do not leave the institution at which they began the tenure process (McElrath 1992). However, this is not always possible. Instead, a "two body problem" is likely to arise when husband or wife is offered a position that requires relocation (Wolf-Wendel et al. 2003). Because a greater percentage of female academics than males are married to other academics (18 percent vs. 13 percent), more women are affected than men (Wolfinger et al. 2008). This is likely a contributing factor in some women's voiced dissatisfaction about lacking personal authority over job decisions (Harper et al. 2001).

Although married women are likely to decline superior job offers in an effort to provide stability for their spouses' tenure prospects, research suggests that they do not expect to be treated in kind. According to Aisenberg and Harrington (1988), female academics are more likely than males to defer to their spouses when making career decisions that require a physical move.

A 1992 study by William and Denise Bielby found that over half of female respondents, but only 16 percent of men, reported a reluctance to relocate because of family considerations. This creates an "accompanying-spouse gap": women are more likely than men to trail along so their husbands can take a desirable job. The accompanying-spouse gap translates very directly into a salary gap (Williams 2003).

In addition, typically, accompanying spouses are considered for only part-time teaching positions at their spouses' new institution. Even under the rare circumstances that a full-time, tenure-track position is made available, tenure-review committees are susceptible to the assumption that an accompanying spouse is not serious about her/his career (Williams 2003). According to Cooke (2001), the gap might more appropriately be called the "accompanying mother gap"; a woman is much more likely to accommodate her spouse's career when children are involved. Overall, 66 percent of married female academics with children and 64 percent of married female academics without children placed greater emphasis upon their husband's career than their own. In fact, of married women with children under six years of age, 72 percent cite family commitments as a limitation to their job search. For males, the most popular answer is "no suitable job" (Mason et al. 2006).

Lack of Dual-Career Accommodations

In performing a large-scale survey of four-year colleges and universities, Raabe (1997) found that 44 percent of institutions offer job assistance to new hires' spouses; such policies were unwritten at 58 percent of those institutions. Additionally, the definition of "domestic partner" varies by institution; at 55 percent of institutions, a "domestic partner" cannot be claimed outside of legal marriage (Wolf-Wendel et al. 2003). Yet, as an increasing number of academic couples are cohabiting, a growing policy problem has resulted. Two-thirds of research institutions use dual-career assistance as a means of recruiting top scholars while engaging in "bidding wars" with other schools (Williams and Norton 2008). However, this practice deprives "lower-profile" spouses of equally needed assistance (McElrath 1992).

Stigma Attached to Dual-Career Accommodations

Despite their helpful intent, dual-career accommodations are often frowned upon by faculty colleagues and administrators. The source of funding for spouses' jobs is often controversial. In order to alleviate such concerns, schools have taken to sharing the burden of related costs. Under this agreement, the dean's office, the desired employee's department, and the accompanying spouse's department each shoulder one-third of a partner's salary (Wolf-Wendel et al. 2003). However, many faculty members look negatively upon couples' "double dipping," so to speak, as it reduces the number of positions that departments can afford to recruit and hire (Ferber and Loeb 1997).

Heightening tensions, the indirect route by which a spouse acquired her/his position is often questioned. In fact, some researchers have even deemed this practice illegal, linking it to nepotism (Shoben 1997). When an accompanying spouse's work is deemed to be of poor quality in relation to her/his department's expectations, additional resentment is likely to emerge (Wolf-Wendel et al. 2003). Should an accommodated couple divorce, institutional and departmental consequences are likely to create further tensions (Williams 2000).

Motherhood

Regardless of marital status, female academics who wish to become mothers must contend with the "simultaneous ticking" of their tenure and biological clocks (Armenti 2004b). According to the 2006 *Survey of Earned Doctorates*, 33.2 marks the median age at which females earn their degrees. Yet, due to publication pressures, many females decide to wait until tenure is secured to begin their families. Although 64 percent of female doctoral students expect to eventually have children, most do not want to raise children while also pursuing their degree (Mason et al. 2009a). However, it is interesting to note that although 33 percent of women consider the tenure fast track to be family friendly at the *start* of their graduate studies, this percentage decreases to 16 percent upon becoming a parent (Mason et al. 2009a).

In making the decision to delay parenthood until after graduate school, however, the complications associated with childbearing increase. Despite attempts to remain healthy, women's fertility markedly decreases each year into their thirties, with significant declines after age forty (Armenti 2004b). Additionally, by becoming pregnant outside of her childbearing prime, a woman places herself and her child at increased health risk for complications such as preterm delivery and low birth weight (Mather 1998). Colbeck and Drago (2005) reported that, among the women faculty they surveyed, 16 percent stayed single because they did not believe they had time for a family and a successful academic career, 25.5 percent had fewer children than they wanted in order to achieve academic success, and nearly 13 percent delayed having a second child until after receiving tenure.

While female faculty with children reported an average total of 101 hours per week engaged in professional, housework, and caregiving activities, male faculty with children reported an average of 88 hours per week engaged in these activities; and men and women faculty without children reported an average of 78 hours per week (Mason and Goulden 2004b). Research has shown that female faculty with dependent children exhibit lower levels of research productivity than their counterparts without dependent children; among men, however, having dependent children is associated with greater research productivity (Sax et al. 2002). In faculty surveys, Davis and Astin (1990) found that women were much more likely than males to view family commitments as an obstacle to research productivity.

Work Constraints Imposed by Pregnancy

Armenti's (2004b) research revealed that young women assistant professors receive three primary messages from their senior women colleagues about motherhood and the tenure track: (1) taking time off from work for child care can be harmful to their career progression; (2) benefits such as maternity leave, child care, and the extension of the tenure clock by one year for the birth of a child do not cover every woman's needs; and (3) having children before tenure can reduce the likelihood of achieving tenure.

Female faculty are frequently urged by both colleagues and advisors to have their children in the month of May. It is at this time, after classes have ended and teaching responsibilities have temporarily ceased, that women may take advantage of a somewhat built-in "mini" maternity leave that will not draw departmental scrutiny (Armenti 2004b). Yet, for many, this desire does not translate into a reality. From a purely biological perspective, impregnation in the month of October is not possible for all females. In reality, the biological and time-related concerns have created the notion of a "child crunch time" that is both unrealistic and an unhealthy pressure (Mather 1998).

The anticipated career "time bind" (Hochschild 1997) factors into female faculty's pregnancy decisions, regardless of fertility issues; nearly half of female academics are both single and childless in comparison to only 30 percent of males (Caplan 1993). According to Phillipsen (2008), although two-thirds of tenure-track women hope to eventually have or adopt children, many are unwilling to do so outside of marriage.

Nearly half of women reported . . . that certain responsibilities—such as attending conferences or giving conference papers (46 percent), other professional work that requires travel away from home (48 percent), and the time-intensive activities of writing and publishing (48 percent)—cause them a great deal of stress in their parenting. In contrast, less than 30 percent of men faculty parents reported that the same activities placed a great deal of stress on their parenting (22 percent experienced a great deal of stress from attending conferences, 29 percent from writing and publishing, and 27 percent from fieldwork away from home). (Mason and Goulden 2004b)

Effect of Parenting on Tenure Outcomes for Females

Regardless of marital status, female academics who are also parents must continually wrestle with maintaining publication productivity. As 27 percent of female academics look toward providing elder care for aging parents (often while also caring for their own children), family demands and pressure are heightened (Drago and Williams 2000). Maintaining high publication rates can prove difficult, especially in light of females' previously discussed "hidden" workload (Kolodny 1998).

While the likelihood of obtaining tenure drastically declines for women who have children within their first five years on the tenure track (Wolfinger et al. 2008), a male academic's likelihood of obtaining tenure increases by 38 percent should he become a father during this period (Mason et al. 2006). And while a woman's odds of achieving tenure further decrease with each subsequent child, the opposite effect is seen among males (Long et. al. 1993). In fact, of parents on the tenure track, men are 20 percent more likely than women to achieve tenure; for couples with children under the age of six, this percentage increases to 50 (Wolfinger et al. 2008).

Yet despite such clear evidence of the negative impact that childbearing has on women's tenure, researchers continue to argue about the relative impact of motherhood on differences in the tenure rate. While some researchers have found motherhood to result in significantly lower publication rates (Sonnert and Holton 1996; Stack 2004), others have found no apparent differences (Kyvik 1990). Others suggest that gender-related discrepancies are largely dependent upon children's ages. When examining tenure-track parents' research productivity in respect to children's ages, mothers of preschool-age children are by far the most productive (Fox 1995a), perhaps because of time-management skills learned in graduate school. To have a child in this age group, a woman either gave birth during graduate school or early in her tenure-track position. Such mothers tend to be very discretionary in their time allocation, drastically limiting any leisure time in order to focus solely upon career and family (Sax et al. 2002). It is perhaps for this reason that, among male and female faculty parents, this group has the strongest likelihood of achieving tenure; in fact, members of this group have better odds of gaining tenure than do their single female counterparts (Fox 2005).

Lack of Accommodations for Faculty Parents

At most schools, campus child care centers do not include extended hours for evening classes (Hornosty 1998). Should a faculty member need to travel or perform service responsibilities, few child care options are made available. In fact, when asked if child care concerns had resulted in missing an overnight conference or bringing a child to work due to a lack of options, women were 28 percent more likely than males to answer yes (Riemenschneider and Harper 1990).

The expenses of child care pose a significant financial issue to tenure-track parents. This is especially true for single-parent females, as, on average, female assistant professors earned lower salaries than their male counterparts (Bellas 1997). Benefits tended to be male-oriented in scope, offering incentives such as reduced tuition rates for faculty children. Yet, of female faculty members who are mothers, four out of ten had a child under the age of eighteen (Civian, 2009). In the short term, such women were more worried about the immediate costs of child care than about future college expenses.

Of those tenure-track women who do become pregnant outside of a May due date, the stakes are raised. Only 58 percent of institutions in the Association of American Universities offer paid parental leave. Furthermore, many policies only cover up to six weeks. Although all schools are required to observe the Federal Anti-discrimination Pregnancy Act, one in three institutions do not (Williams 2000). At odds with Title IX (instituted in1974 to protect against unfriendly family policies in the field of education), few schools comply in treating pregnancy as a disability in terms of benefits and length of leave.

Largely in response to demands to accommodate such absences and to a 2001 addendum to the American Association of University Professors 1974 statement "Leaves of Absence for Child-Bearing, Child-Rearing, and Family Emergencies," called "Statement of Principles on Family Responsibilities and

Academic Work," stop-the-clock tenure policies are now available at most universities. Although regulations vary by institution, faculty members may now stop the tenure clock for a year at a time but generally no more than twice within nine years. In this manner, for each year that the clock is stopped, another year is added before tenure review (AAUP 2001).

While this is a step forward, the AAUP admits in its 2001 statement that "institutional policies may be easier to change than institutional cultures," and therefore, "colleges and universities should monitor the actual use of their policies over time to guarantee that every faculty member—regardless of gender—has a genuine opportunity to benefit from policies encouraging the integration of work and family responsibilities. The goal of every institution should be to create an academic community in which all members are treated equitably, families are supported, and family-care concerns are regarded as legitimate and important." A more responsive climate for integrating work and family responsibilities is essential for women professors to participate on an equal basis with their male colleagues in higher education. Recognizing the need for broader and more inclusive policies represents a historic moment of change. The association encourages both women and men to take advantage of legal and institutional change so that all faculty members may participate more fully in the care of their children and may provide the necessary care for parents and other family members.

Indeed, it remains questionable whether and how the tenure criteria will change should a faculty member choose to stop the clock. Many faculty are fearful that they will be penalized should they present a year of decreased research productivity (Armenti 2004a). Complicating matters, review committees are also uncertain as to how assessment *should* be changed. In fact, less than 5 percent of tenure-review committees are even made aware when a candidate has stopped the tenure clock (Jaschik 2009a).

Biases against Utilizing Family-Friendly Policies

Yoest and Rhodes (2004) discovered that there is a significant relationship between the usage of family-friendly policies and perceptions of departmental supportiveness. In departments thought to be "very supportive" of maternal leave policies, 84 percent of women took a leave after childbirth. At those perceived to be "somewhat supportive" of such policies, the percentage dropped to 57 percent. Violations of family-friendly policies go largely underreported primarily because of fears of institutional reprisal by tenure-review committees. Forty-two percent of tenure-track females report returning to work sooner after childbirth than they would have liked (Mason et al. 2009b).

In the hopes of increasing their tenure chances, women often accept the "ideal worker" (Williams 2000) bias, as in the following.

> The apparent absence of work/family conflict, in tandem with the facts that academic women take on fewer family commitments than academic men, can be explained through appeal to the "ideal worker" norm. . . . In general, the ideal worker is someone who enters a profession immediately upon receiving the relevant academic credential, works her/his way up the career ladder by putting in long hours without interruptions beyond short vacations, and continues in this fashion until retirement age. The ideal worker can contribute financially to the family, but cannot make substantial time commitments to children or other family members without endangering her/his career. Pay and promotion systems, practices, and rules around working time, absence, vacations, and retirement systems, and the beliefs of those from previous generations who have succeeded as ideal workers and currently manage our organizations, are all built upon the presumption that only ideal workers should be hired, retained, and rewarded.
>
> For faculty at U.S. colleges and universities, the ideal worker is someone who goes straight through school and receives the terminal degree (typically a Ph.D.) in their late twenties, and immediately takes a full-time position as an assistant professor on the tenure track. The individual usually receives a mixture of relatively short-term contracts during this time (one to three years), and can be released with few if any penalties for the institution. While on the tenure track, the ideal worker performs a modicum of service work, builds a teaching dossier, and strives to generate research resulting in publication, typically in peer-reviewed journals. At the beginning of the sixth year, the faculty member documents her/his accomplishments; the resulting package is reviewed by faculty at other institutions and at various levels within the college or university. At the end of the academic year (most often in June), the faculty member is notified as to whether s/he will be promoted to the position of associate professor with tenure, or will instead be released by the institution at the end of the seventh year of employment (called the "terminal year" in such cases). (Drago 2002, pp. 4–5)

Female faculty in "women-friendly" departments composed primarily of other females are more likely to utilize the leave options made available to them (Drago et al. 2006). Yet even these women find themselves in the midst of the "mommy wars," constantly defending their actions to those who believe an increased emphasis should be placed on either academia or parenthood (Williams et al. 2006).

As a result of these pressures, many women put their academic careers on hold to spend more time with their children. Unfortunately, however, re-entry into tenure-track positions is unlikely. Once a woman is three years removed from obtaining her doctorate, the likelihood of obtaining such employment substantially decreases each year (Wolfinger et. al. 2009). Yet more and more females are attempting to do so. Attempts to re-enter tenure-track positions are especially common among parents whose children have recently reached school age (Mason and Goulden 2004b). However, most of these parents find that they need to have some sort of recent research experience. As a result, a postdoctorate or other research fellowship first becomes necessary (Mervis 1999).

According to Finkel and Olswang (1996), the majority of female academics are convinced that even taking a short-term parental leave will be detrimental to their tenure prospects. For example, although there were five hundred new parents among Penn State faculty between 1992 and 1999, only seven parental leaves were taken, all by females (Williams et al. 2006). Another study of over thirteen hundred faculty at a large research university (Finkel et al. 1994) showed that immediately following childbirth, 33 percent of women chose to forgo their designated maternity leaves because of tenure-related concerns; only 30 percent of women faculty took the full amount of leave for childbirth allotted by their university. However, 75 percent of women felt that they would take the entire amount of leave if other female colleagues would do the same.

Need for Work-Life Policies
Domestic Partners and Other Situations

Institutions must develop a more inclusive definition of family that extends beyond "a man, a woman, and their children." This is especially true as 27 percent of female academics expect to become elder care providers to their aging parents (Civian 2009). Furthermore, the number of homosexuals represented in academia is nearing 10 percent, and thus more domestic partners are requiring benefits (Miller and Skeen 1997). As such, the need for changes in institutional policy is growing.

Family-Friendliness

In order to encourage family-friendly policies, organizations like the Alfred P. Sloan Foundation have recognized schools that are implementing positive changes to increase work-life balance and financially support tenure-track faculty (Wolf-Wendel et al. 2003). As the majority of these issues relate to marriage and motherhood, improved dual-career and parental assistance are areas that have received great emphasis.

Dual Careers

In providing dual-career assistance, long-term domestic partners (regardless of gender) must be assisted accordingly. Relocation offices should be created to aid in this effort in order to foster collegiality and welcome new hires to the university community (Wolf-Wendel et al. 2003). Additionally, should a spouse require employment, a central financing office should be created in order to fund both short- and long-term academic and administrative positions (Williams and Norton 2008). This takes pressure off of department chairs, who are often blamed for spouses' job outcomes regardless of their personal responsibility in the matter (Wolf-Wendel et al. 2003). For accompanying spouses who seek tenure-track positions, there are certain measures that can be taken in order to avoid a growing accompanying-spouse gap.

Shared Positions

Shared tenure-track positions can be created in which both partners share a single position. This is an especially desirable option should the partners desire to work at the same university. Such an accommodation allows for greater collaboration and, as a result, better work-life balance (Sweet and Moen 2004). Should this not be a possibility, the relocation assistance office can be particularly helpful in supporting the accompanying partner's search for a tenure-track position at another institution, shortening time-consuming job searches (Fleig-Palmer et al. 2003). Finally, should a new position be created for a accompanying spouse, a central funding office should initially pay the new hire's salary in order to alleviate departmental tensions. Then, if the department is satisfied with the hire after one year, the expense of her/his salary could then be shifted to the department itself (Wolf-Wendel et al. 2003).

Child Care

In offering parental assistance, child care is perhaps the easiest and most affordable accommodation that a university can provide. Moreover, it is deemed both most necessary and helpful by faculty. Schools should provide on-site child care facilities with hours that stretch into the evening; ideally, parents should be provided with funded child care provisions during work-related activities such as dinners and overnight conferences (Perna 2001). In addition to regular child care, emergency arrangements should also be made readily available, as a child can easily become too sick for day care or a care-taker's own schedule may change (McGuire et al. 2004).

Automatic Stop-the-Clock Provisions

To avoid the biases associated with needed maternity leaves, a few schools have implemented an automatic stopped tenure clock (Jaschik 2009a). In this manner, the choice to stop the tenure clock is pre-made; as a result, administrators cannot discourage usage. Consequently, parental leave is no longer viewed as a reward reserved for only the most promising faculty. This blankets women from further scrutiny once a woman has made the decision to have a child (Williams and Norton 2008). To complement this deferral, it is necessary that tenure-review committees be well informed as to the uniform implementation of deviations from the traditional assessment process (Drago and Williams 2000).

Part-Time Tenure Track and Modified Duties

Half-time tenure tracks (faculty work part-time and are compensated as such, doubling the amount of time leading up to tenure review) should also be made available to faculty members. Although such arrangements secretively exist at many institutions on a departmental basis, few faculty members are aware of their availability (Drago et al. 2006). These positions would be particularly helpful for dual-career couples and would allow females to work while also attending to extensive caregiving commitments (Mason and Goulden 2004b). Although those who elected to follow this track might be viewed as less serious academics by their colleagues, they should also be held to distinctly different expectations (Williams and Norton 2008).

The Road Ahead

With noted variation between institutions, the tenure track continues to best accommodate the traditional male trajectory, especially at research universities. As a result, due to the competing demands presented by research and home life, women feel obligated to choose between the two. However, with the increasing emergence of family-friendly policies, new stakes have been raised. As females wrestle with departmental pressures, many are hesitant to take advantage of such options. Consequently, younger generations of female academics must push for an acceptance of needed accommodations, pulling in the support of colleagues and administrators in the process. Both women and academia are sure to benefit from this progress toward work-life balance, an entitlement that male academics have long taken for granted.

COACHE Work-Life Data

The COACHE survey asks questions about having and raising children while on the tenure track as well as a couple of broader questions about balancing work and home life. Table 4.1 shows the average agreement scores and table 4.2 shows the average rating for satisfaction with balance.

This score for overall balance, 2.81, and the scores for one's institution doing what it can to make having and raising children and the tenure track compatible are among the lowest ratings on the entire survey. Further, while the focus of this book is not on gender, women rate all of these items significantly lower than men.

The COACHE survey also asks respondents to rate the importance and effectiveness of several policies and practices, including three[2] that have to do with work-life integration. The average policy importance ratings are shown in table 4.3 and the average effectiveness ratings are shown in table 4.4.

Women rated all of these policies as significantly more important and significantly less effective than men. Overall, the gaps between importance and effectiveness are 0.67 for stop-the-clock and 0.65 for personal leave policies; however, the gap on child care is quite large, 1.10, revealing what we know from the literature—that child care provisions on many of our campuses are lacking. In some cases, there is no affordable, quality child care on campus,

Table 4.1. COACHE Survey Average Ratings about Colleague Respect for Work-Family Balance and Compatibility of the Tenure-Track and Having and Raising Children

Please indicate your level of agreement or disagreement with each of the following statements:	Average Rating
My colleagues are respectful of my efforts to balance work and home responsibilities.	3.81
My departmental colleagues do what they can to make *having* children and the tenure track compatible.	3.51
My departmental colleagues do what they can to make *raising* children and the tenure track compatible.	3.47
My institution does what it can to make *having* children and the tenure track compatible.	2.93
My institution does what it can to make *raising* children and the tenure track compatible.	2.76

Scale: 5 = Strongly agree; 4 = Somewhat agree; 3 = Neither agree nor disagree; 2 = Somewhat disagree; and 1 = Strongly disagree

Table 4.2. COACHE Survey Average Rating on Satisfaction with Balance between Work and Home Responsibilities

Please indicate your level of satisfaction or dissatisfaction with . . .	Average Rating
the balance your are able to strike between your professional time and your personal or family time?	2.81

Scale: 5 = Very satisfied; 4 = Satisfied; 3 = Neither satisfied nor dissatisfied; 2 = Dissatisfied; and 1 = Very dissatisfied

Table 4.3. COACHE Survey Average Ratings about the Importance of Work-Life Policies

Please rate how important or unimportant the following policies and practices would be to your success, regardless of whether they currently apply to your institution.	Average Rating
Stop-the-clock for parental or other family reasons	3.98
Paid or unpaid personal leave during the pre-tenure period	3.72
Child care	3.59

Scale: 5 = Very important; 4 = Important; 3 = Neither important nor unimportant; 2 = Unimportant; and 1 = Very unimportant

Table 4.4. COACHE Survey Average Ratings about the Effectiveness of
Work-Life Policies

Please rate the effectiveness or ineffectiveness of the following policies and practices at your institution.	Average Rating
Stop-the-clock for parental or other family reasons	3.31
Paid or unpaid personal leave during the pre-tenure period	3.07
Child care	2.49

Scale: 5 = Very effective; 4 = Effective; 3 = Neither effective nor ineffective; 2 = Ineffective; and 1 = Very ineffective

and in other cases there is not enough to meet demand and waiting lists are long.

In a prior qualitative study at four private and two public research universities (Trower and Gallagher 2008b, p. 28), we explored the issue of child care. Said one provost: "If there's one thing pre-tenure faculty members consistently ask us about, it's child care: Who provides it? Where? How much? Does the university subsidize it? How long is the waiting list? And we just don't have any good answers. This is not an easy problem to solve." A dean said: "If I had a magic wand and could fix one thing that would help us attract, recruit, and retain junior faculty members it would be child care. It's the great leveler—no single institution of which I'm aware has solved this problem satisfactorily . . . or even partially. Sure, we have daycare, but it is inadequate and it doesn't handle sick children."

Several of those interviewed felt that the lack of adequate child care affects women much more so than men. A chair stated, "I believe that a major reason for the paucity of female full professors rests with the issue of getting tenure during the childbearing years; so we can either do away with tenure as we know it (an idea I support) or settle child care issues once and for all." An assistant professor noted that "work-life balance is a big issue, especially for women. There are so many women now with doctorates who are finding that, for a lot of complicated reasons, the [academic] structure is not supporting the various choices they need to make about elder care and child care and there still aren't many remedies." A full professor was particularly direct by saying that the reason she was able to have children and make full professor was because she has a stay-at-home husband: "If not for that, I'm not sure how I would have been able to do it all."

Campuses with High Work-Life Scores

Five universities scored especially well on work-life balance: Auburn, Ohio State, the University of Illinois at Urbana-Champaign, the University of Iowa, and the University of North Carolina at Pembroke. First, some important aspects are noted for each campus followed by factors that make a difference in work-life balance scores that are common to several campuses.

Auburn University

Unlike several other institutions in this study, Auburn did not have a special work-family section on the provost's website, nor could I discern any special policy language around these issues. It was not in regard to policies for having and raising children that Auburn scored well, but it scored in the 97th percentile on work-life balance, primarily because of the quality of life in town, family-friendliness on campus, and flexibility on course scheduling.

Ohio State University

OSU scored really well on the COACHE survey in terms of institutional support for having and raising children and work-life balance. The OSU Office of Human Resources' website is replete with information about work-life integration. The site's numerous pages dedicated to the topic (see hr.osu.edu/worklife/) include "Caring for Children," "Caring for Older Adults," "Domestic Partnership," "Healthy Living," "Education and Training," "Events," "Faculty Resources," "Helpful Policies and Services," "Community Programs and Committees," "Share Your Ideas" (with contact information for a Work Life Specialist), and "Awards and Recognition of OSU" (for quality of work-life integration). The "Caring for Children" page includes a "Parental Care Guidebook" with the following October 2004 quote from then university president Karen Holbrook and then provost Barbara Snyder: "At The Ohio State University, we expect great things and know that these expectations cannot be realized without our greatest assets . . . our faculty and staff. We acknowledge the importance of providing faculty and staff with the ability to better integrate their work/life needs."

In addition, in 2004, the president and provost requested that a committee be formed to review current practices and propose new ones for enhancing faculty careers. The Faculty Career Enhancement Committee's *Final Report* (November 2005) states: "The University at all levels should explicitly acknowledge that faculty members' personal and professional lives intertwine." To that end, the committee made seven recommendations:

1. The Office of Academic Affairs (OAA) should help chairs learn to be alert to the pressures that faculty members' personal lives exert on their professional lives and to communicate that awareness to their faculty.

2. The university should support Human Resources' consideration of further dual-career hiring efforts on and off campus.

3. The university should offer to coordinate the advertising of OSU's Columbus and regional campus vacant faculty positions with hiring opportunities at nearby Ohio colleges and universities in order to widen employment possibilities for all hires with academic partners.

4. The OAA should better publicize internally and to potential faculty the provision that already exists for part-time tenure-track faculty appointments.

5. The university should make emergency drop-in and snow-day day care as well as elder care (or at least elder care referrals) available to faculty.

6. Since faculty also do academic work at home, the university should ensure that they have the technological access in their home workspace that they have at their campus office.

7. The university should create a system that permits gradual retirement that might encourage some faculty to consider retiring sooner (from some if not all aspects of an appointment) and that would assist faculty members in making gradual transitions to retirement.

University of Illinois at Urbana-Champaign

UIUC scored in the 95th and 97th percentile, respectively, on institutional support for raising and having children; in addition, it scored really well in terms of colleague support for raising and having children.

University of Iowa

Iowa scored in the 97th and 98th percentile on institutional support for having and raising children, respectively. In addition, it scored in the 94th percentile on work-life balance and received high marks for the effectiveness of its stop-the-clock policy. Iowa's Faculty Handbook includes an extensive section on work-life balance that includes sixteen links to practices and policies (e.g., adoption resources, domestic partner benefits, dual-career network, elder care and child care, lactation rooms, and a wellness program), which may be found at provost.uiowa.edu/faculty/fachandbk/worklife.htm.

University of North Carolina at Pembroke

UNCP faculty rated theirs among the highest of all institutions in the COACHE survey on a number of work-life dimensions. It was rated in the 100th percentile for both institutional support for raising children and colleague support for having and raising children.

Factors That Matter Most for Work-Life Balance

Factor 1: Quality of Life

Faculty and administrators on all five campuses featured in this chapter talked about the quality of life in the various college towns where each institution is located, and its importance to the satisfaction of tenure-track faculty who choose those locales. A number of dimensions were discussed as helping a location score well for quality of life, including being a place where

- it's safe and relatively easy to raise kids (Auburn, UIUC, Iowa, Ohio State); good schools are available (UIUC, Iowa, Ohio State);
- housing is affordable; the cost of living is low (Auburn, UIUC, Ohio State);
- commuting times are short, making life more hassle-free (Auburn, UIUC, Iowa); and
- many parks and recreation areas are to be found; likewise, cultural centers and programs; boutiques, galleries, and restaurants; and activities for kids (UIUC, Iowa).

For many, high quality of life means a small town where there's a strong sense of community (e.g., "everyone knows everyone here") and where the university figures prominently (Auburn, UIUC, Iowa, UNCP); for some, it means a place where there are lots of young professionals raising families (Ohio State); for others, it means a "low distraction" (UIUC, UNCP), "livable" (Iowa), or "slower-paced" (Auburn) environment. An administrator at Auburn noted,

"There's simply a different concept of time here. There is enough time to spend chatting with your colleagues, especially senior colleagues, about what you need to do [as a junior faculty member], and working with them on research. This is also enough time when the end of the day comes around, to close the door and go home or take the kids to soccer practice or do whatever you've got to do. It's actually possible to have a life here."

On all of the campuses, people articulated the beauty and simplicity of "living in a small college town" or suburbs that allows them to "balance everything that's important in life." Said a faculty member at UIUC, "It's easy to live here . . . to have the lifestyle that you want. You can have kids and have a life here. It's a small enclosed community where your work life and your home life don't necessarily have to be at odds with one another." Said another, "The normal friction of daily living—getting the car fixed, going to the grocery store, taking the kids to the dentist, picking up the dry cleaning—is about as painless as it can be!"

Factor 2: Family-Friendly Campus

Faculty at Auburn, UNCP, Iowa, and Ohio State talked about the family-friendliness on their campuses and articulated why that matters to tenure-track faculty satisfaction. At UNCP and Auburn, the family focus doesn't arise from formal policies but instead from a genuine sense of family in departments and across campus. A department chair at Auburn noted, "There's an appreciation that different people have different priorities at various stages in their lives so it's okay for the younger faculty to have their kids around." At Auburn and UNCP, there "isn't much to do around town, so there are numerous informal, home-like, family kinds of things going on." A senior administrator at Auburn noted, "There's a certain convenience in this small town that has created a very good place for women to succeed, including women who have to balance work and family. People in town pride themselves on Auburn as a good place to live, and because it's very family-friendly, you're expected to take care of your family. Some places aren't like that; they frown on leaving to take care of loved ones, but not here."

A number of interviewees at Ohio State talked about how family-friendly the campus is, including the working mothers support network run by the Work-Life Office, which holds numerous "lunch and learn" sessions as well as informal brown-bag lunches just to talk; lactation rooms (which grew in number from two to seventeen with a stated goal of having one within a five- to ten-minute walk from anywhere on campus); and support in certain departments for balancing work and home life. An associate professor noted that "the barriers to having a good family life just don't exist here like other places; you can have wonderful work-life balance." On-site day care is also available, although space is limited; the president is aware of the situation and is working with Mattel, Nationwide, and Time Warner, which have large child care facilities, to seek spaces for OSU families. Furthermore, in order to show support for faculty with families, one chair noted, "I don't start meetings before 8:30 because I know that a lot of my faculty have to drop kids off at day care. We have been told this in one of our leadership classes . . . and not to have meetings past 4:30 because parents need to pick up their kids."

The University of Iowa likewise has numerous lactation rooms around campus—a relatively new feature. Several of those interviewed mentioned how supportive their departments are for faculty with family obligations. A department chair said, "There's just a wonderful support system on campus, in the departments. People are aware of whose kids play on sports teams and how they're doing or go to the games. I remember department colleagues going to my kid's performances in high school." An assistant professor remarked, "I know a lot of the faculty have kids in my department—men and women—and it's okay. No one makes a big deal about it or worries about everyone working hard enough. We all do and the work gets done, but people also have lives outside of here." Said another tenure-track faculty member, "The culture is very family-oriented . . . when there's a party or an event, grad students and young faculty bring their kids. Maybe it's an Iowa thing, I don't know. But there's this critical mass of families, and that attracts people. My career and my family matter to me, and I need to have balance in my life."

Factor 3: Flexibility

The faculty at Auburn, Ohio State, and the UIUC articulated how flexibility is such an important factor in work-life and family balance. At Auburn, flexibility comes primarily in the form of course and office schedules that match faculty preferences for work-life balance. Said one assistant professor, "It is definitely not an 8 to 5 culture where there are times when you have to be in your office with the door open." Said another tenure-track faculty member, "My department chair asks what days and times work best for all the faculty to teach classes . . . and it's okay if I choose to work at home sometimes . . .

which helps my productivity because there are no interruptions. We have a balance of different styles by which people work based on how they like to interact and what their family requirements are."

Interviewees at OSU also talked about the flexibility afforded by the university, especially in terms of working at home, or at least not always in one's office, and scheduling courses. Said an administrator, "We have built a reward structure that incentivizes people to get out there and work across colleges. In addition, people are working at home more if that enhances their productivity." A chair described his department: "We have one member of the department who has to go home at 2:30 to get a child. Another junior faculty member had a very ill mother and needed to take some time off. So we pitched in and taught her courses for her during this time . . . that's the kind of flexibility we have here. Overall, it's a win-win situation that we're creating. I'm really doing my best to support those faculty members in their family life and the work situation, particularly with aging parents."

A senior administrator noted, "Part of the faculty career flexibility initiative is to create ways for faculty to ramp up and ramp down[3] when needed . . . to take time off—years off, even—and then come back . . . alternative ways that they can get tenure. This career flexibility as a whole is really tied to our culture and our talent initiatives."

Faculty life at UIUC allows flexibility for those who are parents and those who are not. Those interviewed said that it's about getting the work done in whatever manner works best for the individual. A senior administrator recalled that when he was a department head he had two young kids at home and was able to stay home one day a week. On that day, he focused on his research, and had no complaints from the faculty; "as long as you fulfill your responsibilities and you're accessible to your students, you can set up a [work-home] system that works for you," a tenure-track faculty member said, "On Thursdays, no one's at my house, so I work in my office there with no distractions . . . and everyone is fine with that. As long as you get the job done, people are pretty flexible about when and where you do it." Another assistant professor noted that "the institution loves us having children . . . or seems to. The dean has two small kids; the associate dean has two in high school. My wife and I are able to schedule our classes on different days, because of the baby . . . because you never know when he might get sick and one of us has to be there. We have always received remarkable flexibility from this institution. I just have never seen any pressure brought to bear by the institution. Let's face it, we're all Type A's . . . we'll get the job done."

Factor 4: Personnel Dedicated to Work-Life and Family Issues

The Ohio State Office of Human Resources "Education and Training" webpage includes a podcast entitled "Work Life at OSU" that explains benefits, services, and programs offered by the university. (See hr.osu.edu/worklife /education.aspx.) The webpage also includes sections for adoption assistance, breastfeeding/lactation space, child care (there is child care on campus, but with a waiting list), working mothers support network, dependent care task force, teenagers, resources to cope with tragedy, and promoting your child's development. Campus interviews revealed that a woman president and provost had "real impact" because "they put the work-life piece front and center and that has continued for a decade." Numerous policies are in place as well as some staff whose entire focus is the support of work-life integration; there is also the Women's Place, an advocacy center for women, that focuses on writing and promoting policies that are "good not just for women, but for everyone," said a senior administrator.

The staff and faculty were surveyed in 2001 and 2003, respectively, about work-life issues. The surveys revealed, said an administrator, "that everyone wanted dedicated resources to improve the work-life initiative on campus. It was recommended to have an individual tasked with leading these programs . . . she developed a three- to five-year plan that got support from the president, and the provost. We were able to put policies in place like the same-sex domestic partner benefits, and our paid parental leave for both faculty and staff. We did a vacation donation policy and the faculty flexible career initiative; there was some real traction with a woman president and provost—we had the attention of all senior leaders."

Factor 5: Formal Policies and Official Practices

Each of the exemplary institutions featured in this chapter has two or more formal policies for modified duties, tenure clock flexibility (including part-time tenure), dual-career couples, partner benefits, child care, and elder care.

Modified Duties

Faculty at Ohio State may request a reduced teaching load, along with stopping the tenure clock or without. A variety of options are presented in the

"Parental Care Guidebook" (hr.osu.edu/worklife/Parentalcareguidebook .pdf). Requests to modify one's schedule must be discussed with and approved by the head (e.g., department chair, school director, or dean) of the tenure-initiating unit (TIU), are reviewed on a case-by-case basis, and approval is at the discretion of the TIU head (contingent on factors such as the flexibility of course scheduling and available resources). During the quarter(s) before or after the birth or placement of a child, possibilities for schedule modification include but are not limited to

- reducing structured teaching assignment and increasing research or service responsibilities, thereby leaving total workload about the same but creating more flexibility with regards to schedule and work location;
- shifting courses to another quarter such that overall teaching load is unchanged; and
- shifting the off-duty quarter (applies only to nine-month faculty).

UIUC allows new parents to cut back on teaching without a reduction in salary for a specified period of time. Faculty members on modified duties status are relieved of teaching but are "expected to fulfill their other professional responsibilities that can be scheduled around the recuperation/bonding period (e.g., preparation of research proposals, papers, and course materials; supervision of graduate student research)" for a maximum period of one semester. The department is responsible for arranging for coverage of direct teaching responsibilities for the period of modified duties. As at Ohio State, the faculty member must request modified duties status, in writing, from the department head with sufficient time to allow the identification of alternate staff to teach the affected courses. Said a department head, "We have modified duties for men and women and, while it can be a bit of a burden, it's something that nobody hesitates to do . . . it's just expected that if someone has a baby, we'll find a way to give them the time they need. People actually step up to the plate to fill in and cover for colleagues while they're on leave." Said an assistant professor, "I didn't get any flack for modifying my duties when I had a child, only congratulatory energy!"

At Iowa, where there is no formal modified duties policy, departments "make it all work out somehow," said an assistant professor. A chair noted, "I'm not really sure how you would . . . or if you should . . . formalize everything. It's cultural here. The university is very proactive. I remember a young woman faculty member who was going to have a baby and I started getting calls from central administration saying, 'Here's what you need to do. Here's the paperwork she'll need.' She opted out of the stop-the-clock provision but needed to flex her teaching schedule a bit. And the other faculty just jumped in and said, 'Take all the time you need; we'll cover your classes.'" A senior administrator said, "Basically, flexibility happens. We're able to alter people's schedules when it is necessary like when someone's kid is sick or an elderly parent and they're scheduled for a clinic . . . someone steps in for them."

Tenure Clock Flexibility, Including Part-Time Tenure

At UIUC, for candidates "making appropriate, demonstrable progress toward attaining indefinite tenure," the tenure clock may be stopped (or "rolled back," in the university's policy language) for one year, up to two times, by "special written agreement" for "unusual, compelling reasons," including (1) disability or extended and/or severe personal illness; (2) compelling obligations to a member of the family or household that requires significant time away from university duties (e.g., the birth or adoption of a child under six years old); and (3) circumstances beyond the control of the faculty member, such as grave administrative error or other unusual, compelling circumstances beyond the control of the faculty member. Stopping the clock for parental reasons is not automatic at UIUC; it must be requested. A senior administrator said, "We are very flexible in terms of family leave." And a department head noted, "Dads get to take leaves, too. Some choose not to take it, but they can if they so choose."

Ohio State's stop-the-clock provision allows for up to three one-year stoppages for the tenure clock, and the policy has changed from requiring a request to stop for childbirth or adoption to being automatic. Said an associate professor, "We learned that women did not want to have to go to their chair and say, 'Please, may I have an extra year?' They felt like that would have been a sign of weakness . . . so they were hesitant to ask. Therefore, we made it automatic and now you have to opt out of it." Faculty who stop the tenure clock are assumed to be fully engaged in their regular assigned academic responsibilities; any modification to the scheduling of these responsibilities (discussed previously) is an entirely separate matter. It is also possible to stop the tenure clock at OSU in the event of adverse events beyond the faculty member's control that seriously impede academic productivity. In addition, Ohio State has a part-time track that is within the tenure system. According to one administrator, about 13 percent of the faculty members have taken advantage of the policy.

As at Ohio State, stopping the tenure clock (for a two-year period) for parental reasons is automatic at Iowa, although the faculty member may decline the extension by written request. A provision in Iowa's policy that differs from the others is that "if the probationary faculty member has more than two children added to the family during the probationary period or within two years prior to the initial appointment, the faculty member may request a one-year extension for each child beyond the automatic two-year extension." In addition, the probationary period can be extended by mutual agreement of the faculty member, the college, and the provost, "because of a professional or personal impediment, such as the assumption of additional teaching or clinical responsibilities above the normal load at the request of the department or college; the failure of the University to provide resources in a timely manner if the resources are promised in writing; personal health reasons; the assumption of significant ongoing care responsibilities for a spouse, domestic partner, minor or adult child, or parent with a serious health problem; or because of the death of the faculty member's spouse, domestic partner, or minor or adult child" (*Operations Manual,* chapter 10). Further, the policy states that no penalties shall be incurred for extending the tenure clock: "No expansion of a faculty member's probationary period as a result of an extension . . . shall result in any increase in the quantity or quality of the probationary faculty member's expected scholarship from what would have been expected had that faculty member been considered for promotion or tenure in the final year of probationary service as defined by the collegiate norms." Of the policies, a senior administrator pointed out that: "The automatic tenure extension policy is really important to junior faculty. It's something that we promote to new faculty in their initial appointment letter and it's stated at the orientation. We emphasize the automatic nature of it so there's not the politics of choosing."

A formal policy at the University of North Caroline Pembroke that affects flexibility for faculty members, and may allow them more work-life balance, allows faculty to stand for tenure early (www.uncp.edu/aa/handbook/10-11 /10-11.pdf). Under this policy (5-3.C3), faculty members who feel they are ready, can demonstrate exceptional teaching, scholarship, and service, and with a letter of support from the department chair and dean, may stand for tenure early, thus, allowing them to start a family *after* receiving tenure and not be "so old as to make childbearing difficult," said one assistant professor.

Another tenure-track faculty member noted, "Personally, I like the early tenure possibility and plan to shoot for it so I can get past that hurdle and find more balance in my life younger than otherwise." If a candidate is denied early tenure, s/he is not penalized, and may stand again at the usual time. UNCP also has an option for less than full-time status or "relief from all employment obligations for a specific period," while on the tenure track for "compassionate reasons of health, or requirements of childbirth or child care, or similar compelling reasons" (see Policy 5-3.C6[B]). Working less than full time under these conditions also extends the tenure clock.

Provisions for Dual-Career Couples

UIUC has a dual-career couples policy (see appendix G, included here because of its clarity and comprehensiveness) and maintains two websites for dual-career issues and support. The first provides a list of resources available on campus (www.ahr.uiuc.edu/recruiting/dualcareer.htm), including the Dual Career Partners Program, a UIUC Job Registry, and links to the Staff Human Resources Office and the Graduate College Scholars' Program. The second provides brief descriptions of various employment services offered (e.g., "Electronic Career and Employment Center," "Academic Benefits and Services Guide and Recruitment Packets," "Dual Career Couples Program," "Tenure Rollbacks," "Leaves," "Moving Discounts," and the like) and the name of a contact person for each (www.ahr.uiuc.edu/staffandservices/Employment Services.htm).

For dual-career partner hiring, the UIUC provost's office indicates that it "will pay one third, the unit of one spouse will pay one third, and the unit that is hiring the other spouse will pay one third of a salary." Of the dual-career program, a senior administrator reported: "I hear that our dual-career program makes us different, better, and more attractive to candidates because we have a robust program. People tell us that many other places do not have the kind of commitment to the partner as we do on this campus." Another noted, "Our campus has been aggressive in recruiting partners, partly out of necessity, as an excellent institution located as the major employer, and not just Champaign-Urbana but in the surrounding region. Everyone is really open to creative problem-solving, which really contributes to the process." An assistant professor stated that he would not have accepted an offer at UIUC "no matter how attractive," if it hadn't come with an equally attractive offer for his wife.

Iowa has an office, called the Dual Career Network, with personnel who help faculty and staff members secure employment in the area, but the university does not have an official policy, as at UIUC. "We admire Illinois' generous support for dual career couples, but we just don't have the funding. We do have some dual academic career salary support from the provost's office, and the pool of money has increased in the last couple of years, but not as much as we'd like," said one senior administrator.

Ohio State has an official dual-career hiring program. While brief, the policy[4] makes explicit that "deans and department chairs cooperate willingly, constructively and in good faith" to accommodate academic couples. A full professor noted that, within his department and college, there are five dual-career couples, and that this policy has been instrumental in getting new faculty to come to Columbus.

Child Care, Elder Care, and Domestic Partner Benefits

Iowa subsidizes a portion of child care as part of a cafeteria-style benefits package. In addition, faculty may use flexible spending accounts to pay for child care, elder care, and health, vision, and dental coverage. Said one assistant professor, "We actually have in-home care because both of our kids have some health issues; the flex account allows us to afford this." UI also offers health care coverage for domestic partners.

Policy and Practice Implications

An examination of the five institutions with high work-life scores yields several action items for administrators.

Personnel

1. Hire personnel to staff work-life services offices. This is important not only to get the job done but also for symbolic reasons. Putting physical resources into something signifies that it matters, well beyond the typical rhetoric. It is extremely unlikely that universities will need fewer personnel in the future to attend to these matters.

Policies

2. Have written policies. If it were ever the case, it is no longer that junior faculty will be placated by hearing, "This is a family-friendly

place" or, "There's plenty of work-life balance here." In addition to assuring pre-tenure faculty that the institution is doing more than just paying lip-service to work-life balance, written policies provide clarity, consistency, and transparency which leads to greater fairness and equity. Written policies are also a primary indicator of how family-friendly a campus actually is.

Policy areas for written codification include

A. dual-career couples hiring;

B. early promotion and tenure;

C. parental leave;

D. modified duties;

E. part-time tenure option; and

F. stop-the-tenure-clock provisions.

3. Ensure that written policies are communicated to everyone— pre-tenure *and* senior faculty members, department chairs, heads, *and* deans.

4. Ensure that written policies are easily accessible on a user-friendly website.

Practices and Other Accommodations

5. Provide child care, elder care, lactation rooms, flexibility, and opportunities for social occasions in which kids can be included—all relevant practices that help ensure a viable workplace for the future.

CHAPTER FIVE

Support for Research and Teaching

An Ideal World

The workplace demands of today's college and university faculty are ever increasing.[1] This is especially true for junior faculty on the tenure track, where pressure to acquire grants and to publish in top journals is mounting (O'Meara et al. 2008). Although obtaining research funding can be a painstaking process, it is critical nonetheless. Hermanowicz (2009) captures the importance of funding to faculty members by describing it as "nothing short of a lifeline that enables scientists to advance in a career" (p. 96). Despite this reality of faculty work, the percentage of faculty research funded by the U.S. government has steadily declined over the last several decades (Schuster and Finkelstein 2006). In addition, many faculty members continue to be inundated with heavy teaching loads, even at research intensive universities (O'Meara et al. 2008).

The institutional support provided to junior faculty members for teaching and research varies depending on the type of institution. Some elite, well-resourced institutions provide ample sources of support and funding to their junior faculty, while others fail to meet demand. All institutions, however, struggle to identify the most effective means of support for their junior faculty, given budget restrictions (Hermanowicz 2009). This chapter begins with a discussion of protecting faculty time, followed by a look at research-specific support mechanisms such as travel funds and grant assistance. The efficacy of workshops and teaching and learning centers and support in the form of staff and facilities are addressed.

Protecting Faculty Time

One of the common ways that junior faculty are supported on the tenure track is by protecting their time so that they have sufficient opportunity to obtain grant funding, conduct research, and to publish. Although considered one of the three staples of the junior faculty diet, service on committees is often given less weight during the tenure evaluation process (Rosser 2004). Rosenthal et al. (1994) found that "faculty members without tenure are often warned to concentrate on other forms of endeavor, to keep service to a minimum and to focus on activities that will count more when they are being evaluated" (p. 46). In other words, senior faculty and institutional leaders admonish junior faculty regarding too much service work but too often leave it to them to decide how much to take on. Institutions must make a concerted effort to protect their junior faculty from service work because many young academics are unprepared for the demands of the tenure track (Rosser 2004); "there may be a conflict between the socialization processes of doctoral students with the expectations (e.g., external funding, service work) and reality that confront new faculty members. . . . Although departments expect a new faculty member to 'hit the ground running,' these same departments must also protect new faculty members' time and the amount of service activities they contribute" (Rosser 2004, p. 303).

Rosser's argument suggests that newly minted Ph.D.s may not be experienced enough to manage their service workload by themselves and that it is the hiring institution's job to ensure that these faculty are protected. However, because explicit institutional policies and practices that place a cap on service work for junior faculty are a rarity, Beloit College dean and psychology professor Dave Burrows has suggested, in *Balancing Teaching, Scholarship, and Service* (2005), that senior faculty provide support for junior faculty by voluntarily taking on more committee work and the like. Burrows argues that junior faculty are a precious resource for institutions and that they bring fresh ideas and perspectives to their research. Although senior faculty espouse a culture where junior faculty have limited service work, it is up to them to take action and ensure that young scholars do indeed have their time protected.

Some junior faculty also have their time protected when it comes to teaching load, one of the greatest sources of stress for tenure-track faculty. Menges and Associates (1999) found that the teaching-related stress of junior faculty increased from the first year to the third year. "Because teaching-related activities were bound by specific dates by which classes had to be prepared, by which papers had to be marked, and by which grades had to be submitted, teaching-related activities were not tasks that could be put off" (Menges and Associates 1999, p. 315). Due to the time commitment and stress of teaching, some institutions provide release time that allows junior faculty to teach one or two fewer courses per semester while spending more time on their research. Schuster and Finkelstein (2006) found that 54 percent of tenure-track and tenured faculty reported the availability of release time from teaching in 1998; however, only 22 percent reported using it, suggesting that many junior faculty may hesitate to request it, believing that this practice might be frowned upon by senior colleagues. Teaching releases are only effective and well received if such practices fit with the institution's goals and mission (Miner et al. 2003). At large research universities, teaching releases are necessary to allow junior faculty to apply for grants and publish articles. At liberal arts colleges with teaching as the primary mission, teaching releases are less useful and can often cause strife when faculty members feel that allowing course releases takes away from the student-centered goals of the school.

In some cases, teaching releases depend on the academic discipline of the junior faculty member. Some researchers suggest that junior faculty in fields that are typically awarded grants (i.e., chemistry and psychology) earn teaching releases, whereas faculty in fields with less access to external funding (e.g., English) have course loads well above their institution's average (Carroll 2003; Blackburn and Lawrence 1995). In addition, interest and engagement in teaching rises and declines in cycles over the course of a faculty member's career and there is no general pattern by age (Blackburn and Lawrence 1995). Therefore, instead of having all faculty members teach the same number of credits per semester, "What would be more effective for the individual faculty member and for the organization would be to have faculty teach more when that is in their interest and desire and to teach less when other activities hold a higher value" (Blackburn and Lawrence 1995, p. 205). Such ideas are most likely to be successful when they sprout organically from within the faculty and involve multiple constituents in the planning process (McMillin and Berberet 2002). Further, such policies can receive pushback from

non-tenured faculty if they are not afforded the same luxuries as their tenured and tenure-track counterparts.

Although some institutions protect their junior faculty from heavy teaching duties, this practice has not been commensurate with the substantial
growth in research demands for faculty on the tenure track over the last couple of decades (Schuster and Finkelstein 2006), suggesting that there is a
need for teaching release policies at many institutions and most especially at
research-intensive universities. Writes one researcher in reference to an un-
named college of education, "The most significant commitment of this college to junior faculty was the agreement to offer a single course release for
each year the faculty member is not tenured" (Bailey et al. 2007, p. 261). Even
when teaching releases are not granted, however, junior faculty can be supported in their teaching when they are allowed to teach smaller seminar
courses (as opposed to large introductory courses), so they can better integrate their research and teaching and be more productive researchers in
general (Blackburn and Lawrence 1995).

Support for Research
Research Leaves

Research leaves are also enormously helpful for junior faculty. Research leave
is incredibly attractive to faculty members at all types of institutions, even
for those focused more on teaching than research (Hamilton 2000). In some
cases, release time is awarded only to faculty who bring in large grants, effectively buying out of teaching. Such incentives may help to control faculty
turnover. "Funding that supports faculty members' professional development
and research activities through travel, release time, and sabbatical leave, have
been shown to be important factors in the retention of faculty members"
(Rosser 2004, p. 302). When faculty members have more time for research,
they are generally more productive scholars (March and Hattie 2002); however, the same is not true for teaching, where more time spent does not necessarily equate to more effective teaching. Accordingly, Toews and Yazedjian
(2007) have suggested that junior faculty members negotiate research leave
into their contracts before accepting tenure-track employment.

Despite the overwhelming desire for research leave and sabbaticals, the
percent of tenure-track and tenured faculty who reported the availability of
sabbaticals dropped from 60.4 percent in 1992 to 55.7 percent in 1998, and
the percentage of faculty who actually took a sabbatical dropped from 18.4

percent in 1992 to 9.0 percent in 1998 (Schuster and Finkelsten 2006). Although there is demand for research leave and agreement that it is an effective provision for enhancing faculty productivity, one might infer from these data that academic culture dissuades the use of such policies or that faculty members are simply too busy with teaching and service duties to take a research leave.

Start-up Packages

Finding quality time to produce "tenure worthy" research is just part of the arduous tenure-track experience. Funding this research is another challenge altogether. Most newly hired junior faculty, especially those in the sciences, receive a start-up package from their employer that includes lab space, equipment, and other resources designed to attract talent and enable productive research. In fact, start-up packages significantly impact junior faculty workplace satisfaction (Hermanowicz 2009). Many institutions are using start-up packages to emphasize their investment in junior faculty success (Clayton 2007). Start-up packages can, however, highlight the inequity of resources across institutions in higher education. While some junior faculty enjoy the "platinum" start-up package common to well-resourced institutions, others struggle to excel in research given the meager resources at their disposal. Science faculty members at lower-ranked institutions view their workplaces as stymieing because of the financial and structural constraints (Hermanowicz 2009, p. 86); they feel they must lower the bar on their professional goals. Furthermore, faculty members in the humanities often do not receive start-up packages at all. This inequity within institutions has prompted researchers to suggest innovative plans, such as giving non-science junior faculty members start-up packages that include book subsidies and computers. Another idea is for institutions to take a small percentage of all faculty salaries in order to fund a "publishing subsidy pool" where both junior and senior faculty could be guaranteed a publishing subsidy once they have completed a book that has navigated the review process of a university press (Davidson 2004, p. 137). Although implementing such a plan would require no significant institutional costs, it presents at least two barriers: that faculty from all fields be willing to lower their salaries and that junior faculty get a book through the review process of a university press before qualifying to receive a subsidy.

Travel Funds

The availability of travel funds is another important form of junior faculty support. Indeed, institutional travel funds for research symposiums and fieldwork are essential ingredients in the tenure bids of many junior faculty. Travel funds for junior faculty to attend national conferences and discipline meetings can help to develop their teaching skills and increase their workplace satisfaction (Menges and Associates1999). The percentage of tenure-track and tenured faculty that reported the availability of professional travel funds at their institution grew from 80.5 in 1992 to 90.3 in 1998, however, the percentage who actually went on professional trips dropped slightly from 76.0 in 1992 to 74.4 in 1998 (Schuster and Finkelstein 2006). Over the last decade, the availability of travel funds for research is perceived by the faculty to be declining and they are right; institutions have not been as generous with travel funds as they used to be (Hermanowicz 2009). Providing travel funds for junior faculty to share, expand, and explore their research not only increases satisfaction but also increases their chances for tenure. When economic realities result in the restricted availability of travel funds, institutions can obviate the potential pushback from faculty by communicating openly and unequivocally instead of letting intimations and perceptions infect the faculty and potentially increase attrition

Pre- and Post-Award Support

The pre- and post-award support provided by institutions to junior faculty during the grant procurement process is another important factor in the satisfaction and success of tenure track faculty. "The strong role that having grants has in predicting faculty publication rate suggests that those institutions that want to increase this kind of output need to consider ways they can assist faculty members prepare acceptable proposals . . . the faculty member needs time and assistance. Relief from an assignment, help from advanced students who can locate key resources, and some seed money to gather critical pilot data and equipment are some of the things the institution can supply at a relatively low cost. . . . Receiving support challenges them to deliver" (Blackburn and Lawrence 1995, pp. 149–50).

Grant support can take many forms—administrative grants offices, money, technology, equipment, and research assistants. Faculty members in the hard sciences tend to feel more confident in their grant-writing abilities, perhaps because of the relatively high availability of funding in the sciences. Still, many junior faculty enter these same disciplines thinking that they have to quickly prove their "fundability" and end up prematurely writing grants that are underdeveloped (Gaugler 2004, p. 525). Further, if junior faculty do not establish sound, disciplined grant-writing habits early in their career, they are unlikely ever to do so (Porter 2004).

It is critical, therefore, that grant support be organized in such a way that junior faculty can easily identify and access the help they need. Miner et al. (2003) have suggested a reorganization of the grant-writing process as it exists at most universities: "Researchers consistently express a strong desire for centralization of knowledge and assistance in all facets of grant seeking and proposal preparation. Further, most faculty agree that the repository for this central core should be located in the grants office" (p. 19). The reason, they argue, is so that faculty do not have to waste time searching. Effective communication makes effective grants offices; efficiently managing the flow of grant information through their offices minimizes the uncertainty and confusion of the faculty (Miner et al. 2003). This point seems particularly important as one considers the value of faculty time, an issue highlighted by Amy and Crow (2005), who underscored how tedious and time-consuming the grant process can be. Although providing grant support requires an investment in personnel and resources, researchers agree that it is necessary and vital to the health of both faculty and institution.

Graduate Assistance

Graduate students and research assistants constitute another important form of support in the work of junior faculty. Without question, junior faculty benefit immensely from having graduate students and research assistants help them with their teaching and research (Schuster and Finkelstein 2006; Rosser 2004; Blackburn and Lawrence 1995). "The notion that good graduate assistants are priceless to faculty members cannot be more applicable. . . . They often provide faculty members with much of the foundational work (e.g., pulling citations, reviewing the literature, grading papers, lab work) to keep them productive in their teaching and writing" (Rosser 2004, p. 302). The number of research assistants grew at about double the rate of faculty at colleges and universities from 1989 to 2001. However, during that period, about 40 percent of junior faculty at research universities rated the availability of research assistants poor or very poor (Finkelstein et al. 1998). The disparity between the growth of research assistants and their availability as perceived by junior faculty could be due to financial differences between the haves and the have-nots of higher education. Some of the better-resourced institutions may have hired disproportionate numbers of research assistants, thereby skewing the data. Furthermore, within institutions, some academic disciplines may have ample support from research personnel while others lack the availability of such support. In addition, women tend to be more critical of the availability of research assistants, perhaps signifying unequal resources and support along gender lines (Finkelstein et al. 1998).

The amount of funding for graduate students is perceived by department chairs to be declining. The funding for post-doctoral researchers, however, is seen as generous by some department chairs but insufficient by others, further suggesting that some institutions are able to fund such personnel while others are not (Hermonwicz 2009). Although the availability of and perceptions of this form of faculty support have waxed and waned over the years, one fact has remained true: research assistants and graduate students are invaluable resources for junior faculty that enable them to manage their course loads and expand their research capabilities.

Professional Development

Faculty members on the tenure track are also supported through the use of professional development programs that range from workshops on grant writing and starting a lab to teaching and learning centers that perform theatrical role-playing skits. McMillin and Berberet (2002) defined faculty development as "the process of nurturing the continuous learning, growth, and vitality of the faculty person (in all his or her roles) as a key member in meeting the aims/goals of the organization, including long-lasting student learning and institutional agility in responding to internal and external forces" (p. 34). The goal of professional development is not only to promote learning but also to enable and bolster the faculty member's role as an integral contributor to the university's mission.

Faculty development programs, such as time-management training, research workshops, grant-writing workshops, web page development, multimedia, and distance-learning training are important for the growth of junior faculty (Price and Cotten 2006). They help acculturate junior faculty members to their school and to build professional relationships with their junior and senior faculty colleagues. Bailey et al. (2007) provided the example of a successful integrative program at a college of education that shifted its focus to become more research oriented and ran a rigorous three-day workshop where senior faculty helped junior faculty develop their research agendas. Institution-driven research circles have contributed immensely to the research skills of junior faculty. Gillespie et al. (2005) describe the benefits of the research circles; "For the new faculty, especially, the circles strengthen scholarly identity in the context of collegial interaction and engagement. And the same reflective process—preparation, feedback, revision—can be used to strengthen teaching and service" (p. 161).

Professional development activities that mix together junior and senior faculty are especially effective because of the mentoring and role modeling that senior faculty provide (Porter 2004). Workshops offer "superior capabilities to provide learning opportunities in several domains at once—knowledge, skills, and attitudes. Properly designed, an interactive workshop combines the immediacy of problem-centered instruction with opportunities for reflection, analysis and discussion" (Porter 2004, p. 7). Workshops that provide talks by past grant winners in addition to providing concrete examples of successful grants and their accompanying paperwork are some of the development opportunities most valued by junior faculty; for workshops to have the most impact, written and oral feedback must be provided to junior faculty throughout the process (Porter 2004).

Activities and workshops specifically attuned to the needs of minority and women faculty (groups that continue to have distinctive, challenging tenure-track experiences) should be offered (Price and Cotten 2006). For example, an Office of Faculty Development created a convenient in-house leadership program that has resulted in an increasing number of women in leadership roles (Emans et al. 2008). Even those who did not attend the workshops reported that they benefited by reading the faculty development newsletters that are published and distributed to all faculty. In another example, Belcher (2009) noted that "a preponderance of my students were women, people of color, non-Americans, and/or first-generation academics. This workshop has been responsible for helping many on the margins—racially, economically, internationally, and theoretically—to feel more confident and to frame their fascinating work in ways that would be acceptable to mainstream journals" (p. xii).

This quote illuminates a fundamental reality of contemporary higher education: supporting a diverse faculty is an ongoing process that continues long after staff have been recruited and hired. As institutions strive to increase the diversity of their faculty, professional development programs may become more and more necessary.

The use of professional development as a means of supporting and valuing faculty has grown over the years. The percentage of tenure-track and tenured faculty who reported the availability of training to improve research or teaching skills grew from 51.2 in 1992 to 74.4 in 1998; however, the percentage that actually used the training programs dropped from 38.8 in 1992 to 34.5 in 1998 (Schuster and Finkelstein 2006). These data could indicate that high teaching and research expectations preclude faculty from participating in the very training opportunities designed to assist them in performing and managing their workload. Another possible diagnosis is that institutions are offering more teaching-specific development opportunities but many faculty are not taking advantage, feeling that their existing pedagogical skills render the time-consuming development opportunities unnecessary (McMillin and Berberet 2002; Blackburn and Lawrence 1995).

For professional development in teaching to be effective, it must be intrinsically motivated (Blackburn and Lawrence 1995): "We saw that a combination of teaching self-efficacy, personal valuation of teaching, and perceived institutional valuation of teaching is what led to variation in teaching effort" (p. 205). Faculty members are more likely to leave an institution when they perceive their teaching to be undervalued (Menges and Associates 1999). Offering teaching development workshops and seminars may symbolically represent an institution's values, but faculty will only participate if such values are embedded in institutional culture. If junior faculty are given the message that research is valued over teaching in the tenure-review process, they are unlikely to take advantage of programs designed to improve their pedagogy. And it is important for institutions to remember that research and teaching are inextricably linked; successful scholarship provides fodder for successful teaching (Menges and Associates 1999).

Successful teaching development programs must also combine motivation with feedback; to that end, Menges and Associates (1999) argued that hiring teaching consultants can supplement workshops by providing faculty with feedback and guidance on course plans, organization of materials, and presentation techniques. Marsh and Hattie (2002) supported the use of teaching consultants: "Randomly assigned groups of teachers who met with external consultants to discuss specific strategies to improve their teaching effectiveness in areas selected by the teachers did significantly improve their teaching effectiveness (in relation to pretests and to a randomly assigned control group)" (p. 635). The fact that the teachers in Marsh and Hattie's (2002) study worked with consultants on selected areas of focus further supports Blackburn and Lawrence's (1995) argument that teaching development is most effective when driven internally by faculty. When properly administered within a culture of support, teaching consultants challenge faculty to break ineffective teaching habits and expose them to techniques and practices that can drastically improve the learning of their students and the feedback they provide (Marsh and Hattie 2002).

Administrative Personnel, Facilities, and Equipment

The personnel who work in university administration represent another critical element of the junior faculty experience, as they can greatly enhance or inhibit workplace satisfaction on the tenure track. The retention and attrition of faculty members is often directly impacted by the support of administrative personnel (Rosser 2004). On the one hand, nothing perturbs faculty more than when administrative personnel increase the bureaucratic red tape. "The filling out of perceived needless or senseless forms, adhering to absurd or outdated policies, and the duplicating of materials and paperwork seems to pick constantly at the faculty member's time and worklife" (Rosser 2004, p. 301). On the other hand, when administrative support staff expedite otherwise time-consuming tasks for faculty and enable them to focus on their teaching and research, faculty tend to be more satisfied with their work. This form of support can come in many forms, including library staff, secretarial assistants, and audiovisual technicians.

It is the role of campus leadership, Rosser (2004) argued, to ensure that the right number of support staff are in place so that faculty feel supported but not impeded in their work. Many faculty feel that chairs, deans, and other administrative leaders have little influence on their research success and that faculty members often do not recognize the important contributions and assistance the administration provides for their research (Blackburn and Lawrence 1995). This could be, in part, a failure of the institution to properly communicate the different roles and functions of the administration. Institutions have created numerous administrative leadership positions designed to support the faculty that range from the dean of administration to the director of the office of educational outreach (Bailey et al. 2007). Unless the purposes of these new positions are clearly delineated to the faculty, most will assume the administration is fattening itself unnecessarily and diverting resources from the institution's main objectives of teaching and research.

Access to facilities and equipment also greatly impact the satisfaction of junior faculty on the tenure track. Finkelstein et al. (1998) found that about 74 percent of early career faculty at research universities rated their research facilities either good or very good, 68 percent rated their classroom space good or very good, and 85 percent rated their research equipment and instruments good or very good. "New career entrants are somewhat less satisfied than their senior colleagues in some areas: Mainframe computer facilities, library holdings, and office space. . . . This finding probably reflects the numbers of new faculty who trained in relatively computer-rich graduate programs but who now find themselves at institutions with fewer computing resources" (Finkelstein et al. 1998, pp. 97–98). The authors further posit that the concern of junior faculty over the extensiveness of library holdings could be due to the fact that early career faculty were trained at research universities with large library collections. The amount of resources available or perceived to be available not only impacts faculty satisfaction but productivity as well. In his study of science departments, Hermanowicz (2009) found that scientists with stronger, more well-funded research facilities were more likely to believe it is easier to publish in top-tier science journals, suggesting that research facilities increase the publishing confidence of professors (p. 67). Blackburn and Lawrence (1995) found that faculty at larger, wealthier institutions are more likely to publish more, as compared with faculty at smaller, more modest institutions. They contend that institutions with larger library resources (larger collections and more professional librarians) enable faculty to publish in larger numbers. As one might expect, however, even within highly resourced campuses there is perceived inequality by faculty who feel that some departments have more access to administrative resources than others. And the perception of administration is almost always at odds with that of faculty when it comes to resource availability, as administrators tend to see resources as more abundant than do faculty (Blackburn and Lawrence 1995).

Increasing access to resources is not always the best plan of action for administrators who want to support and satisfy their junior faculty. In some cases, new facilities and adding state-of-the-art technology equipment can create more work for faculty (O'Meara et al. 2008; Schuster and Finkelstein 2006; Rosser 2004). "While most faculty members perceive the use and application of technology as paramount, technology does come with a cost, and usually that cost amounts to faculty members' time, and often the price is scholarship or student advising and mentoring" (Rosser 2004, p. 301).

Whenever a new technology is introduced, faculty must make adjustments to their routine and spend time learning how to use it. New technologies including web-based course platforms and social networking tools have made faculty members accessible to students around the clock and are often accompanied by numerous technical difficulties (Schuster and Finkelstein 2006). When implementing new technologies and equipment designed to support faculty work, it is of the upmost importance that institutions provide the training and support necessary to ensure the smoothest transition possible. Without it, faculty, and particularly those struggling to survive the demands of the tenure track, will likely become frustrated and less satisfied with their work (Rosser 2004).

COACHE Faculty Support Data

A number of COACHE survey questions are germane to the topic of support for faculty work, most especially practices that may affect a faculty member's ability to conduct effective research and teaching. Survey respondents to rated the importance and effectiveness of several policies and practices, including seven about support for faculty work (see table 5.1).

The most important policies or practices for pre-tenure faculty are those that impose upper limits on teaching loads and committee assignments, and those that provide for travel funds and research leave. The least effective practice is professional assistance in obtaining external grants. The largest gaps between policy importance and effectiveness relate to professional assistance in obtaining external grants (1.48 points) and upper limits on committee assignments (1.25 points).

In addition to policy ratings, COACHE data reveal satisfaction with several dimensions of the workplace related to research and teaching. Table 5.2 shows the average agreement ratings on survey items.

Overall, junior faculty are most satisfied with their autonomy surrounding their teaching and research; they are most dissatisfied with the amount of time they have for scholarly work, their access to graduate assistance, the

Table 5.1. COACHE Average Ratings on Importance and Effectiveness of Faculty Work Policies and the Difference between Importance and Effectiveness

Policy	Average Importance	Average Effectiveness	Difference
Upper limits on teaching assignments	4.61	3.49	1.12
Travel funds to present papers or conduct research	4.59	3.50	1.09
Upper limits on committee assignments	4.36	3.11	1.25
Paid or unpaid research leave during the probationary period	4.33	3.23	1.10
Professional assistance in obtaining external grants	4.19	2.71	1.48
Peer reviews of teaching or research/creative work	4.10	3.17	.93
Professional assistance for improving teaching	3.73	3.32	.41

Importance Scale: 5 = Very important; 4 = Important; 3 = Neither important nor unimportant; 2 = Unimportant; and 1 = Very unimportant

Effectiveness Scale: 5 = Very effective; 4 = Effective; 3 = Neither effective nor ineffective; 2 = Ineffective; and 1 = Very ineffective

amount of external funding they need to find to support their work, and the quality of research support services.

Prior research (Trower and Gallagher 2008b, p. 16) showed that there are a number of professional development barriers to success for new faculty, including

- difficulties related to the transition from a doctoral program or post-doc experience;
- department chairs and senior faculty who lack experience providing, or are unwilling to provide, guidance and mentorship (the subject of chapter 6);
- uncertainty as to how to run a lab, manage a research program/large grant, and obtain external funding;
- lack of adequate prior teaching experience and a lot of learning on the job;
- fear of taking intellectual risks; fair of failure;

Table 5.2. COACHE Survey Average Satisfaction Ratings on Research and Teaching

Please indicate your level of satisfaction or dissatisfaction with each of the following items:	Average Rating
Discretion you have over the content of the courses you teach	4.62
Influence you have over the focus of your research/creative work	4.43
Influence you have over which courses you teach	4.21
Level of courses you teach	4.16
Number of students you teach	3.90
Number of courses you teach	3.84
Quality of graduate students	3.63
Quality of teaching support services	3.61
Quality of clerical/administrative support services	3.58
Quality of computing support services	3.57
Quality of undergraduate students	3.51
Quality of facilities (i.e., office, labs, classrooms)	3.37
Quality of research support services	3.20
Amount of external funding you are expected to find	3.00
Amount of access to teaching Fellows, graduate assistants, and the like	2.96
Amount of time to conduct research/produce creative work	2.78

Scale: 5 = Very satisfied; 4 = Satisfied; 3 = Neither satisfied nor dissatisfied; 2 = Dissatisfied; and 1 = Very dissatisfied

- pressure to be visible and make a name for oneself in one's discipline; and
- uncertainty about how to navigate university politics and departmental factions.

In this study, junior faculty told us that there are numerous ways their campuses could help them succeed, including providing assistance identifying potential sources for grant funding and writing grants; training on how to start and manage lab and personnel; space, equipment, and administrative support; and opportunities to present their scholarship to senior departmental colleagues and outside scholars in their discipline. On the teaching front, some appreciate teaching and learning center support, opportunities to team-teach, and feedback on pedagogy and classroom performance by experienced teacher-scholars (Trower and Gallagher 2008b, p. 17).

Campuses with High Scores on Support for Research and/or Teaching

Four public research universities that scored well on aspects of support for research and/or teaching were Auburn, Ohio State, the University of Illinois at Urbana-Champaign, and the University of Kansas.

Auburn

Auburn scored in the 92nd percentile on quality of facilities, in the 84th percentile on support services for teaching, and the 100th percentile for computing services. Interviews revealed several key programs at Auburn for supporting research and teaching, including a major center for teaching and learning, grants, and workshops.

Ohio State

OSU scored in the 92nd percentile on quality of facilities and in the 89th percentile on the amount of time for research. Interviews revealed the Ohio State is very serious about funding research and giving junior faculty time to do it. The Faculty Career Enhancement Committee Final Report (November 2005) stated, "The University and its colleges and departments have made notable strides in providing start-up and seed funding for beginning faculty, and many departments have reduced the service responsibilities of assistant professors as they start their careers" (p. 4). While the focus of this analysis is on pre-tenure faculty, the report is clear about assisting faculty at all career stages, and this tone that permeates the institution and reveals its intentionality about faculty success and satisfaction.

> Faculty career enhancement is a positive, future-oriented process that addresses all aspects and stages of faculty careers and work life—helping faculty remain productive, satisfied with their work, significantly connected to their university and its mission, and supported in the conduct of their interdependent professional and personal lives. It should not be thought of as merely a means to assist faculty in meeting criteria for promotion and tenure. An outstanding faculty comes about from recruiting the best candidates and then assuring that they have the opportunities to succeed, and so career enhancement ought to begin at the time of hiring and extend fully across faculty members' careers—even, for active colleagues, into retirement. (pp. 3–4)

University of Illinois at Urbana-Champaign

UIUC pre-tenured faculty ratings placed the institution in the 97th percentile for satisfaction with research services, the 95th for the amount of outside funding faculty are expected to find, the 92nd for the amount of time for research, and the 92nd for access to teaching and research assistants. UIUC also scored well for the quality of graduate students (84th percentile) and computing services (86th percentile).

University of Kansas

Re-tenured faculty at KU rated research services in the 89th percentile, the influence faculty have over their research agenda in the 84th, what's expected for research in the 84th, and the amount of funding expected in the 81st.

Effective Practice 1: Provide Strong Presidential and Provostial Leadership on Faculty Issues

Ohio State and UIUC are noteworthy in terms of leadership focused on faculty excellence. Ohio State has received a great deal of press about President Gordon Gee's push to move the institution from excellence to eminence, to be "the nation's leading public land-grant university." Said a senior administrator, "Excellence is not enough; it must be eminence. The top quartile is not good enough; it must be the top 10 percent. The University of Michigan tries to compete with the best private universities in the country, but we want to be the best public university in the country, with the mission that that entails."

A goal of the academic plan is to "build a world class faculty" with a strategy to "significantly increase the space dedicated to funded research" including a "multidisciplinary building devoted to high-quality research space as well as to office and meeting space." The plan also specifies "facilitating actions" that include increasing organizational flexibility and improving the faculty work environment. Improving that work environment means encouraging individualized faculty workloads; recognizing the workload efforts of faculty who supervise large numbers of doctoral students; enhancing the professional leave opportunities by encouraging faculty participation in the leave system and rewarding faculty who use this time productively; and encouraging faculty entrepreneurship through opportunities in areas where external funding sources are limited (www.osu.edu/academicplan/action.php). Said an associate professor, "For the past four or five years, the administration has been very specific about putting money into interdisciplinary programs rather than departments or colleges. The purpose is very explicit; it's transparent and it's working."

In addition, the OSU president and provost are intentional about strategic and academic planning. The institution was described as having a highly decentralized, hierarchical, top-down structure but not as "command and control." Instead, leaders are data-driven and realize that one size does not fit all when it comes to working with different colleges, centers, deans, and departments. Vastly different cultures exist on campus department by department. The provost shares effective practices and approaches discovered from department to department and college to college, which is important because a cornerstone of transformation at OSU is to push for more collaboration to break down barriers across campus.

The UIUC provost discussed the university's Faculty Excellence Program (FEP) "to get the best faculty anywhere—faculty who will be transformative." Specifically, the Office of the Provost supports three programs in which partial or total central financial support for academic positions may be provided: the FEP; the Targets of Opportunity Program; and the Dual Career Program (described in chapter 4). While the FEP is used to hire faculty at the full-professor rank, its impact is felt by all faculty because senior faculty mentor junior faculty, lead interdisciplinary centers that engage junior faculty, and build rich scholarly communities where junior faculty thrive.

> The primary purpose of this program is to recruit individuals who will contribute to transformation and positive change, within their units and across the institution. Individuals recruited through the FEP will have an outstanding record of accomplishment and will be able to provide scholarly leadership from the outset of their appointment at Illinois. Faculty Excellence hires should clearly enhance our capacity to achieve strategic objectives and promote interdisciplinary research activities; these individuals may also strengthen undergraduate teaching capacity in critical areas, promote the University's engagement and outreach missions, and meet other objectives of the University and its academic units. The focus is on experienced faculty with established records of excellence in their area of scholarly or research inquiry.

The provost believes strongly in the African proverb "If you want to go fast, go alone; if you want to go far, go together" and that is how she works with deans and department heads. Perhaps in part because of this belief, deans and heads take their respective roles very seriously and think about their own legacy by pondering the question, "What will I do to take my department/school to the next level?" The provost does not encourage competition among deans for a bigger piece of the pie; rather, "It is all about team-building: how do we grow the pie so everyone has more?" She continued, "We all care about everyone else. If one needs more funding, we figure out how to get more for all; we trust each other, which defeats internal competition. If the environment isn't good for one, it isn't good for anyone. I provide the mission, framework, and strategic approach but the deans have the authority to run their colleges and control their own destinies." For example, the College of Liberal Arts and Sciences has fifty-eight units with very different cultures, so the dean works very closely with the heads regarding how they think their junior faculty are doing and to give her feedback about how the dean's office is doing. She has individual meetings with department heads and holds monthly Town Halls for group meetings.

In addition, said the provost, "We value and use data here so the COACHE survey is one important piece of that. We use data to inform decision-making starting with the board and working through the faculty ranks."

Effective Practice 2: Have Formal Offices and Programs to Support Faculty Work
Support for Grant Writing and Faculty Research

Auburn's Office of Sponsored Programs provides links to various funding opportunities; the links are updated monthly. The office also offered a "Proposal Preparation Workshop Series" in 2008; the site includes links to information and PowerPoint presentations used in those workshops. In addition to the assistance on campus, an assistant professor at Auburn noted that the institution encouraged him to "go to any kind of grant-writing program he could find," even if that meant traveling to find one, because getting outside funding is crucial in his department. Auburn also offers internal grants to faculty members including the Daniel F. Breeden Endowed Grant Program, which supports teaching and learning projects that directly benefit the instructor, students, and AU's overall teaching program. Approximately $30,000 is available each academic year for awards of up to $3,000 each.

Ohio State's Faculty Career Enhancement (FCE) Committee Report makes recommendations regarding the chair's and dean's roles in supporting faculty research. Chairs should (1) require faculty to develop and update plans for their career enhancement in annual review dossiers and reward meaningful activity, (2) identify resources available to faculty for career enhancement, and (3) address FCE in departmental patterns of administration. Deans should (1) reserve funds for departments to use for FCE; (2) require chairs to report on FCE efforts in their annual reports to the college; and (3) establish minimum expectations for departmental funding of the scholarly work of faculty members and report annually on those levels to the provost. Because of the centrality of research for tenure and promotion, "there's an up-front expectation that we provide significant start-up dollars for new faculty to get their labs started," said a senior administrator. "The support packages for new faculty say, 'We expect you to do well and we will support you in doing well,' rather than making this a competitive thing where they have to apply for limited dollars," said a full professor. In engineering, for example, a department chair noted that new faculty members receive summer support in the first two years, as well as money to buy computers, furnish their office, outfit their lab, or use for travel. An assistant professor noted that there are daylong sessions for new faculty on preparing grants and the grant review process, which were very helpful.

At UIUC, faculty members and administrators alike echoed the sentiments of one department head who said, "It's all about the work. And the work here is research, period. If you do the research, get funding, get published, you get tenure." And there is "plenty of support" for research. "Some schools and departments have their own grants office for pre- and post-award support. You give them an idea or outline, they'll write the proposal and budget, find potential funders, and even go with you to the potential funder!" remarked a senior administrator. Said a full professor and department head, "We have a large business office that supports the grants machine. Because we process so many grants, there are two parts—pre-award and post-award. On the pre-award side there are two people, one of whom is a CPA and has an MS in human resources management; this person is an unbelievably strong advocate and support person for the faculty to polish budgets and justifications for budgets, making sure compliance is met with all the granting agency requirement and actually getting everything through on time."

At Kansas, the single most discussed aspect of research support was the professional assistance for grant writing. The KU Writing Center provides thorough instruction for writing grant proposals (www.writing.ku.edu/instructors /guides/grants.shtml). The KU Institute for Policy and Social Research provides pre- and post-award grant support (www.ipsr.ku.edu/grantsup/), and the Hall Center for the Humanities was noted for its internal awards as well as support for finding external funding, as well as its proposal-writing workshops (www.hallcenter.ku.edu/~hallcenter/). Said an assistant professor, "The Hall Center for the Humanities is excellent. In particular, there's a grant-writing specialist who provides fantastic support." And a senior administrator commented, "The Hall Center does so much across the university including facilitating grant development or any kind of humanistic scholarship." An assistant professor noted, "It was critical for me to hear about all the grant services provided here; I might have found that all out through mentoring, but they told us exactly how it all worked so when I submitted my NIH grant two months later I knew what the university provided in terms of support and who to go to. This was crucial in allowing me to finish on time to get the grant."

Teaching and Learning Centers

Several of those interviewed at Auburn discussed the importance of the campus's Biggio Center for the Enhancement of Teaching and Learning. A senior administrator explained the center's inception: "It was an initiative of the Provost's Office and has been in place for about seven years. A former provost formed a faculty committee with a representative from each of the colleges and schools and charged them to develop a vision for a teaching and learning center; then he identified a donor and it was built. It is very successful and well-attended by faculty and students." The center is fully staffed with professionals and offers programs including two specifically for new faculty. An orientation to teaching occurs prior to the start of classes during the new faculty convocation. (The program may be found at www.auburn.edu/aca demic/other/biggio/programs/convocationschedule.pdf.) This full-day event, in 2009, included sessions on strategies for becoming an excellent teacher, using groups effectively, Blackboard and support for online learning, and much more.

The New Faculty Scholars program at Auburn requires nominations to take part in two retreats—one in the fall focusing on the professoriate and best practices for teaching effectiveness and one in the spring focusing on portfolio construction (www.auburn.edu/academic/other/biggio/programs /for_faculty/new_faculty_scholars/nfs_2009_overview.pdf).

Research Institutes

A cornerstone of the cultural transformation process at Ohio State is to break down barriers to interdisciplinary research across campus by creating a number of centers and institutes. While on campus, we learned about TIE—Targeted Investments in Excellence, a program begun in 2005 and sponsored by the provost's office that provided $100 million to ten programs across the university that would move their teaching and research into the top ten or twenty among world peers. An associate professor commented: "A tremendous amount of cash has gone into the TIEs—money to conduct research. It's internal money, so no overhead is taken out. I was an assistant professor at the time and working with full professors . . . this was very helpful for me getting started." Another said, "The administration is offering money explicitly for what they're calling centers for innovation. Rather than dictating a process, this is a call to the faculty directly. Give us your ideas; write a proposal. The money goes straight into the faculty members' hands—to fund salaries, to buy equipment—whatever it takes."

The University of Illinois at Urbana-Champaign has a number of interdisciplinary research centers, including the Beckman Institute for Advanced Science and Technology, the Center for Advanced Studies, Institute for Genomic Biology, the iCAT Imaging Institute, and the Center for Informatics Research in Science and Scholarship, that are a part of the "research engine" of the institution. A senior administrator noted: "Our institutes provide an excellent source of internal funding for faculty research including seed funding for junior faculty. The Beckman Center, for example, provides funding for student fellowships and faculty scholarships. All of our centers and institutes provide a scholarly environment and support for interdisciplinary endeavors."

Colloquia, Workshops, and Seminars

Auburn offers numerous professional development seminars and symposia to all faculty each year; in the spring of 2010 (www.auburn.edu/academic/other /biggio/programs/spring_2010_pds_and_eventsf.pdf), various topics included getting published in peer review journals, mentoring undergraduate researchers, and building scholarship from outreach efforts. In addition to faculty development workshops, according to a senior level administrator: "The Provost's Office developed several mandatory development programs for department chairs. These covered everything chairs need to know about how to deal with faculty problems, annual evaluations and feedback, hiring, diversity, and budgets. Now the programs are offered to each incoming class of new chairs."

Ohio State offers numerous opportunities for pre-tenure faculty to enhance their research, writing, and teaching skills. An associate professor mentioned a roundtable where everyone reviews each other's work and gives feedback to those who are trying to revise their manuscripts to submit them as books. Group members provide suggestions about publishers and negotiating that process. In addition, there are forums in the department where junior faculty can get their work profiled so everyone can see what they're doing and ask questions, give feedback, and support them in that way. A senior administrator spoke about the importance placed on quality teaching: "In addition to providing support for research and scholarship, we offer teaching workshops for new faculty and post-docs. We ran a weeklong program this past summer followed up by brown bag discussion groups on various aspects of teaching, and while optional, there is an unwritten expectation that new faculty attend as many as they can."

UIUC offers numerous programs and workshops for administrators throughout the year focusing on research, engagement, advancement, tenure and promotion. "It's important for new administrators to know the policies and rules, and also what's important to the faculty," said one senior administrator. For new faculty, there's an orientation to teaching. "The reflective teaching seminars were really helpful when I first got here. The senior faculty make it clear that if you don't cut it as a scholar you won't stay here, but you also have to be a good teacher—that's the message from the start," said one assistant professor. The Center for Teaching Excellence, said a full professor and department head, "really helps new faculty who are struggling with teaching to improve. I know of a couple of cases where someone was scoring in the 2-range, in a 5-point scale, and with the help of the CTE, those scores are now up where they should be."

At KU, the Hall Center offers a new faculty orientation to help faculty members negotiate their first three years. New faculty are afforded an opportunity to meet each other and also to ask the senior faculty about teaching, research, and service expectations. Said an assistant professor, "Every January, the dean sponsors a workshop on best teaching practices that is well attended and very helpful." A senior administrator commented that "there's a workshop where the provost, vice provost, two or three chairs, a member of the University Committee on Promotion & Tenure, and a faculty member who has recently gone through promotion talk about their experiences and the expectations." A full professor and department chair informed us that there are "colloquia where we invite junior faculty to present their work to other scholars who give them feedback. It's really great for pre-conference planning—you've got a paper to present somewhere—you can run it by us first."

Effective Practice 3: Ensure that Tenure-Track Faculty Can Focus on What Matters Most to Achieve Tenure
Equitable Workload

Maybe it's part of the "one big happy family" culture at Auburn, or the Auburn Creed[2] manifested, but there's a sense of equity among the faculty. A senior administrator remarked, "You just don't see the senior faculty here teaching all the graduate courses and the junior faculty with the undergraduate or leftover courses. Individuals are hired into their field of specialization . . . maybe we're a thin faculty . . . we don't have a lot of duplicates. But the senior faculty don't get all the Ph.D. courses; they teach the whole range. The senior faculty don't take all the plum assignments; there are senior faculty teaching freshmen seminars." And a department chair noted, "There's no 'ownership' of courses where senior faculty say, 'We teach the graduate seminars and you junior faculty teach the freshmen and sophomores because you are young and don't know what you're doing.' We'll have none of that mentality. We want the pre-tenure faculty to come in and know that they have an enormous contribution to make. This enables the new faculty to integrate quickly into the culture as equal players whose opinions and contributions are valued."

Protection from Too Much Teaching and Service

Beyond establishing formal offices, centers, and programs to assist pre-tenure faculty, like many research universities, Auburn makes efforts to lighten the service load for junior faculty. An assistant professor remarked, "The senior faculty really step up and play a role, so at the department level, especially early in my tenure process, I was protected from service. I was told to focus on teaching and research and that, as those looked fine, I could expect more service. The senior faculty not only talked about helping me, they really did!"

At Ohio State, department chairs and senior faculty ensure that junior faculty have time to conduct and publish scholarly work; it's part of the ethos of OSU. Said a professor, "There is a lot of concern for protecting junior faculty—minimizing the number of course preps they have to do." Said another professor, "We believe that service is important, but not the first year." A department chair noted that he is "very protective of junior faculty time—no committees whatsoever; we have very clear guidelines and dos and don'ts to protect their time." A senior administrator said that there is "very low" service expectation and a "light teaching load" for tenure-track faculty for the first couple of years. A department chair noted that tenure-track faculty have a quarter off just to get acclimated followed by a light teaching and service load until they make associate; "research is essential to achieving tenure so they need time to do it."

The senior faculty at UIUC are credited for protecting the junior faculty from commitments that take them away from research. Said one assistant professor, "The tenured faculty are extremely protective of making sure that our focus is on what counts for tenure; there's lots of time for research." A full professor and department head noted that because tenure-track faculty need to "hit the ground running" they are protected from committee work and have a light teaching load in the first three years.

Effective Practice 4: Provide Professional Development Leave

Recognizing that "faculty need large blocks of uninterrupted time to develop and complete their work," the Faculty Career Enhancement Committee report for November 2005 at Ohio State noted, "The University should better publicize its current faculty leave programs and make them more flexible." The specific recommendations were as follows:

1. Applications for faculty leave—time away from academic responsibilities—should be a routine part of each faculty member's career enhancement plans, and chairs should regularly encourage faculty to apply for leaves.
2. Faculty should be routinely notified that they are eligible for FPLs (Faculty Professional Leaves—leave devoted to enhancing one's research skills and knowledge).
3. The Office of Academic Affairs should investigate whether it is possible for FPLs to be taken for shorter periods of time but (as, for

example, at the University of Iowa) more frequently. Similarly, to acquire the time needed to complete new and ongoing projects that can enhance one's career, departments and colleges should be encouraged to permit faculty to combine an SRA (Special Research Assignment—to facilitate research and writing) with an FPL, thereby enabling faculty to accumulate extended leave time with reduced financial liability.

4. Given salary disparities among colleges across campus, faculty who are paid 25 percent less than the mean university salaries at each rank should be able to commit to two- and three-quarter FPLs at no cost to themselves (i.e., without taking a reduction in salary).

5. The OAA should facilitate leaves by maintaining an informational website with appropriate links that assist in the mechanics of a leave (e.g., connect faculty applying for leaves with new hires and visiting scholars looking for housing).

6. The OAA should remind all colleges that there is no longer a 10 percent-of-faculty limit on SRAs per college.

7. Faculty should be encouraged to take SRAs for teaching purposes and for major outreach/engagement projects as well as for research.

Described as "very generous," the University of Illinois at Urbana-Champaign provides research leave and course reduction for tenure-track faculty members. The idea is to "ensure the success of early career scholars, and get their work off the ground" said a senior administrator. "When we hire someone in their first year on the tenure track, we give them a two-course release for them to use as they like," said a full professor and department head. "And because the fourth year is so critical, we give them a semester off. This campus is amazing in terms of the opportunities for course release. Humanities faculty are eligible for release time through the Illinois Release Time in the Humanities Fellowships; Beckman has fellowships and also the Center for Advanced Studies."

An assistant professor at UIUC explained that she is expected to teach three courses per year and can "bank" those course credits so that in another year she'll have enough banked to take a semester completely off from teaching. She said, "Compared to our peers, this is a very reasonable teaching load and a big selling point when we recruit new junior faculty members."

Effective Practice 5: Provide Travel Support and Research Assistants

Assistant professors at Auburn talked about the multiple forms of support they found in their early years at the university, including research assistance in the first two years; one noted, "This form of support was invaluable. It was offered through my own department where there's money available for grad students, which makes a big difference in the quality of students you can attract."

An assistant professor at UIUC said that the "absolutely phenomenal graduate student" support offered, which guarantees six years of support, is "very attractive in a very competitive situation when you're competing for the very best." An associate professor remarked, "I came here as an assistant professor and I've stayed because they gave me more access to research funds, the opportunity to work with graduate students, have RA funding, and discretionary funds for research through a research expense account."

Policy and Practice Implications

In summary, the following conclusions may be drawn about how university administrations can best provide the support for teaching and research.

1. Provide leadership from the top. Presidential and provostial leadership in stressing the importance of excellence in research and teaching is crucial substantively and symbolically. At Ohio State, the president has set a high bar to build a world-class faculty through providing space for interdisciplinary research and improving the faculty work environment. To that end, the president and provost work hard to ensure that various schools and divisions have the necessary autonomy to decide what will work best in their culture and the provost spreads best practices by word of mouth across the campus. The provost at UIUC provides financial support for a Faculty Excellence Program and empowers the deans and department heads to build effectiveness through teamwork.
2. Have formal offices and programs to support faculty work. Dedication of resources to supporting faculty work is one clear indicator of how important faculty are to institutional success. All

campuses visited for this project have established programs to support faculty research and teaching.

- Grant support. Many universities offer pre-award support to faculty preparing proposals for outside funding and this is good practice. What's less common, but equally important, is post-award support.
- Internal grants. Faculty are grateful for internal funding, even in small amounts, especially in the humanities where typically less money is needed to support faculty research.
- Teaching and learning centers. Many pre-tenure faculty are better researchers than teachers, in part because they may not have teaching experience, depending on their graduate training. Even if they have experience, they may need additional pointers to improve; thus, they find on-campus support extremely helpful.
- Research institutes. Such institutes may be a source of internal grant support, but beyond that, they are places where pre-tenure faculty can find collaborators and engage in interdisciplinary work—something many find especially fulfilling.
- Colloquia, workshops, and seminars. Pre-tenure faculty appreciate opportunities to present their research at colloquia on campus, receive feedback, and fine-tune prior to presenting at a national conference. Workshops and seminars for writing grants, running a lab, getting published, mentoring undergraduates and graduates, improving teaching, and getting tenure are all typically well-received by pre-tenure faculty.

3. Ensure that pre-tenure faculty can focus on what matters most to achieve tenure; if that's research, then minimize the teaching and service requirements.
   - Ensure equity of workload. Auburn, in particular, was noted for ensuring that the junior and senior faculty alike teach introductory courses and large seminars.
   - Protection from too much teaching or service. Pre-tenure faculty at Auburn, OSU, and UIUC mentioned their appreciation of course load reduction and relief from burdensome committee service during the early years so that they can get their research program off the ground in order to be on track for tenure.

4. Provide professional development leave. At OSU and UIUC, pre-tenure faculty discussed the importance of research leaves during their probationary years.

5. Provide travel support and research assistants. At most universities, outside letters of recommendation are required to gain tenure and promotion; therefore, it is necessary to become known outside one's own institution, which often requires traveling to conferences or to conduct research remotely. Thus, pre-tenured faculty members require funding for such purposes and are grateful for internal travel stipends (along with that provided in grants). Research assistants are also highly valued.

CHAPTER SIX

Culture, Climate, and Collegiality

The Toughest Topic of All

Getting one's mind and arms around institutional climate, departmental culture, and camaraderie among colleagues is challenging yet crucial to understanding pre-tenure faculty workplace satisfaction.[1] In fact, no other measures have greater impact on global satisfaction and intention to stay (Chaffee and Tierney 1988; Tierney and Rhoads 1993; Trower and Gallagher 2008b, 2008c; Trower 2009).

Culture and Climate: An Overview

It is useful to begin this analysis with a broad yet cogent definition of culture that will help to guide further discussion. The culture of an organization or group can be defined as "a pattern of shared basic assumptions that the group learned as it solved its problems of external adaptation and internal integration, that has worked well enough to be considered valid and, therefore, to be taught to new members as the correct way to perceive, think, and feel in relation to those problems" (Schein 1992, p. 12).

Culture is immeasurable and not readily observable, even by the very members that create and embody it (Van Maanen 1984). The shared assumptions that serve as the backbone of a culture can be inferred when considering the norms, ideology, artifacts, and stories of a person or group (Chaffee et al. 1988). These shared assumptions are not born and adopted in a vacuum, as external influences such as the media, religion, and politics create unique cultural experiences that individuals bring into the workplace.

With regard to academe, college and university faculty members operate within multiple cultures at once. Consider that the academic profession has its own shared assumptions, some of which can be inferred through the actions and ideology of organizations such as the American Association of University Professors. In addition, each discipline (e.g., mathematics; theology) has its own norms and practices. Now take into account that institutions, whether they are community colleges or large research universities, also have their own shared assumptions. Furthermore, within these institutions, separate departments or units have their own unique cultural attributes (Austin 1994). Although many of these cultures overlap in their norms and beliefs, faculty members inevitably play favorites and assimilate to some cultures more strongly than others. For instance, some faculty identify most strongly with their institutional culture, whereas others do so more with their discipline's culture, sometimes resulting in cultural divides between members of the faculty that can impact their sense of community and shared purpose (Tierney and Rhoads 1993). Regardless of their cultural bent, however, all faculty operate within multiple cultures and must continually negotiate their different attributes on a daily basis (Austin 1994).

That faculty juggle multiple cultures in their work becomes more significant when one considers this factor's effect on workplace satisfaction. When faculty feel misaligned with one of academe's cultures, they tend to feel less satisfied with their job. Faculty who perceive themselves to be at odds with their department or institution's perceived organizational culture indicate higher levels of job-related stress, report less overall satisfaction with their positions, and spend less time on teaching (Wright 2005, p. 332).

The reverse is true when faculty feel that their beliefs fit with the cultures they experience at work; they generally stay longer in their jobs, are more satisfied with their position, and are more committed to their institution (Wright 2005). Faculty play a critical role in the health and vitality of institutions because they teach and advise students, conduct research, serve on committees, and offer knowledge for the betterment of society as advisers and consultants. Indeed, understanding the relationship between faculty and culture is critical if these essential participants of higher education are to perform at their best (Tierney and Rhoads 1993).

When one investigates the important link between faculty satisfaction and culture, it becomes apparent that climate is an integral component. Climate, described as a "surface manifestation of culture" (Schein 1990, p. 109), can be thought of as the general feeling or attitude that members of an organization have in relation to the culture (Austin 1994). It is a ubiquitous cultural force that can make a group member experience an array of feelings from welcomed, included, and respected to tense, excluded, and singled out.

The choice of the word *climate* is appropriate given that people often describe their workplace using expressions such as cold or warm (Piercy et al. 2005; Somers et al. 1998); such perceptions are, however, not static. Whether at the institutional or departmental level, perceptions of climate can shift depending on how much positivity or negativity one encounters, and also may vary from one individual to another. When noxious issues such as sexual harassment or bigotry infect a campus, school, or department, the climate can quickly turn cold and unwelcoming (Bond et al. 1993). However, when faculty are engaged in open and communicative dialogue, they often experience a more friendly and helpful climate with their colleagues (Fritschler and Smith 2009). For example, Virginia Tech ran university-wide workshops to address campus climate and improve retention. They involved diverse panels of administrators and faculty members, small group exercises, and discussions of national data trends related to culture and climate. Such efforts have helped faculty to get involved in the discussion of inclusion and support on their campus, thereby improving their perception of the climate (Piercy et al. 2005).

Although the climate at the campus-wide level is important, the effects of climate on faculty workplace satisfaction are particularly pronounced within the departments where faculty spend most of their time. Faculty are accustomed to and immersed in the culture and day-to-day life of their department or unit and are greatly affected by its climate (Austin 1994). The climate they associate with their department can influence the decisions faculty make, particularly when it comes to sensitive policies like stopping the tenure clock. When faculty feel that taking advantage of such policies is frowned upon by their departmental peers, they forgo such avenues altogether in fear for hindering their chances of promotion—known as bias or discrimination avoidance (Drago et al. 2006). As a result, many faculty members postpone starting a family, hide the fact that they have children, or attempt to balance the tenure track with family life, situations that can cause significant stress and pressure, thereby negatively impacting workplace satisfaction (Marcus 2007). The departmental climate can also turn cold when faculty disagree on a department's primary emphasis: research or teaching.

Socialization

The many cultures of higher education and their associated climates are typically unfamiliar territory for newly hired faculty members. Assimilating to these new surroundings is referred to as socialization, a process over time that enables faculty to understand the norms, attitudes, and beliefs of a group. When faculty are socialized, they begin to recognize what is expected of them and what is customary behavior within the group. In essence, it is during this process that faculty members become acculturated members of the organization (Austin 2002; Bauer et al. 2007; Schrodt et al. 2003; Van Maanen and Schein 1979).

Socializing new faculty members is critically important as institutions perpetually work through the necessary and expensive process of hiring and training new faculty. Today's new faculty are under tremendous pressure from multiple angles. At many institutions, they are expected to produce work that contributes to institutional prestige and that bolsters the economic and social well-being of society, to bring in grant dollars to support research, to produce and publish scholarly work, to teach and advise students, and to be good members of the campus community through committee service. Depending on the discipline, creative production or outreach may also apply. However, such expectations can quickly overburden faculty if they are not made to feel welcomed and to be productive members of their organization. New faculty are particularly susceptible to pressure and stress as they may feel isolated in their new surroundings, often because there are few other junior faculty nearby (Cawyer and Friedrich 1998; Cawyer et al. 2002). Therefore, acculturating new faculty members is essential if they are to feel comfortable, focused, and confident in their ability to perform at the level expected by their peers and the public (Austin 2002). The socialization process can ease new faculty members' transition and help to build and maintain their allegiance, make them feel included, and boost their morale (Chaffee and Tierney 1988).

The socialization of new faculty members to the many cultures of higher education is vitally important for their workplace satisfaction, productivity, and retention. It is important to note, however, that young scholars begin their socialization to academe during graduate school (Austin 2002; Austin 1994; Gaff 2002; Van Maanen 1984). As newly minted doctoral graduates enter the workplace, they bring with them bits and pieces of the cultural attributes gleaned during their graduate school experience. The manner in which graduate students are socialized to academe affects the manner in which they handle their responsibilities as faculty members (Van Maanen 1984); therefore, it is worth considering the graduate school socialization process and its effectiveness in preparing new faculty. Many graduate students are socialized through the lens of the research university, and while they are exposed to some of the norms of research, they often lack cultural experiences regarding teaching and service. One study of graduate student socialization found that "experience and training in advising, institutional service, outreach and public service, and ethical aspects of the faculty role were generally not part of the experience" (Austin 2002, p. 112). Furthermore, the students in this study felt as though they had no time for reflection on their graduate school socialization, making it more difficult to understand the academic culture. As a result, many felt unprepared and uncertain regarding the faculty role they aspired to. Although graduate students are socialized to some of the norms, beliefs, and attitudes of faculty work, there are many aspects of the professoriate that are foreign and intimidating. Therefore, it is during this formative stage of academic incubation that graduate students should be exposed to broad cultural attributes of higher education in order to better prepare them for the difficult tenure track ahead (Austin 2002; Gaff 2002).

Fortunately, the socialization process for scholars at the graduate school level and as new faculty members is not a fixed entity. Like culture and climate, the socialization process is a living organism that changes over time and can be improved. Both organizational veterans and newcomers shape and are shaped by the socialization process. However, socializing newcomers is only effective if the attributes one is being socialized to are desirable and represent cultural norms that foster workplace satisfaction and productivity (Tierney 1997). One of the keys to an effective and successful socialization process is sound leadership that is intentional in its efforts to understand and improve the experience of newcomers. To this end, department chairs and other academic leaders must be cognizant of socialization indicators such as newcomer self-efficacy, social integration, and role awareness. The extent to which early career faculty show signs of development in these areas can inform leadership as to the effectiveness of its socialization processes (Bauer et al. 2007). Leaders can also monitor and adjust the socialization process by taking the perspective of the new faculty member, anticipating potential barriers to their acculturation, and linking their unique cultural experiences with the organization's culture (Bensimon et al. 2000). Furthermore, leaders that are effective at managing socialization consider how the newcomer can contribute to the learning and cultural development of both the organization and its veteran participants (Tierney 1997).

Leaders can also use specific tactical strategies to improve the socialization of new faculty members. For example, training activities and workshops with other new faculty members can combat the feeling of loneliness and detachment that often plagues new hires. Also, communicating a clear timetable of events during the first weeks on the job can give newcomers a sense of certainty and order to their new surroundings (Cooper-Thomas and Anderson 2002). This point is supported by Van Maanen (1984), who wrote, "If the socialization machinery of the recruit is of the ceremonial, confirmatory sort, the culture of orientation offers the person in transition knowledge, technique, and value, all of which are helpful in making the transition a smooth one by providing a strong link in the socialization chain" (p. 217).

Another study found that socialization tactics such as training sessions, orientation events, and scheduled social gatherings tended to have the strongest correlation with the cultural assimilation of new faculty members (Bauer et al. 2007). While tactical solutions are not infallible methods of socialization, they do help to open the lines of communication across the organization and send the message to new recruits that they are not alone.

Although organizational leadership plays a critical role in the socialization process, part of the responsibility lies with the new faculty member. New faculty members can reduce uncertainty in their work by actively seeking information from others. Communicating openly and often with senior faculty colleagues enables new faculty members to build relationships and solicit feedback regarding their work performance. The communication, however, will be most effective if it can lead to the formation of reciprocal relationships between newcomers and veterans. In other words, both junior and senior faculty must be sociable, open their doors, and provide honest feedback to each other. When this relationship is healthy, senior faculty colleagues can affirm the socialization of junior faculty and junior faculty can contribute to the cultural development of senior faculty (Bauer et al. 2007). It is this relationship that we will explore in the following section on mentoring, a critical component of the socialization process.

Mentoring

One of the most effective and popular methods of socializing new faculty members is through both formal and informal mentoring. Viewing mentoring as a right rather than a privilege, many of today's tenure-track faculty are eager to receive it and to reap its associated benefits. Despite the apparent demand, less than half of junior faculty feel adequately mentored (Bickel and Brown 2005; Chew 2003). In 2007, less than 20 percent of the junior faculty in some disciplines reported having a mentor (Brown 2007). For many junior faculty, this lack of mentoring can be traced back to their graduate school experiences, a critical starting point of the socialization process. Although 95 percent of graduate students deem mentoring to be essential for professional development, only one-third to one-half ever receive mentoring (Aagard and Hauer 2003; Boyle and Boice 1998).

Unfortunately, when mentoring is absent, potential mentors and mentees are denied its vast benefits to individuals. Typically in the form of a senior faculty mentor and a junior faculty mentee, mentoring can mitigate junior faculty isolation, alleviate their anxieties and uncertainties, and help them to understand their new surroundings (Cawyer et al. 2002). Mentored junior faculty also tend to have increased job satisfaction, leadership capacity, and productivity, as measured by the submission of journal manuscripts and new project undertakings (Carr et al. 2004; Gunn 1995; Johnson 2007; Jossi 1997; Luecke 2004; Murray 2001; Ragins and Kram 2007; Zellers et al. 2008). Mentoring has also been shown to increase the tenure and promotion prospects of junior faculty, partly because mentors can act as advocates for mentees during key promotional milestones (Johnson 2007; Kosoko-Lasaki et al. 2006; Stanley and Lincoln 2005). Additionally, as junior faculty begin to form professional identities, they often see "possible selves" in their senior faculty colleagues; they visualize their own potential in the attributes and skills of their mentors (Johnson 2007, p. 10). In addition, when junior faculty have multiple mentors, they are exposed to various perspectives, professional identities, and personal stories of development. Such arrangements can offer a more diverse mentee experience and increase dialogue between junior faculty members and their senior colleagues (Bickel and Brown 2005). Also, when junior faculty mentor each other (referred to as peer mentoring), they are better able to normalize their experiences and decrease feelings of professional isolation. In addition to providing support, peer-mentoring programs can serve as a catalyst for developing relationships and initiating collaborative projects (Santucci et al. 2008).

Although junior faculty socialization is often the primary goal of mentoring, senior faculty also benefit from the process. Upon jointly determining a junior faculty member's specific needs and goals (both career-oriented and psychosocial), a senior faculty mentor properly aligns himself or herself by taking one or more of the following roles: friend, career guide, information source, and intellectual guide (Sands et al. 1991). Within these roles, senior faculty can experience the intrinsic satisfaction of aiding in a colleague's development. Mentoring also helps senior faculty to foster professional and personal relationships in the workplace and enables an increased awareness of the professional interests and personalities of other colleagues.

Despite these potential benefits, heightened work demands have limited senior faculty time for informal exchanges and one-on-one interactions (Bickel and Brown 2005). Furthermore, some senior faculty are unlikely to view mentorship as being mutually beneficial. The inherent satisfaction and professional opportunities (e.g., collaborative research projects) that stem from mentoring are often overlooked by senior faculty because autonomous work remains highly rewarded and recognized in academe (Johnson-Bailey and Cervero 2004; Zellers et al. 2008).

Junior and senior faculty members are not the only potential beneficiaries of mentoring; institutions also have a lot to gain. Mentorship often serves as the best means for institutions to impart their organizational culture to faculty members (Gibson 2004). One of the primary benefits to institutions is the increased organizational loyalty and devotion that mentoring can foster in junior faculty. In essence, mentoring helps junior faculty to transition from institutional newcomers to institutional citizens (Bickel and Brown 2005; Johnson 2007). As a result, mentoring helps to retain junior faculty because there is a sense of shared commitment; the institution is invested in the faculty member and the faculty member in the institution (Bickel and Brown 2005; Kosoko-Lasaki et al. 2006). Furthermore, some of the individualized benefits of mentoring double as perquisites for the institution. For instance, that mentoring makes junior faculty more productive and satisfied scholars means that institutions with mentoring programs are likely to see more fruitful scholarly returns from their junior faculty. And because mentoring junior faculty makes them more likely to be promoted, it also makes institutional investment in resources to support the tenure and promotion processes more worthwhile (Johnson 2007).

The many benefits of mentoring are also accompanied by potential pitfalls that individuals and institutions should be aware of. At the beginning of a mentoring relationship, it is important that the expectations of the mentor and mentee are aligned (Sorcinelli and Yun 2007). In cases where the expectations are misaligned, deleterious effects can occur. For instance, because many senior faculty are attracted to junior faculty members who conjure images of themselves, a "cloning phenomenon" may result (Johnson 2007, p. 28). In this manner, a junior faculty member's individual goals are stifled when a senior faculty mentor "projects" onto her/his mentee. Similarly, junior faculty are often afraid to disappoint senior faculty members who view mentorship as an arranged marriage meant primarily to promote the mentor's personal agenda (Pololi et al. 2002, p. 867); therefore, junior faculty sometimes abandon their own ambitions in order to please their mentors and follow directly in the mentor's footsteps. Traditional, dyadic mentoring relationships may also transgress into a "sponsor-protégé" model, in which junior faculty's psychosocial needs are overlooked in favor of a strictly career-focused relationship (Hill and Kamprath 2008). This model sometimes creates tension when an organization uses mentorship as a means to "changing the individual" (Smith et al. 2000, p. 260). In this manner, a focus is placed on molding junior faculty to fit an institution's culture rather than allowing individuals to bring some of their own culture to the institution (Smith et al. 2000).

How then can an institution design its mentoring program to capitalize on the potential benefits and limit the potential pitfalls? Ensuring that a formal mentoring program is in place is the first step. This allows incoming junior faculty members to receive support from the start of their career (Fuller et al. 2008). The stakes are simply too high to assume that effective relationships will be "formed by osmosis" (Wilson et al. 2002, p. 317). Raising campus awareness about the importance of mentoring is crucial to garnering sufficient faculty assistance and input. Research on the organizational benefits of mentoring has shown that mentoring programs are most effective when integrated within an institution's larger human resource management system, allowing for interdisciplinary exchanges (Zellers et al. 2008). Department chairs are also instrumental in this process, organizing events within and outside of departments (Sorcinelli and Yun 2007). Many schools partner in offering symposia that aid in peer networking while also cultivating relationships with senior faculty. Senior faculty may also be more inclined to participate in such initiatives, attaching personal and professional benefit to feedback received from other faculty representatives of different departments and pedagogical approaches (Katz 2008).

With regard to the number of mentors that a junior faculty member has, more is often better. One mentor is insufficient to introduce a new faculty member to the multidimensional complexities of an institutional culture (Chapman and Guay-Woodford 2008) and places enormous pressure on that one individual and a single relationship. Consequently, a need has developed for university-wide mentorship programs, both formal and voluntary, intended to acquaint junior faculty members with a "portfolio" of mentors that span the course of their careers (de Janasz and Sullivan 2004, p. 273). Access to separate mentors has shown to increase faculty morale and decrease workload fatigue (Fuller et al. 2008). Additionally, should an individual mentor prove to be ineffective or absent, there is little disruption made to a faculty members' mentorship construct (Wasburn 2007). As junior faculty progress through the tenure track, separate learning phases will undoubtedly present different needs. A diverse group of mentors can help in serving different roles as faculty members' respective situations evolve (de Janasz and Sullivan 2004). Having a developmental network can allow junior faculty to access "mentors of the moment" whose knowledge or expertise is most apropos (de Janasz and Sullivan 2004, p. 269). Ultimately, the professional and personal benefits accrued through mentoring relationships are dependent upon the investment made by both the mentor and mentee (Zellers et al. 2008).

Wasburn (2007) made a strong case for multiple mentors, arguing that networking mentoring, or peer mentoring (which is nonhierarchical and involves building a community of more than two participants), is more flexible and less intense than traditional "grooming mentoring models" (one mentor and one protégé) and offer the additional benefit of less concern over whether participants will be compatible over the long period of time (p. 60). Wasburn calls her model "strategic collaboration" as it combines features of networking or peer mentoring and developmental networks; "The resulting model provides two mentors and creates a peer group of support as well. If properly managed, strategic collaboration teams can help to ensure that all faculty, women and minorities in particular, are mentored for success" (pp. 60–61).

Collegiality

When discussing the culture, climate, and socialization of faculty, collegiality plays an integral role. Defined here as amicable interaction and coexistence between members of an organizational setting, collegiality is nothing less than the linchpin of a healthy climate and culture in academe. For a collegial atmosphere to exist at a college or university, faculty members must feel like members of a community in relative accord regarding their principles and ideals (Birnbaum 1988). When collegiality is lacking, faculty members report being less satisfied with their job; in surveys, pre-tenure faculty place its importance above tenure clarity and compensation (Trower and Gallagher 2008b). The repercussions of a noncollegial environment can include isolation, detachment, dissatisfaction, and higher attrition rates (Bensimon et al. 2000).

Although collegiality is an essential ingredient in the workplace satisfaction of faculty, the current state of collegiality in higher education looks bleak. One study reported that "higher education suffers deeply from a loss of community . . . professors report that they rarely engage in conversations about ideas or teaching. They feel uncertain about their performance, but have no one with whom to discuss their problems (Bensimon et al. 2000, p. 122). The authors reported that collegiality is rare in academic departments, and when collegiality is absent new faculty tended to endure increased stress. They also found that the nature of academic work actually impedes collegial relationships because faculty members are naturally separated by their specialties and thus may have few chances to build relationships with colleagues across their department and institution. Other barriers to community building include gender, race, sexual orientation, belief systems, and generational gaps (Bensimon et al. 2000).

Despite academe's inherent obstacles to collegiality, there are techniques that can help to foster and protect it. When a new faculty member arrives on campus, a department- or institution-wide announcement to colleagues will not suffice for community building. Department chairs and mentors should make a concerted effort to communicate the newcomer's research interests beyond the departmental level in order that others at the institution may make relevant connections with their own work. Also, it is important to help new faculty members to translate and make meaning of the institutional conversation that is ongoing when they begin their job. In that way they can contribute and not feel lost. On a related note, talking to new faculty members about existing political feuds can help them to avoid getting swept into an atmosphere of divisiveness. Moreover, competitiveness, a sometimes viral threat to collegiality, can be maintained at healthy levels by evaluating a faculty member's work in relation to her/his past performance and not in relation to the work of others (Neumann in Bensimon et al. 2000).

Techniques that encourage a collegial faculty work environment can also generate the proper conditions for collaboration. A collaborative culture is described as one in which "faculty members, regardless of age, rank, experience, and tenure, all support one another and co-exist in a cooperative, friendly, nurturing environment" (Edmondson et al. 2002, p. 10). For such a collegial environment to thrive, certain elements must be present. To begin with, the physical layout of offices and the distance between colleagues matters. Offices that surround an open space can facilitate more communication and interaction because faculty members can open their door and see who is in the office and available for asking a question or simply having a chat. Also, an atmosphere of teamwork and cooperation is important; back-stabbing and infighting can be damaging to a collaborative culture. Effective leadership can help to foster a common vision for the department and help to build consensus regarding collaborative work standards and expectations. By including all faculty members in decision-making processes, everyone becomes responsible for the results. Furthermore, faculty tend to feel a greater sense of team membership and belonging when they make decisions as a group. And, because all ranks are allowed to be involved in the decision-making process, there is limited division or disrespect along seniority lines (Edmondson et al. 2002; Quinland and Ackerlind 2000).

One may ask if collaboration among colleagues is necessary or feasible, given that most academics work within a very specific field and because single-author work is still highly rewarded. Institutions are now finding that more and more of society's demands—whether they be health related, economic, or otherwise—require the fusion of multiple disciplines thereby necessitating faculty collaboration (Biggs 2008; Frost and Jean 2002). Collaboration can take more forms than simply the coauthored paper. One study found that faculty who were promoted and recognized and had strong teaching and publication records had informally consulted with their colleagues on a more frequent basis than their less successful colleagues. Furthermore, when these faculty members collaborated, they often developed lasting bonds that benefited their careers further down the road (Hitchcock et al. 1995).

While faculty collaborations come in many forms, the newcomer's collaborative experience is often with a senior faculty member; when successful, these collaborative partnerships frequently morph into mentoring relationships (Quinland and Ackerlind 2000). There are differences, though, in the collaborative experiences and preferences of junior and senior faculty that can impede the development of such relationships. Junior faculty are typically focused on achieving tenure and therefore want to collaborate on projects that will get them closer to their goal. Senior faculty, however, often prefer longitudinal studies that allow them to investigate experimental hypotheses and venture into unknown territory (Frost and Jean 2003). The structure of an organization can also impact the frequency and success of junior and senior faculty collaborations. If the institution is overly hierarchical in its decision making, then inequities can result "between faculty generations and classifications" often causing "a climate of distrust" (Quinland and Ackerlind 2000, p. 45). When an organization is flatter in its power structure, the probability of successful junior-senior collaborations is higher. Junior faculty are more trusting and open to working with senior faculty when they do not feel that their academic freedom will be threatened by an imbalance of power (Quinland and Ackerlind 2000).

When collaborations between junior and senior faculty members develop, there are important issues related to the junior faculty member's career progression that warrant discussion. In the case of interdisciplinary collaboration, faculty develop knowledge of multiple academic units and are often solicited for committee work and the task of building their interdisciplinary field. Senior faculty should be cognizant of these demands and make sure that they encourage interdisciplinary junior faculty to complete the necessary research for tenure. Furthermore, in the case of interdisciplinary collaboration, it is useful to discuss common tenure and promotion concerns early on. Such concerns include how much a junior faculty member contributed to a multiple-author study and why leaders in individual disciplines are not as familiar with a junior faculty member's interdisciplinary work. Although interdisciplinary collaborations are becoming more frequent, conversations regarding junior faculty development and success must accompany them (Pfirman et al. 2005a).

COACHE Climate Data

The COACHE survey includes ten measures of climate, culture, and collegiality, including nine satisfaction questions and one agreement item (see tables 6.1 and 6.2).

Overall, pre-tenure faculty are most satisfied with the fairness with which their immediate supervisor evaluates their work and the amount of personal interaction they have with other pre-tenure colleagues. They are least satisfied with three factors concerning tenured colleagues: opportunities to collaborate with them, their intellectual vitality, and the amount of professional interaction they have with them.

In addition, the COACHE survey has pre-tenure faculty rate the importance and effectiveness of formal and informal mentoring. Formal mentoring

Table 6.1. COACHE Survey Average Ratings on Climate, Culture, and Collegiality Items

Please indicate your level of satisfaction or dissatisfaction with each of the following items:	Average Rating
The fairness with which your immediate supervisor evaluates your work	4.02
The amount of personal interaction you have with pre-tenure colleagues	4.00
The amount of professional interaction you have with pre-tenure colleagues	3.87
How well you fit (e.g., your sense of belonging, your comfort level) in your department	3.81
The amount of personal interaction you have with tenured colleagues	3.70
The interest tenured faculty take in your professional development	3.53
The amount of professional interaction you have with tenured colleagues	3.49
The intellectual vitality if the tenured colleagues in your department	3.43
Your opportunities to collaborate with tenured faculty	3.35

Scale: 5 = Very satisfied; 4 = Satisfied; 3 = Neither satisfied nor dissatisfied; 2 = Dissatisfied; and 1 = Very dissatisfied

Table 6.2. COACHE Survey Average Rating on Departmental Fair Treatment of Pre-Tenure Faculty

Please indicate your level of agreement or disagreement with the following statement:	Average Rating
On the whole, my department treats pre-tenure faculty fairly compared to one another	3.79

Scale: 5 = Strongly agree; 4 = Somewhat agree; 3 = Neither agree nor disagree; 2 = Somewhat disagree; and 1 = Strongly disagree

Table 6.3. COACHE Survey Average Ratings of the Importance of Informal and Formal Mentoring

Please rate how important or unimportant the following policies and practices would be to your success, regardless of whether they currently apply to your institution.	Average Rating
Informal mentoring	4.44
Formal mentoring	3.97

Scale: 5 = Very important; 4 = Important; 3 = Neither important nor unimportant; 2 = Unimportant; and 1 = Very unimportant

Table 6.4. COACHE Average Ratings on the Effectiveness of Informal and Formal Mentoring

Please rate the effectiveness or ineffectiveness of the following policies and practices at your institution.	Average Rating
Informal mentoring	3.56
Formal mentoring	2.90

Scale: 5 = Very effective; 4 = Effective; 3 = Neither effective nor ineffective; 2 = Ineffective; and 1 = Very ineffective

programs match protégés with a mentor or team of mentors, while informal mentoring happens naturally, or organically. Average importance results are shown in table 6.3 and mean effectiveness ratings in table 6.4.

The data show that pre-tenure faculty find informal mentoring more important to their success than formal, and also find it more effective. A number of pre-tenure faculty with whom we have spoken reported a certain ambivalence or even skepticism about formal mentoring programs, preferring instead to find their own mentor(s).

COACHE research (Trower and Gallagher 2008b, 2008c) demonstrated that pre-tenure faculty face a number of challenges related to culture and climate in their early years. One frequently mentioned issue was isolation resulting from (1) a lack of colleagues with similar interests, demographic characteristics, or at the same career stage in the department; (2) a culture where everyone is very busy with little time for face-to-face, quality interaction with colleagues; (3) not knowing how to navigate interdepartmental politics and uncertainty with whom to align oneself if there are departmental factions; and (4) a lack of freedom to express one's opinions, especially those that conflict with senior departmental colleagues. Therefore, pre-tenure faculty would like a chair who is "demonstrably" invested in their success and an open-door environment where they can have informal conversations and license to ask "stupid questions" (p. 20).

Pre-tenure faculty were clear about what they want in terms of a campus and departmental support. First, they would like to feel supported, respected, and valued for their contributions. Second, they would like to see departmental cultures of shared responsibility for early career faculty success and a sense that the institution really wants pre-tenure faculty to succeed (Trower and Gallagher 2008b, p. 23). In terms of collegiality and collaboration, pre-tenure faculty would like more opportunities to engage with colleagues intellectually and professionally.

Campuses with High Climate Scores

The four public research universities that scored well on some aspects of climate, culture, and collegiality were Auburn, Ohio State, the University of Iowa, and the University of Kansas.

Auburn University

Auburn scored in the 84th percentile for fair departmental treatment for junior faculty, the interest senior faculty take in the professional development of junior faculty, and opportunities for junior faculty to collaborate with senior colleagues. Auburn also scored quite well for the effectiveness of informal mentoring offered. Interviews shed light on reasons for these high scores.

The creed[2] was mentioned in chapter 5 as it related to faculty support and the sense of equity among the university's faculty, but it also has relevance in terms of creating a campus culture of community that includes everyone— faculty, administrators, staff, students, and alumni. Said a senior administrator, "There is the Auburn creed on the campus; the alumni cling to it . . . the President brings it up now and then . . . it is part of the culture here to buy into the creed and culture of family and it makes it much more of a statement about what Auburn is. We believe in hard work." Said another administrator, "My translation of the creed, and the collegiality statement, is basically—are you ready to pitch in and be part of the team? If not, this is not the place for you." The creed was described as a "tool to help build the Auburn family idea" that helps generate a "huge sense of loyalty among our alumni and our students and most of the faculty who believe that you can advance together. It's somewhat of a Utopian view of what this university is, but it provides a unifying factor."

Ohio State University

OSU scored in the 97th percentile on supervisor fairness, the 89th for the interest senior faculty take in the professional development of junior faculty, and the 81st for opportunities for junior faculty to collaborate with senior colleagues. The university also scored quite well for effectiveness of informal mentoring.

University of Iowa

Iowa's scores placed it in the 94th percentile for opportunities for junior faculty to collaborate with senior colleagues, the 92nd for professional interaction with senior colleagues, the 91st for the intellectual vitality of the senior faculty, and the 80th for the interest senior faculty take in the professional development of junior faculty. Three overarching themes were found to sum up what's happening at Iowa—a Germanic and Midwest climate that is supportive; the deans and chairs take an active role in creating a supportive workplace; and there is mentoring, formal in some departments and informal in others. These three factors are intertwined and define the university's culture.

University of Kansas

Pre-tenure faculty ratings at KU placed their sense of fit and their professional interactions with senior colleagues in 89th percentile, with scores for personal interaction with senior faculty placing it in the 84th percentile. Informal mentoring received a net effectiveness rating of 74 percent. Based on interviews, it seems that there are three primary aspects of culture that differentiate KU: (1) a long-standing tradition of shared governance where all faculty, including tenure-track, have a voice and where the junior faculty's opinions are respected; (2) a sense of "Midwest niceness," in that trust and fairness are very important and people are genuinely nice; and (3) a climate where tenure-track faculty are encouraged to ask questions and seek answers of mentors and at workshops and seminars.

Effective Practice 1: Ensure Formal or Informal Mentoring as Well as Opportunities to Form Networks and Collaborations for All Tenure-Track Faculty Members

Cultures are created through relationships, and relationships are developed through networking and mentoring. At Auburn, although some of those interviewed mentioned a formalized matching system, most mentoring tends to happen most often on an informal basis. A senior administrator remarked that most department have senior faculty who feel it is part of their responsibility to bring junior faculty along. "It's a fairly standard practice here for a senior faculty member to put junior faculty members on grants as PI and take the secondary role as co-PI. Mentoring is just part of the culture here." A full professor and department chair put it this way, "The culture in our department is simple—if we hire someone on the tenure track, we want them to succeed. We're responsible for doing everything we can to ensure their success when they stand for tenure and promotion. The associate and full professors discuss what they can contribute to mentoring the assistant professors whether that collaborating in the lab or on grants, providing feedback on articles or grant proposals, or helping out with a syllabus or teaching. There are countless ways for senior faculty to mentor the assistant professors—all done informally." Another chair stated, "We are clear when we hire a new faculty member that there's going to be some natural mentoring and numerous collaborative opportunities with the senior faculty. This helps both the junior and senior faculty and builds the quality of the department. We have to always ensure that everyone is willing to be part of the greater good and working as a team."

Auburn rewards senior faculty during the review process for mentoring tenure-track faculty and for research collaborations and interdisciplinary work. During the first semester on campus, tenure-track faculty are encouraged to "look around and decide who they want for a mentor; all of them have more than one, actually," said a department chair. An assistant professor exclaimed about how active the senior faculty are in her department in terms of formal and informal advice for publishing, getting grants, handing service requests on campus, and for making connections in the discipline. Another assistant professor talked about how collegial Auburn is, describing it as a "work hard and play hard environment." He elaborated by saying that there are plenty of social activities but also research support for collaborating on projects. "There are numerous internal and external support networks. Internally, the senior faculty have been very active in making recommendations. They spend a lot of time talking to me about what the market is like, what we need to do with the students, and then stepping up with advice about achieving tenure; they offer guidance and mentoring. There is this wonderful interplay between junior and senior faculty." A department chair elaborated:

> There's a lot of informal mentoring going on. Once you start here on the tenure track, you're seen as an equal player; there is no hierarchy. There is not a pecking order, which is unique to Auburn, from what I've heard. I can't overemphasize how much we try to sell that to incoming faculty—if you like that, and can live up to that, this is the place for you. You simply have to be a team player here; collegiality is a requirement for achieving tenure, and it's difficult to be on a team where the playing field isn't even. The greatest strength we have in our department is the collegiality of our faculty.

At Kansas, as at Auburn, much of the mentoring is "unstructured" and "informal." However, the School of Medicine has a formal process that includes one-on-one (career) mentoring, team mentoring (for research), and layered and group mentoring, described in a document (see www.kumc.edu/som/facdev/mentoring/kusommentoringbooklet.pdf) that covers definitions; goals and objectives; benefits for junior faculty, senior faculty, and the school; the process—including tasks for leadership and the faculty, how mentors are matched, orientation, how to change mentors, meetings, confidentiality, guidelines, and training; expectations; the impact of race and gender; challenges; and evaluation.

Whether the subset under consideration was formal or informal mentoring, those with whom we spoke had good things to say about mentoring at

KU. An assistant professor noted that he was assigned an official mentor—a senior faculty member—but also received mentoring from the chair and another senior member of the department. He met with them several times before his third-year review and they were "very clear" about what he needed to do. Another tenure-track faculty member said that there is a different formal mentor assigned every year: "Some are better than others, but I liked switching because you figure out who to go to for research and who to talk to about teaching. Some of the best advice I got was in my first year when my mentor told me to get on a plane and meet with my NSF program officer in person to discuss my grant submission—to personally show up. And that has made a big difference."

In the humanities, an important function of an official, assigned mentor is to serve as a peer reviewer for the tenure-track faculty member's teaching. A department chair in the College of Liberal Arts and Sciences discussed how every young faculty member has to have a mentor: "In consultation with the new faculty member, they are assigned someone; we ask them who they would like as their mentor, who they would feel comfortable asking questions and not being judged, who they think can help them. But that mentor is not always the person who actually stays their mentor. The faculty member will usually seek out whomever they have affinity with—someone from whom they think they can get the best information and that's more fluid." According to a department chair and full professor,

> There are incredible demands on the senior faculty to do mentoring work. We assign two official full professor mentors to each junior faculty member. We used to let people choose their mentor(s), but then some people end up always being selected and doing all this work, so now we assign and spread the work around. We tell everyone that it's not permanent, but to just see how it goes for a couple of years. If personality-wise, it's not clicking, I tell the junior faculty members to come to me and tell me so I can figure something else out. As chair, I just try to create a supportive environment, and everyone tends to pitch in with that.

At OSU, some departments have established formal mentoring processes for junior faculty and to encourage interdisciplinary collaboration across campus, while others rely more on informal connections. A full professor described a formal mentoring process that has been in place for several years whereby senior faculty members are assigned to a junior faculty member for regular meetings. A department chair noted that, as soon as assistant professors are hired, he works with them to establish a mentoring committee of three to four people. The committee meets with the mentee every quarter and the committee chair provides a written review to the chair and to the assistant professor. In addition, the chair takes each junior faculty member to lunch once a quarter so they can talk about their frustrations and whatever else seems important. Another department chair said that junior faculty members are advised to have more than one mentor. "The risk is confusion if they tell you different things, but on balance, we discovered that risk is worth taking because the real benefit is having more than one person as your advocate."

A dean said that an informal approach to mentoring has worked well. "We encourage the junior faculty to seek the advice of their senior colleagues before submitting a grant proposal; and the senior faculty members are happy to take a look and give them feedback." Similarly, a full professor noted, "My department didn't like the word 'mentor'; it sounds too paternalistic, so we use 'resource partner.' A resource partner for assistant professors is someone who helps you navigate this place, reads your work, checks in on you now and then, and is just someone you can trust to talk to openly. We also have groups of faculty who meet for readings, social events, brown bag discussions, meeting about pedagogy—all of that. The tenure-track faculty take part and feel this is an effective part of learning the culture."

Ohio State also has a Diversity Enhancement Program (DEP) in the College of Humanities; it has four parts including mentoring, described in table 6.5. It is important to note that mentees in this program "are relieved from other departmental service for at least one quarter during the first year here, ideally for longer."

In addition to mentoring, the other components of the DEP are (1) an Ethnic Studies Research Working Group to which junior faculty of color in the College of Humanities bring their work-in-progress, thus providing a forum for feedback for papers and talks; (2) a Teaching for Diversity pedagogy group for faculty and graduate students who wish to discuss teaching ideas and strategies; and (3) a Faculty of Color Caucus (FCC) "for the general purpose of providing professional and collegial support," and whose objectives are to

- assist the COH Dean and Diversity Committee in assessing and, if necessary, adjusting the Diversity Enhancement Program by providing feedback about the experiences of involved faculty;

Table 6.5. Ohio State University, Statement from the Diversity Enhancement Program on Mentoring

---

A mentoring model, which provides Humanities faculty of color with a mentor who assists the faculty member with substantial and sustained support throughout his/her first four years at the university. In the first year, the faculty member is assigned a mentor from among a group of interested faculty from the College of Humanities or other Colleges in the Arts and Sciences who have undergone sustained training for effective mentoring (described below). After the first year, the faculty member may choose a new mentor or continue with the assigned mentor.

This mentoring program coexists with and supplements existing departmental mentoring programs which assign a senior member, perhaps with overlapping intellectual interests, to assist the new faculty member in navigating departmental procedures, service, and intellectual expectations. However, because the College mentor (who might but need not belong to the same department as the new faculty member) undergoes training and provides substantial mentoring support throughout the faculty member's early years at the university, he or she is given departmental support as well as professional recognition for this significant mentoring responsibility.

In addition, because the new faculty member of color is expected to commit some time to the mentor as well as to participate in some of the training sessions, the Faculty of Color Caucus, the Ethnic Studies Research group, and the Teaching for Diversity Pedagogy group, he or she is to be relieved from other departmental service for at least one quarter during the first year here, ideally for longer.

Source: humanities.osu.edu/cohi/InterAdministration/committees/diversity/yr2005 -06/enhancementProgram.cfm

- meet regularly to discuss quality of life and professional development issues;
- provide networking, both within and outside the university, that will enhance recruitment and retention of minority faculty to Ohio State;
- provide a setting wherein mentoring can take place in a group format; and
- strengthen connection with external professional networks of scholars of color and faculty teaching in Ethnic and Area Studies.

Said one associate professor of the DEP:

A big piece of the mentoring for me has been my involvement in the FCC. We meet regularly with the junior faculty—especially at the time of annual review— and go over those review documents with them. We've been reading each other's work and giving feedback on that; we give suggestions on possible publishers and how to negotiate that process. We provide forums where the junior faculty can get their work profiled—so people in the department can see what they're doing and ask questions, and give them feedback and support them in that way. A lot of it has to do with helping them structure their annual reports and prepare them for their sixth-year review when they stand for tenure. I'm a mentor through the DEP where I am matched with a junior faculty member and you do these same sorts of things for someone in another department—read work, help them get published, and all that.

At the University of Iowa, a Mentoring Task Force composed of ten faculty members from across the campus, and one administrator was established by the provost's office in 2006 and charged with making recommendations for the purpose of supporting and enhancing faculty mentoring. Overarching purposes were to increase the rate at which qualified faculty achieve tenure, to improve the retention rate of qualified tenured faculty, and to improve and enhance the UI environment by making it more supportive and welcoming.

The task force felt that "central mandates for specific forms of mentoring programs would be resented by both mentor and mentee and thus would not be as successful as the continuation of the current voluntary mentoring practices" (Report of the Mentoring Task Force, p. 1, provost.uiowa.edu/docs/reports/mentoring.pdf). The task force made five short-term and three long-term recommendations to enhance mentoring, without prescribing mandatory mentoring. Short term recommendations of the report included making provisions for

1. an electronic newsletter focused on the needs of new faculty, including mentoring, issued by the provost's office;
2. a centralized website/clearinghouse to provide information and web links to a variety of university resources for faculty (mentor and mentee);
3. a listserv for interchange among mentors on campus;
4. a workshop on mentoring for the Departmental Executive Officers (DEOs), and to other faculty who serve as mentors; and
5. policy changes (see table 6.6) that would incorporate mentoring into the written framework of institutional goals and expectations.

The long-term recommendations included

Table 6.6. University of Iowa, Recommendations on Mentoring Plans

- Require that the offer letter to new faculty include a detailed mentoring plan that would be in place for the new faculty member coming to campus.
- Require that a developmental plan (potentially developed by the candidate) and as assessment of mentoring to date, be included in the annual review of the faculty member, with documentation of the nature of mentoring that was received and of the mentoring plan for the next year.
- Require an assessment at the three-year review of the probationary faculty member regarding mentoring received to date.
- Require that as part of their reviews, Deans and DEOs would be evaluated on how successful their mentoring programs are.
- Require that annual faculty reports on accomplishments solicit description of mentoring activities similarly to requests for description of service activities.
- Require that the DEO regularly and at least annually communicate to faculty, e.g., via annual DEO address or newsletter, information about mentoring and mentoring expectations for post-tenure reviews.

6. requiring each college to have a mentoring plan, incorporating centralized mentoring support programs, or identifying initiatives designed to meet the unique needs and characteristics of the college;

7. creating a Mentoring Advisory Board based in the provost's office that would have long-term responsibility for monitoring and evaluating mentoring; for development of additional mentoring initiatives; and for identifying two or three departments or colleges as the site for decentralized pilot projects that would serve as a parallel avenue for gathering experiential data on mentoring; and

8. monitoring the outcomes of mentoring initiatives over the short and long term should be monitored.

Iowa now has a website for mentoring (provost.uiowa.edu/mentoring/index .html) that includes information about mentoring for staff, students, and faculty and describes a number of mentoring awards (see table 6.7).

At least three UI colleges—education, dentistry, and law—have developed formalized mentoring programs for junior faculty. Business has a program that is "formal, but voluntary." Appendix H provides brief descriptions of each college's mentoring programs and policies.

A senior administrator mentioned that the provost's office supports the junior faculty socially for the "cost of pizza once a month"; the junior faculty

Table 6.7. University of Iowa Recognition, Awards, and Grants for Mentoring

- Carver College of Medicine Distinguished Mentoring Award. This award is intended to honor Carver College of Medicine faculty members whose distinguished careers have resulted in the mentoring of individuals who went on to their own distinguished careers. In its broadest sense, mentoring is meant to include research training, classroom teaching, clinical training and faculty career development.
- Dewey Stuit Fund in Liberal Arts and Sciences. The Dewey Stuit Fund in Liberal Arts and Sciences is an endowed fund created by friends and former colleagues of the UI College of Liberal Arts and Sciences long-term (1948–1977) former dean, Professor Dewey Stuit. Its purpose is to promote the development of mentor-protégé relationships between undergraduate students and faculty members.
- Graduate College Outstanding Mentor Award. The Graduate College Outstanding Mentor Award recognizes and rewards exemplary mentoring efforts. Each year, the Graduate College gives two $2,500 awards.
- Hubert E. Storer Engineering Student Entrepreneurial Start-Up Award. Undergraduate student recipients will be allowed to register their award as a qualified internship on their transcript. Each student recipient will have access to an entrepreneurial mentor, provided by the John Pappajohn Entrepreneurial Center.
- MBA Alumni Mentor of the Year Award. The MBA Alumni Mentoring Program is designed to match incoming MBA students with alumni whose backgrounds and career interests are similar. The alumni then provide the students with advice regarding career direction, critique their résumés and general academic and professional insights.

get together and talk about issues and then they can bring forth concerns en masse. "No one is exposed personally. Some have decided to form their own writing support group to help them keep focused. Sometimes they ask senior faculty members to join them to just talk." A full professor said, "We assign mentors from the get-go and there's rigor in our mentoring system. Protégés are expected to meet with their mentors three, four times per year and we require a written report."

A formal mentoring system "works well for us," remarked an associate professor. "The senior faculty interact very directly with the junior faculty and look out for them, work on research with them, make sure they aren't overburdened with service make sure they get their fair share of the best incoming graduate students. As an assistant professor here, I worked with one faculty member directly who agreed to be my productivity mentor; we met regularly to discuss my progress and she asked how she could facilitate that. In the first year, everybody works closely with two or three mentors."

A dean talked about have monthly meetings with all the junior faculty and any senior faculty who want to come. A lunch is provided, along with a program outlining university resources that are available to junior faculty. "At the heart of several sessions we cover what is needed for promotion and tenure. I hand out a checklist for meeting with the department head for annual reviews; this is very important because each individual needs feedback from their head on how their progressing toward promotion, not just the day-to-day stuff. It's all formalized and we find it effective."

Another dean talked about a more informal approach to mentoring saying:

> We encourage junior faculty to not just rely on one mentor but to have several and some outside the department. We don't have a formal program because I'm a little uncomfortable assigning people—that just doesn't always work out and then the protégé is kind of stuck. I do ask every junior faculty member every year to name their mentor . . . everyone to whom they feel comfortable going to for help or advice . . . and then I encourage them to do that. It is my expectation that a junior faculty member from one department can walk into the office of a senior faculty member in another department and either ask a question or propose a project, or talk about collaborating, and that there would be no barriers to that.

An assistant professor explained that he prefers the informal nature of mentoring in his department.

> My colleagues are fantastic! They are productive, they're working hard, but they're also genuinely supportive. You can ask them to read your work and they'll say yes. There's a very good vibe for a junior faculty member that we really appreciate. If this were somehow to be mandated, I don't think it would work as well. I also think that the mentoring workshops are excellent, as is the provost's mentoring website. You can go there and click away and learn all about mentoring across campus, and there are resources beyond . . . best practices at other campuses, too. It's a great resource.

Effective Practice 2: Stress the Importance of Community and Provide a Culture of Support

The creed is certainly part of what makes Auburn feel like a family, but there's more to it than that. Those interviewed spoke of social gatherings at faculty homes, of a culture of support, and of a "liberal arts college feel" at this public university. Said a senior administrator,

We have a very strong culture at Auburn; I've been at other universities and they just don't have that. This is the Auburn family—people refer to us as that. I haven't been anywhere else where they have referred to themselves, the campus, as you are part of a family. So we want people to come, be productive and happy, and we want to nurture them to stay. I think that it is part of the culture to make sure that someone becomes part of the family and feels like part of the family and understands that we want them to be successful in staying.

Another senior administrator put it this way: "I've heard from others who are not from the South either say that what's unique about Auburn is that we are a public institution that has the feel of a small liberal arts college and that's all to the good." A full professor and department chair noted that there is no "philosophy of sink or swim" at the campus; instead, it's "just part of the culture" that the senior faculty members do everything they can to help ensure the success of junior faculty to be successful.

An assistant professor noted, "Recently tenured and tenure-track faculty have our own special support system that's become an important part of the culture of community here. And in speaking with several colleagues elsewhere, I think this is unique to Auburn." And a department chair said, "You can't walk through our building without seeing somebody from other departments— there's an internal, open staircase that creates a wonderful community atmosphere. I think this builds community amongst our faculty."

As on most campuses, there's a certain amount of self-selection that occurs when faculty are interviewed and offers made. Apparently, those who will be happy at Iowa, and stay for their entire career, like the culture that characterizes this small, Midwestern town. A full professor mentioned that Iowa City's population is around 75,000 and that "you have to be someone who can be happy in this rather homogeneous place. The nearest big city is a long drive from here. You have to fit the culture; recruiting new faculty is very much a two-way process."

Others talked about the "Iowa Way," which they described as being based on self-sacrifice and a distaste for self-promotion. "People here are pretty humble so leave your ego at the door. There's a certain circumspect nature to the Iowa way" said a senior administrator. Two others elaborated: "The 'Iowa Way' is this cultural frame throughout the state around humility; even if you are excellent, you don't promote that—you don't say it. It's not that you don't strive for excellence; it's just that you don't toot your own horn. You still strive. There's a really strong work ethic in Iowa . . . it's a kind of Germanic thing about working hard, being great, and being humble, too"; and "There is this Midwest sort of 'no bones about it' way of being here . . . people are casual but have high standards . . . and they are generally honest and polite." An assistant professor said that, to him, the "Iowa Way" is about hard work—nose to the grindstone—but where people help their neighbors when they need it. He said, "People work hard and get along; it's an amazing work ethic where people are nice and honest and what you see is what you get—no artifice."

A department chair talked about the support structures at Iowa and said that there's no sense of anyone being "cutthroat or out to get you"; instead, "There's an attitude where 'your success is my success,' and everyone's individual success is the college's success." An assistant professor remarked that "collaborations are just a natural part of the culture here—they're an outgrowth of the Iowa Way. I've co-authored with a senior faculty member, I've co-advised graduate students, and I've also co-taught a graduate course. I doubt these things would have happened if I working someplace else, but here it's encouraged and certainly not frowned upon. I think we all benefit because breakthroughs happen more frequently."

The small town feel of Iowa City means that everyone gets to know most everyone else—faculty, students, staff, and administrators. "Because of the culture of the college, which tends to be very collaborative, and very supportive, there are lots of conversations between senior and junior faculty just to make sure that the junior faculty are satisfied, productive, and supported," said a senior administrator. An associate professor echoed this theme, saying, "There's a general sense of fairness here that I like . . . it comes from the central administration and permeates the place. The central administration makes it clear that the work is hard, we take it seriously, and we're going to push you to be your best, but also that 'we're here to help.'"

As at Iowa, people at KU were often described as being really nice—in fact, "Midwest nice." "There's a Midwestern niceness here—a climate of friendliness; people who visit are always struck by this. There's a sense of wanting to be a part, to pitch in, and volunteer and work hard," said one senior administrator. Another administrator talked about the work ethic culture that is also one where people genuinely care for each other. "It's not at all about lowering standards so people can get tenure; obviously, we don't hire people who we don't think can go all the way and be promoted. It's that the culture here is: 'Join us. Do everything that we say you need to do and you'll get tenure.' And we have a very welcoming atmosphere. This place becomes home. The university sets high expectations, but we're not neurotic about it." Said a senior administrator,

> It feels like a nice family from the get-go. When we being prospective faculty in for interviews, we hold receptions at faculty houses; we want to establish good interpersonal relationships from the beginning. This way, faculty feel like they're joining a family and we carry that through to new faculty orientation which is also very social in its feel. We introduce faculty across campus so that people can get to know others with similar research interests and those networks are very important to everyone. The provost has lunches. Each school has a social event for new faculty, as do the research centers.

An assistant professor talked about having a sense from the start that her department wanted her to get tenure and that there was no competition among assistant professors. "That's very different from what I hear it's like elsewhere—that feeling is that if we hire someone, we want to tenure them. It's not easy but it's not cutthroat; the standards are high, but it feels fair and you feel supported." Another assistant professor noted that, despite having had three different chairs so far, he has found them all to be "really nice and tremendously supportive of the junior faculty. They understand that the success of the junior faculty is critical to the success of the department. The senior faculty work hard to lighten the (teaching and service) burden for the junior faculty."

Effective Practice 3: Stress the Importance of Shared Governance and Level the Playing Field

Several of those we interviewed talked about the faculty's strong role in governance at the University of Kansas and its firm place in the institution's history and culture. Said an associate professor, "Some would say that KU has an over-developed sense of democratic governance; each department has its own bylaws and each meeting is run according to Robert's Rules. Governance is taken very seriously here, and not only among its faculty, but also its students and this is good for the faculty culture." A senior administrator elaborated, "There's a very strong faculty governance system of input here. The faculty's views play an important role in the administration's decision-making, and this includes the tenure-track faculty members who all have a voice."

A department chair noted that the faculty function as a team and that means that the junior faculty get the same vote as the senior faculty. "It's very democratic. We all want to move forward together and the way we do that is for our young faculty to be successful and to be a part of the enterprise from the start." A full professor and department chair commented that, "We have a long-standing culture of respecting junior faculty as being equal and part of the department. If I could put my finger on what's maybe different here (from other large publics) is that there is a sense of treating junior people as an investment, as important, and as equals."

Effective Practice 4: Lead From the Top; Develop Other Leaders; Engage Chairs and Deans

As discussed previously, Ohio State is engaged in numerous campus initiatives to move from "excellence to eminence" per university president Gordon Gee. A large portion of that cultural transformation involves a focus on the faculty and academic personnel planning. In addition, Gee has stressed the importance of breaking down departmental silos and increasing opportunities for interdisciplinary work. This focus on campus culture was mentioned in several interviews. "Keeping a focus on the junior faculty experience, as a very important part of our human capital, has been very important across the campus," said a senior administrator.

> We have committee after committee after committee looking at various faculty issues including whether we have an environment that is supportive of junior faculty. Some departments have hired a lot of junior faculty recently and so we ask them what the senior leadership is doing to help develop these faculty. It is not about 'command and control' here; it is about how the president and provost meet with every dean and every department chair to remind them about paying attention to these issues. We do that through our planning and annual evaluation processes. This all takes time, but we are highly decentralized so this is the best way. It gives central administration a way to say, "We expect you to address such and such issue," and then hold people accountable.

Said another senior administrator,

> The president has been a very forceful advocate for collaborative work across the campus. We have retreats for senior administrators and the idea to talk about culture and climate will be pushed out to the rest of the campus. The top

administration is looking at colleges that are really high performers and the idea is that they will then encourage the deans to talk together and share the best ideas. This is all part of transforming the culture of OSU from "excellence to eminence." A key will be to break down barriers and silos because we believe that the problems of the 21st century are not disciplinary-bound and won't be solved unless we collaborate.

Another OSU administrator noted that provost meets with deans and chairs to discuss annual evaluations of faculty and issues of fairness. "We have a president who has said over and over again that supporting faculty—paying attention to the needs of junior faculty as well as the senior faculty—is absolutely critical to the institution. It has become part of our culture to do so." A full professor stated, "Our president's leadership style is that he wants to hear from the faculty. He has become much more proactive in his relationships with the faculty and there has been an enormous increase in the invitations for faculty to participate in things. We also have some wonderful leadership on the faculty senate side at this time, and that matters, too."

OSU is noteworthy in its efforts to engage the deans and chairs in the culture change process. The Office of Human Resources offers numerous seminars and workshops for academic leaders (see hr.osu.edu/ohrc/learningdevel opment.aspx). One department chair commented, "We have two groups of chairs mentoring chairs right now . . . about 10 chairs get together once a month like a big therapy session. We just share everything—our successes and failures—there's a lot of trust that develops. Each meeting has a theme of something we've all decided we'd like to discuss." Another said, "A program called 'Collaborating among Chairs' is a work group set up by Human Resources where chairs across campus meet once a month to talk about issues. Whatever is said in the room stays in the room. It's a peer mentoring circle."

A full professor and former department chair discussed the instrumentality of chairs in setting department tone and culture, reinforcing the need for these education session for chairs, "The better the chair are, the better the faculty, the greater the likelihood that junior faculty will succeed—it's all related."

A dean said that he always spends time with early career faculty soon after they arrive on campus; typically he takes them to lunch to talk about the college and expectations, how things are going, how they're settling in. And once or twice a year, he meets with the faculty individually just to ask how it's going and maybe to "just chat a bit informally." He noted that "face-to-face is key to establishing a strong culture of support for junior faculty as they are an integral part of the division, of the teaching and research enterprise—we're all in this together."

An associate professor and chair mentioned that too often "there can be little fiefdoms within schools and disciplines and so it's rare when all of the faculty get together." So he started a series of department seminars, called "Cookies and Conversation," where they showcase those who are going up for tenure or who recently published books in order to "celebrate our intellectual accomplishments and have great intellectual conversations. It helps build a more cohesive culture."

At the University of Iowa, a number of those interviewed spoke about the importance of dean and chairs in establishing and maintaining a culture of "seamless support" for junior faculty from the provost's office, to the deans, to the department chairs. A full professor described a culture where department heads or chairs "expend a lot of effort, and try to nurture the junior faculty . . . and I think that for many, and I would certainly include myself, that's probably one of the most rewarding experiences of a faculty job—ensuring the success of the next generation of faculty."

A senior administrator noted it is crucial for deans to select for chair positions those senior faculty members who "understand the importance of creating a healthy climate for pre-tenure faculty." One assistant professor told a story about her second year, when there was an opportunity in the college to apply for internal funding, "My chair suggested we write an application to start a speaker's series in our research area. We got that grant and we've invited the most amazing people! So we keep getting this funded. I'm so fortunate to be where I can go to my chair and say what I'd like to do and request supplemental funding, and there's never been a problem; the answer is always, 'Yes'!"

A dean said that much time is spent discussing the welfare of the faculty: "It makes a big difference when you can approach the chair of a department and say, 'We're seeing the following pattern among faculty in the sciences, and I wonder if your department can do something to address the issue.'" In addition, the dean meets with each faculty member one-on-one to discuss their career and professional development. As a supplement to numerous workshops, the dean spends an hour with 90 to 120 faculty every year to discern how they're doing and to help them think through preparing for promotion or tenure.

Another UI dean spoke about playing an active role in building connections and fostering collaborations. "I'll connect someone in the humanities with someone in the sciences by saying, 'How about talking with X of Y?' And I'll personally call the senior faculty member and say, 'I have a junior faculty member who would benefit from having a cup of coffee with you.' And this really works! So many collaborations have emerged as a result and the informal type of mentoring that magically happens is gratifying." An assistant professor talked about how the dean met with him and provided a notebook to help him collect everything needed for the third-year review and encouraged him to ask any questions that he had about that notebook's content and the tenure process.

An associate professor said, "The dean sets the tone and that tone is one of mutual respect and ensuring that the senior faculty look out for the junior faculty and help them to succeed." He noted that the dean meets regularly with the junior faculty for lunch to discuss how everything's going and if there are any issues or challenges they're facing. "The dean deserves a lot of the credit because a lot of the positive climate comes from her. She also does a great job of using every bit of funding that she has available to provide extra research assistants or TAs, particularly to the junior faculty. And we all make a concerted effort to encourage the pre-tenure faculty at every turn—asking, 'What do you need?' and encouraging them to just stick their heads into our offices and keep in touch."

Auburn, too, recognizes the importance of chairs in creating and maintaining supportive work environments for pre-tenure faculty. The provost's office developed a mandatory training program for chairs and heads in which they learn how to (1) conduct annual faculty evaluations, (2) deal with problems, (3) conduct searches and hires, (4) think about diversity, and (5) look at budgets.

Policy and Practice Implications

In summary, to promote campus-wide cultures and departmental climates that are supportive of tenure-track faculty, it is recommended that institutions take these actions:

1. Ensure instrumental mentoring for all tenure-track faculty. According to JoAnn Moody (2004), the best mentors provide psychological

support as well as instrumental assistance. She noted: "Instrumental mentoring occurs when senior colleagues take the time to critique the scholarly work of junior faculty, nominate them for career-enhancing awards, include them in valuable networks and circles, collaborate with them on research or teaching projects, and arrange for them to chair conference sessions or submit invited manuscripts."

Tenure-track faculty at the four campuses highlighted in this chapter are mentored, some formally and others informally, but the common denominator is that early career faculty are looked after by senior faculty members. Ideally, mentors should be rewarded for this work, and the quality of mentoring should be evaluated. Importantly, mentoring should meet the individual's needs; don't make assumptions about what type of mentoring early career faculty will want (or even if they'll want it at all). Mentoring should be tailored to individual needs. Written, departmental guidelines can be helpful for both mentors and protégés.

2. Ensure opportunities for faculty to form networks and collaborate. The best campus climates for pre-tenure faculty are ones where there are many prospects for faculty to interact in a variety of settings. Faculty at Auburn and Ohio State were grateful for the many forums, both social and in work settings, for tenure-track and tenured faculty to interact.

3. Stress the importance of community. Faculty at Auburn, Iowa, and Kansas all talked about their tight-knit faculties—that the campus feels like "home" and their colleagues, by and large, feel like "family." Faculty and administrators on these campuses are deliberate about supporting social interactions among colleagues

4. Stress the importance of shared governance and level the playing field. At Kansas, people talked about how engaged faculty are in governance, and a common refrain at Auburn was that there really is no hierarchy—senior and junior faculty are "all in it together."

5. Lead from the top and develop other leaders. At Ohio State, the messaging is clear from the central administration that the faculty are of paramount importance to advancing the academic mission. Rather than leaving leadership development to chance, deans and chairs are engaged through conversations, workshops, brown-bag lunches, and other forums.

CHAPTER SEVEN

Engaging Leaders across the Campus

This chapter offers ideas for university leaders (the president and provost, deans, department heads and chairs, and senior faculty) to make progress on improving the workplace for pre-tenure faculty in order to help ensure their satisfaction, success, productivity, and intentions to stay. In order to effectively do so, it is necessary to reflect on both leadership and academic culture because universities are complex entities from both perspectives.

I share Schein's (1992) view that culture and leadership "are two sides of the same coin in that leaders first create cultures when they create groups and organizations. Once cultures exist, they determine the criteria for leadership and thus determine who will or will not be a leader. . . . The bottom line for leaders is that if they do not become conscious of the cultures in which they are embedded, those cultures will manage them. Cultural understanding is desirable for all of us, but it is essential to leaders if they are to lead" (p. 15).

And I agree with Birnbaum's (1988) point that "the important thing about colleges and universities is not the choices that administrators are presumed to make but the agreement people reach about the nature of reality. People create organizations as they come over time to agree that certain aspects of the environment are more important and that some kinds of interaction are more sensible than others. These agreements coalesce in institutional cultures that exert profound influence on what people see, the interpretations they make, and how they behave" (p. 2).

Organizational Culture

Culture was defined in the last chapter as "a pattern of shared basic assumptions that the group learned as it solved its problems of external adaptation and internal integration, that has worked well enough to be considered valid and, therefore, to be taught to new members as the correct way to perceive, think, and feel in relation to those problems" (Schein 1992, p. 12).

Three layers of culture may be analyzed in order to begin to understand an organization: (1) artifacts (visible organizational structures and processes); (2) espoused values (stated strategies, goals, philosophies); and (3) basic underlying assumptions (unconscious, taken-for-granted beliefs, perceptions, thoughts, and feelings—the ultimate source of values and actions) (Schein 1992, p. 17).

Artifacts

In the academy, artifacts would include everything from how buildings are laid out on campus (open spaces, green areas, sidewalks, architecture), to what it's like inside the buildings (and those might be quite different across a campus), to rituals like commencement and new student orientation, to the structure and reporting relationships of senior administrative posts, to the tenure and promotion processes and the policies that guide tenure and promotion practices. According to Schein, artifacts are easy to observe but difficult to decipher (p. 17); he argued that "it is especially dangerous to infer deeper assumptions from artifacts alone because one's interpretations will inevitably be projections of one's own feelings and reactions" (p. 18). Therefore, one must go deeper to examine the values that organizational members say are important.

Espoused Values

"All group learning reflects someone's original values, someone's sense of what ought to be as distinct from what is" (p. 19). Over time, the values that are acted upon and achieve desired results become part of a group's shared meaning and understanding. Eventually, the most successful strategies become shared assumptions of what is good and correct. The prevailing espoused values "gradually become transformed into nondiscussable assumptions supported by articulated sets of beliefs, norms, and operational rules of behavior" (p. 20). Schein pointed out an important distinction between what people say they value (espoused values) and values that have actually transformed into basic assumptions. Espoused values "predict well enough what people will *say* in a variety of situations but which may be out of line with what they will actually *do* in situations where those values should, in fact, be operating" (p. 21).

In academe, for example, there are many things we value, including academic freedom, autonomy, knowledge production, peer review, and lifetime job security (tenure). There are also things we say we value, such as diversity, inclusiveness, community service, and interdisciplinary research. But not everything we say we value in academe is rewarded equally or even rewarded at all—something I'll address later in this chapter.

Basic Assumptions

If a basic assumption of a group is strongly held, members will find any other premise to be "inconceivable" (p. 22). Argyris (1976) called these basic assumptions the "theories-in-use" and found that they actually guide behavior. Because basic assumptions are so widely held, we neither confront nor debate them; they truly are taken for granted and are therefore extremely difficult to change. Schein argued that, viewed this way, learning (as in changing) is very difficult because it requires us to "resurrect, reexamine, and possibly change some of the more stable portions of our cognitive structure, something that Argyris and others have called double-loop learning or frame breaking" (p. 22). To challenge strongly held assumptions would be to "destabilize our cognitive and interpersonal world" (p. 22), which goes beyond producing cognitive dissonance—the uncomfortable tension that comes from holding two conflicting thoughts in the mind at the same time—to causing great anxiety. "Rather than tolerating such anxiety levels we tend to want to perceive the events around us as congruent with our assumptions, even if that means distorting, projecting, or in other ways falsifying to ourselves what is going on around us. It is in this psychological process that culture has its ultimate power" (p. 22).

Cultures are, thus, pervasive, stable, and extremely resistant to change for reasons Schein explained:

- The human mind needs cognitive stability which comes, in part, from basic underlying beliefs about what is good and right.
- Challenges to such stability produce anxiety and defensiveness for individuals and for groups.
- Defense mechanisms kick in that can distort data by denial, rejection, rationalization, or other defensive means; we would rather *defend* than *change* basic assumptions.
- The power of culture is that assumptions are implicit, unconscious, and shared, and therefore mutually reinforced.

- Even if assumptions are somehow surfaced, or exposed, they still operate.

Leadership

Whether a leader wants to overhaul culture, or work at the margins within an existing culture, s/he will do well to heed the advice of experts.

Changing Culture

For leaders, the key issues are how to get at the deeper levels of a culture, how to assess the functionality of assumptions made at each level, and how to deal with the anxiety that is unleashed when those levels are challenged (Schein 1992, p. 27). None of these is a simple task!

I have argued elsewhere that academic cultures are difficult to change because the faculty have "deeply held rules, beliefs and values embedded in the culture of the dominant coalition which wishes to preserve its power base at almost any cost and operates largely in its own best interest, with little understanding or, of interest in, the university writ large" (Trower 2006, p. 152). In the academy, we have structured "intentional continuity." The status quo is maintained because (1) tenure shields faculty from the vicissitudes of the marketplace; (2) shared governance shields faculty from leaders who may wish to make changes; (3) decisions happen by accretion because of decentralization and loose coupling (Birnbaum 1988; Weick 1976), and thus, accountability is lacking; and (4) the market is fine with that. Therefore, to lead is challenging, to change a culture even more so.

Without going into the vast literature on changing organizational culture, I'll mention here just a few ideas for leaders writ large.

Making Incremental Changes

The first ideas come from Rosabeth Moss Kanter (1983), who suggested that salable projects share several characteristics. They must be

- trial-able (able to be demonstrated on a pilot basis);
- reversible (allowing the organization to go back to pre-project status if it doesn't work);
- divisible (able to be done in steps or phases);
- consistent with sunk costs (build on prior resource commitments);

- familiar (consistent with a successful past experience);
- congruent (fit with the organization's direction); and
- valuable as publicity(have visibility potential) (Kanter 1983, p. 221)

"But," notes Kanter, "when these features are not present—as they are un-likely to be in more 'radical' innovations—then projects are likely to move ahead if they are either *marginal* (appear off-to-the-side so they can slip in unnoticed) or *idiosyncratic* (can be accepted by a few people with power with-out requiring much additional support)" (p. 221).

Making More Radical Change

Edgar Schein (1993) discussed three types of organizational learning and the role of anxiety in facilitating organizational change.

The first is knowledge acquisition and insight learning, such as when a leader articulates a new vision or direction. But insight does not automatically change behavior; indeed, if the new direction is viewed as too disruptive to existing routines and too difficult to achieve, people become frustrated and anxious—what Schein calls "anxiety 1": "To avoid this anxiety 1, we deny the problem, or simplify it to something we can cope with, even if it distorts the problem" (p. 86), and thus we do not change/learn.

Schein's second type of learning is the acquisition of habits and skills, most often symbolized by the carrot and stick, where errors are punished and positive behaviors are rewarded. This type of learning takes a long time be-cause we must practice and receive carrots or sticks consistently for good or poor performance. We have to unlearn old behaviors, and "unlearning is emotionally difficult because the old way of doing things . . . has worked for a while and become embedded" (p. 87).

Schein's third kind of learning—called emotional conditioning and learned anxiety (most often associated with Pavlov's dogs)—is the "most potent" (p. 87) because it is based primarily on sticks and becomes so deeply engrained that even when the stick is removed (no punishment), the behavior won't change.

The idea for leaders, according to Schein, is to produce "anxiety 2"—the fear, shame, or guilt associated with *not* learning anything new (Schein 1993, p. 88)—and anxiety 2 must be greater than anxiety 1 for change to occur. Because humans seek homeostasis and equilibrium and prefer a stable environment, for an organization to change, it must first be destabilized, or "unfrozen" (Lewin 2009). Unfreezing, according to Schein, requires three simultaneous processes: (1) producing convincing *and* disconfirming data that forces organizational members to perceive that the current way of doing things is no longer working well; (2) inducing guilt anxiety because the problem cannot be deflected or blamed on someone else (e.g., small sample size; the data are incorrect; it's someone else's responsibility—any number of defensive mechanisms that people use as excuses *not* to learn—see Argyris 1993)—in Schein's terms, anxiety 2/not doing anything; and (3) creating psychological safety whereby people see a manageable path forward that (a) is not catastrophic, (b) will not jeopardize anyone's sense of identity and wholeness; and (c) is possible (meaning that anxiety ultimately will be reduced). Writes Schein: "To put all of this in very plain language, the problem of organizational learning and transformation is to overcome the negative effects of past carrots and sticks, especially past sticks. To make people feel safe in learning, they must have a motive, a sense of direction, and the opportunity to try new things without fear of punishment. Sticks are not very useful during the learning process. Once the learning is underway, the carrot is the essential learning tool. The environment will take care of providing the sticks if the organization is on the wrong path" (Schein 1993, p. 91).

For others to learn, leaders must learn. Schein advises leaders, therefore, to ask themselves (1) What are my *own* learning needs? (2) What anxieties, defenses, and cultural assumptions stand in my way? (3) How can I create psychological safety for people? and (4) How might I create a parallel learning system to build a culture conducive to perpetual learning? (Schein 1993, p. 92).

Leaders are typically the ones to provide the disconfirming information or data (a strategy that COACHE employs) that initiates the change process, and they have to induce the anxiety and guilt to motivate change while at the same time providing enough psychological safety to allow change to happen— quite the balancing act.

Ultimately, leaders must be effective orchestrators of data collection, dissemination, and use in the complex, loosely coupled world that is an academic institution. This requires (1) political readiness (helping people understand who want to know what and why); (2) technical and operational readiness (an infrastructure to support data gathering and effective dissemination); and (3) agreement on definitions (a common vocabulary so everyone is measuring the same things) (Trower and Honan 2002).

But leaders should be careful not to assume that the data provided will actually be used in decision making. This is true for a host of reasons, including these:

- Much of the information gathered and communicated by individuals and organizations bears little relevance to the decision.
- Much of the information used to justify a decision is collected and interpreted after the decision has in effect been made.
- Much of the information gathered in response to requests for information is overlooked when making the decision for which it was requested.
- Regardless of how much information is available at the time a decision is first considered, more information is requested.
- The relevance of the information provided is less conspicuous than is the insistence on information. (Feldman and March 1981, p. 174)

This does not, however, refute the need for data or take away from the multiple functions that data do play, including to catalyze, compare, identify and warn, illuminate and enlighten, influence, inform, monitor, orchestrate, signal, socialize, substantiate, and symbolize (Trower and Honan 2002, pp. 290–92). Our advice to leaders was as follows:

- Be careful what data you ask for because anxieties will rise (in Schein's view—that's a good thing).
- Remember that data are not neutral.
- Clarify your data and analysis needs with data providers prior to collecting and displaying data.
- Model the behavior that you want others to show.
- Recognize the symbolic functions data serve that are not directly tied to decision. (Trower and Honan 2002, pp. 299–301)

Cohen and March (1974) provide further advice for leaders based on five properties of decision making in organized anarchies: (1) most issues most of the time have low salience for most people; (2) the total system has high inertia; (3) any decision can become a *garbage can*[1] for almost any problem; (4) the processes of choice are easily subject to overload; and (5) the organization has a *weak information base* (pp. 206–7). Therefore, leaders need to (1) spend time; (2) persist; (3) exchanges status for substance; (4) facilitate opposition participation; (5) overload the system (because in an organized anarchy, it is a mistake to become absolutely committed to any one project; (6) provide garbage cans; (7) manage unobtrusively; and (8) interpret history (pp. 207–15).

And Birnbaum (1988) reminded us that "good cybernetic leaders are modest. Recognizing that they preside over black boxes whose internal operations are not fully understood, they adopt three laws of medicine (Konner, 1987, p. 21): 'If it's working, keep doing it. If it's not working, stop doing it. If you don't know what to do, don't do anything'" (p. 200).

Presidents, in particular, should (1) be certain that data are collected that serve as indicators of the issues with which they are most concerned; (2) pay attention to the processes through which information is disseminated on campus; and (3) provide campus forums for interaction (Birnbaum 1988, pp. 218–20).

Starting from Scratch

Occasionally in academe, albeit rarely, leaders have opportunities to create cultures from scratch—when new institutions or centers open or new departments are formed. In these cases, leaders have more leeway to produce radically new cultural expectations, however, the academy's traditions—even here—may prove difficult to surmount. Importantly, "Culture change also occurs as a result of the entry of new people with new assumptions and different experiences" (Schein 1992, p. 333).

Recommendations for Leaders

Leadership may be exhibited by people at all levels in organizations, a notion advanced in academia by Wergin (2007). Leaders "in place," whether they hold formal leadership positions or not, do the following:

- recognize the potential for leadership throughout the institution;
- build relationships of trust that transcend organizational boundaries;
- frame problems in ways that challenge conventional thinking while also acknowledging the need to work within the existing structure and culture;
- are not afraid to take reasonable risks;
- give voice to a sense of shared purpose and future; and
- exhibit patience and persistence, knowing that real change is neither predictable no linear. (pp. 225–26)

The sections that follow offer advice to those who hold formal positions of leadership as well as those who do not.

For Presidents and Provosts

- Use the strategic planning process to signal intent concerning the faculty and the faculty's importance in achieving institutional objectives and goals.
- Be in sync about academic goals and the importance of faculty in achieving outcomes.
- Ensure that institutions adopt an academic plan that makes goals explicit and provides means for holding divisions and departments accountable by setting measureable targets with internal and/or external benchmarks.
- Set realistic timeframes to realize goals and report annually progress against stated goals
- Provide opportunities for organizational, double-loop learning where errors are detected and corrected.

Using three examples from the COACHE institutions featured in this book, it is possible to compare a variety of approaches to setting targets and reporting progress, ranging from the specific and faculty-focused imperative (OSU's "Build a World-Class Faculty") to less specific (Auburn's "Support, Develop, and Strengthen Our People") to fuzzy (Iowa's "Vitality"). The three institutions also show differences in terms of stated goals and outcomes measures, from the clearest and most direct (OSU's scorecard) to moderately direct (Iowa's key performance indicators) to opaque (Auburn's "progress" report).

Ohio State University

In 2000, Ohio State's board approved its strategic plan, known as the Academic Plan—an initial roadmap for the journey to academic excellence, with an ambitious goal of being attainable in five years. The plan had 6 core strategies and 14 initiatives; a scorecard (see appendix I) was designed that graphically displays OSU's data compared to that of peers as well as increases or decreases in performance over the previous year.

The first strategy was to "build a world-class faculty," and the corresponding two initiatives for implementation were as follows:

1. Over the next three to five years, recruit at least 12 faculty members
    who have attained or have the potential to attain the highest honors
    in their disciplines, concentrating these appointments in areas of
    strategic focus.
    *   Implementation: Begin immediately to recruit two to three
        internationally eminent, National Academy–caliber faculty
        members per year.
    *   Cost: $3.6M in continuing funding for salary and benefits and
        $15M in one-time funding for start-up packages.
2. Implement a faculty recruitment, retention, and development
    plan—including a competitive, merit-based compensation
    structure—that is in line with benchmark institutions (Arizona,
    UIUC, Michigan, Minnesota, Penn State, Texas, UCLA, Washington,
    and Wisconsin).
    *   Implementation: Adopt a two- to three year merit-based plan to
        match the average faculty salaries at our benchmark institutions,
        which requires an increase of 2.5 percent beyond the 4 percent
        baseline. Provide competitively funded enhanced support for the
        most promising junior and senior faculty.
    *   Cost: $13.5M in continuing funding over the next five years

Over the next several years, and under the leadership of two different
presidents, OSU made steady progress against the plan (see www.osu.edu/aca
demicplan/preface.php):

• In 2003, it was reported that four eminent scholars had been hired and
that while efforts had been made to restore compensation to competitive levels, little progress had been made. In addition, the Offices of Academic Affairs
and Research joined with a wide variety of colleges in funding 19 successful
counteroffers to retain valuable Ohio State faculty. For the first time, recipients of University Distinguished Teaching, Scholar, and Service Awards were
recognized during halftime of an Ohio State football game.

• The 2004 report indicated that OSU had improved its competitive faculty salary ranking among the benchmark institutions by three places, placing it 1.7 percent below the benchmark average. In addition, three Eminent
Scholars were hired along with a world-renowned physician-researcher and
member of the National Academy of Sciences. For the second year in a row,
more Ohio State University faculty members earned the rank of Fellow from

the American Association for the Advancement of Science (AAAS) than any other single institution. With 15 faculty members earning the rank of Fellow in 2003–4 and 14 faculty members earning the rank in 2004–5, Ohio State now has 90 Fellows.

• Pursuant to the second initiative, the board affirmed the administration's decision to include sponsored dependents in our benefit package. A new parental leave program provides new parents with paid time off after the birth or adoption of a child. And, in response to the results of the Faculty Work/Life survey, the Faculty Career Enhancement Committee was created to recommend positive and practical ways to support the professional development of women and minority faculty members, and associate professors especially.

• In 2005, President Karen Holbrook reported that OSU had hired 60 faculty members at senior rank and that the institution ranked sixth among the 10 benchmark institutions in average faculty salary. Further, central and college-level support made it possible to fund a number of successful counteroffers; a newly designed Plan for Health was implemented to promote personal health awareness and management; and the Faculty Career Enhancement Committee had developed recommendations to support the professional development of women and minority faculty members and faculty at associate rank providing guidance on mentoring, peer evaluation, professional leave, recruitment, and support for interdisciplinary activities (discussed in chapter 4).

• The 2006 report showed that OSU had hired forty-eight faculty members at senior rank and that faculty salaries were within $500 of our benchmarks, compared with a $5,000 gap in 2002. The university provided nearly $1 million in 2006, making it possible to fund a number of successful counteroffers. And new and enhanced programs within Ohio State's comprehensive Plan for Health were promoting the health of the university community "as never before."

• The year 2007 marked the end of the academic plan, and OSU hired a new president who stated his vision and six initiatives for the institution, including "retaining world-class faculty and staff as we create a high-performance culture" (discussed in chapter 5).

University of Iowa

The University of Iowa's 2005–10 plan, called "The Iowa Promise" (www.uiowa.edu/homepage/news/strategic-plans/strat-plan-05-10/index.html), has five primary goal areas—undergraduate education, graduate and professional education and research, diversity, vitality, and engagement—with 19 corresponding strategies and 44 key performance indicators (some internal and some benchmarked against peers).

It is more difficult to discern the strategies and indicators directly affecting faculty in the Iowa plan than in the Ohio State plan because there is no single strategy devoted to faculty (e.g., OSU's "Build a World-Class Faculty"). Still more challenging is to find specific performance indicators *directly* linked to these goals.

Iowa has delineated several core strategic areas, including graduate and professional education and research, diversity, vitality, and engagement with faculty-related goals for each. The university's documentation also shows performance indicators that can at least be *indirectly* linked to the stated goals. See tables 7.1 to 7.4.

Table 7.1. University of Iowa, Faculty-Related Goals, Targets, and Indicators for Graduate and Professional Education and Research

Goals
• Recruit and retain excellent faculty and research staff.
• Provide faculty and research staff with the research support appropriate at a comprehensive research university.

Target	Indicator
Total sponsored funding by fiscal year, in millions of dollars	Increase external funding 2.5% per year (P)
Sponsored research applications	Increase the number of annual external grant applications from 3,041 to 3,200 (I)
Fellowships and scholarships	Increase to 10 the average number of national faculty fellowships and scholarships awarded per year (e.g., Guggenheim, Fulbright, NEA, and NEH) (I)
Graduate assistant salary and tuition scholarship levels	Increase to top third of peer group (P)
Graduate fellowships and scholarships	Redeploy block allocation to support the recruitment of higher quality graduate students (I)

Key: (P) to be benchmarked against peers; (I) internal target

Table 7.2. University of Iowa, Goals, Targets, and Indicators for Faculty and Executive Diversity

Goals
- Increase the diversity of the faculty, especially in tenured and tenure-track positions.
- Increase the diversity of those in executive positions.

Target	Indicator
Women tenured/tenure-track faculty as a percentage of total tenured/tenure-track faculty	Increase from 27.7% to 32.0% (P)
Women in executive positions	Increase from 32.1% to 37.0% (I)
Racial/ethnic minorities in executive positions	Increase from 6.7% to 8.0% (I)

Key: (P) to be benchmarked against peers; (I) internal target

Auburn University

At Auburn, the strategic planning process began in 2006–7, and the plan was posted in 2008 (ocm.auburn.edu/strategic_plan/original_plan.html). It had six strategic priorities: the first three reflect Auburn's "historic, enduring commitment to the mission elements of instruction, research, and extension," and the last three deal with "imperatives for the future." The priorities are

1. elevating academics and enriching the undergraduate experience;
2. building the foundation for a stronger and larger research enterprise;
3. redesigning extension and outreach for greater impact;
4. supporting, developing, and strengthening our people;
5. committing to continuous improvement; and
6. building the financial resources needed to advance

As at Iowa, many of these priorities might encompass the faculty (1 through 4), but one (4) is specific to Auburn's "people," meaning faculty and staff. Four initiatives support strategic priority number 4:

• Strengthening faculty recruiting and retention. Auburn will take steps to ensure that it is appropriately supporting faculty in their teaching, research, and other endeavors. It will also confirm that we have the proper approaches in place to continue to recruit a diverse and high-quality faculty who will

Table 7.3. University of Iowa, Goals, Targets, and Indicators for Faculty Salaries, Health, Equity, Development, and Rewards

Goals
- Provide nationally competitive faculty salaries and establishing new faculty positions in critical areas.
- Promote the health, well-being, and professional growth of all members of the University community.
- Attain and maintain gender and racial equity in opportunities and compensation.
- Increase opportunities and support for leadership development.
- Encourage and reward innovation, flexibility, and collaboration.

Target	Indicator
Faculty salaries as compared to peer institutions	Increase nonclinical tenured/tenure-track faculty salaries to top third of peer group (P); increase clinical medicine faculty salaries to 50th percentile in AAMC (P)
Health risk assessment	50% participation of faculty and staff in survey (I); 50% participation of identified at-risk individuals in campus health programs (I)
Faculty/staff participation in development and leadership programs	Increase annual enrollment in programs from 9,300 to 10,250 (I)
Gender equity	Appoint committee to study gender equity and develop action plan if deficiencies are found (I)

Key: (P) to be benchmarked against peers; (I) internal target

Table 7.4. University of Iowa, Goal, Target, and Indicator for Faculty Engagement

Goal
- Recognize faculty, staff, and student contributions to the external community through, for example, performance evaluations, transcripts, and public recognition.

Target	Indicator
UI contributions to external community	Develop recognition program for faculty, staff, and students who make significant external contributions (I)

Key: (P) to be benchmarked against peers; (I) internal target make significant long-term contributions to the Auburn experience and help us carry out our strategic directives.

• Enhancing faculty professional development. Ongoing professional development is a shared responsibility of the faculty member and the University. Auburn will implement several proven approaches to enrich professional-development opportunities for our faculty. As we increase calls on faculty to design innovative teaching approaches and incorporate new material on global and sustainability issues into appropriate courses, it must provide them with best-practice tools, content, and experiences.

• Better developing university staff to enable them to fulfill their potential, raise their productivity, and make a greater contribution. Auburn benefits daily from the collective activities of our dedicated and committed staff. Further developing university staff and building their capabilities is a win-win for each individual and Auburn, and the university will accelerate its activities in this area.

• Reinforcing faculty and staff recognition and rewards. The university will acknowledge the valuable contributions of our employees through appropriate recognition and reward programs.

For each initiative, Auburn listed action steps as follows:

Initiative 1: Strengthen Faculty Recruiting and Retention

Faculty Positions. Increase the number of faculty positions for those departments that are 20 percent or more above the norm for student credit-hour production. Similarly, those departments that are less productive in credit hour terms than the norm (adjusted for sponsored research productivity) will see a lower rate of faculty replacement than others.

New Professorships. Within the next year, create 80 new professorships for existing faculty with exceptional merit. The salary support should be approximately $12,500 annually.

Planning for Retirements. Initiate planning for anticipated retirements of senior faculty and deans.

Initiative 2: Enhance Faculty Professional Development

Faculty Study Opportunities. Development and implementation of a faculty study policy will encourage further faculty skill development. Very few faculty members have had the opportunity for a study leave, and Auburn is atypical in this respect. Auburn's policy should allow faculty to take one semester every seventh year at full pay or two semesters at half pay. With the large number of faculty who would be eligible based on national standards, interim policies will be developed to address the backlog over time.

Faculty Consulting. AU encourages faculty consulting and will annually recognize engaged faculty who are contributing to professional organizations, business and industry, state and federal agencies, etc.

Teaching Reviews. Auburn is designing improved reviews of teaching, performed by faculty peers as well as students.

Faculty Study and Work Abroad. As part of Auburn's study leave program for faculty, the institution will design a structured, university-wide program that encourages faculty to work and study internationally.

Initiative 3: Better Develop Employees to Enable Them to Fulfill their Potential, Raise their Productivity and Make a Greater Contribution

Online Courses. Online credit courses will be made available to employees as part of our existing policies. Any additional costs will be incurred centrally. In addition, 50 online continuing education courses (ranging in duration from a few hours to several days) will be developed. Completion of these courses will compose a portion of the annual review process for staff. Finally, online Spanish language training will be made available to employees at no cost.

Initiative 4: Reinforce Recognition and Rewards

Faculty and Staff Salaries. The Auburn campus will maintain faculty and staff salaries, in general, at national norms based on merit. The Auburn Montgomery campus will maintain faculty salaries, in general, at regional or local norms based on merit.

Faculty Recognition. AU will design and implement a program for recognizing and rewarding faculty who demonstrate superior performance based on accepted reviews and measures. The program will devote particular recognition to faculty who make outstanding and innovative contributions within the strategic priorities of elevating academics and strengthening research.

Staff Recognition. We will develop and implement a strong staff recognition program based on ideas to make Auburn more efficient. To ensure that this effort generates the desired results, we will designate cash awards of up to $20,000.

Rather than use a scorecard (OSU) or benchmarks (Iowa), Auburn provided an update of goals completed in 2008–9 (ocm.auburn.edu/strategic _plan/2008-2009_strategic_goals_completed.pdf) and has an interactive website providing information on goals completed in 2009–10 and stated goals for 2010–11 (ocm.auburn.edu/strategic_plan/sg1011_100927.pdf). Pursuant to faculty goals, for 2010–11, Auburn will

- develop and implement a comprehensive diversity plan;
- improve the promotion and tenure process; and
- implement faculty/staff initiatives in the strategic diversity plan and report on progress.

Because there is no scorecard, let alone benchmarks directly linked to each goal, it is impossible to tell precisely what progress has been made against the plan.

For Provosts/VPs for Academic Affairs

As the chief academic officer, the provost or vice president for academic affairs is typically looked to as an advocate for the faculty. Newcomers, in particular, will want to know that the CAO cares about the quality of work life for faculty.

Starting broadly, and getting more specific, the CAO should consider

- having a one-stop website where faculty can find links to everything they need to know. Among the institutions in this book, three are noteworthy.
  - The University of Iowa's provost's website (provost.uiowa.edu /faculty/index.html) has links for faculty development (including an orientation, workshops, and a newsletter specifically designed for new faculty); faculty organizations and governance; policies and procedures (including the *Faculty Handbook* and all associated forms); and faculty human resources information (including recruitment process, annual reviews, promotion and tenure guidelines, and key contacts).
  - The provost's website at North Carolina State (www.provost.ncsu .edu/) has links for governance; faculty development (where there are 15 links for such items as new faculty orientation, new faculty, and work-life integration—with guidance for family

assistance, automatic stop-the-clock provisions, and a seminar on integrating faculty work and personal responsibilities); and a very thorough promotion and tenure section, discussed in chapter 3.

o The Ohio State University Provost's website's (oaa.osu.edu/) "For Faculty" tab sends viewers to additional information on faculty governance, faculty development, and a faculty "toolkit" (with information on new faculty orientation, benefits like child care and tuition assistance, work life policies and the Parental Care Guidebook—discussed in chapter 4, mentoring, research, and promotion and tenure (with the handbook of policies, forms, deadlines, etc.). There is also a list of topics and dates for the provost's monthly lunches with new faculty.

- providing an informative and thorough New Faculty Orientation Program that not only covers all the basics (e.g., library, email, parking, computing services, etc.) and the rules and guidelines for promotion and tenure, but also opportunities to network and form relationships across campus with administrators and other faculty. See links to new faculty orientation programs at institutions discussed in this book:

  o Auburn: www.auburn.edu/academic/other/biggio/programs/new _faculty_gta_orientation.pdf
  o UIUC: www.provost.illinois.edu/inforientation/
  o Iowa: www.clas.uiowa.edu/faculty/new_faculty/index.shtml
  o Kansas: www.hreo.ku.edu/new_faculty_staff
  o North Carolina State: www.provost.ncsu.edu/faculty-dev/new -faculty-orientation/
  o Ohio State: oaa.osu.edu/assets/files/documents/AgendaNFO2010 .pdf
  o UNCP: www.uncp.edu/tlc/

- sponsoring brown-bag lunches and other events for new faculty to ask questions of senior faculty and administrators.

- providing safe opportunities (without senior faculty present) for pre-tenure faculty members to ask about and discuss issues that concern them.

- encouraging written policies for dual-career hiring, faculty evaluation, leaves, mentoring.

- providing opportunities for the deans to gather (e.g., establish a council of deans) to discuss issues especially relevant to new faculty, to inform them of new policies and practices for early career faculty, and to allow them to ask questions of the provost and each other for cross-fertilization of ideas. Showcase successes.
- ensuring appropriate education (e.g., about providing feedback, creating a culture of support for early career faculty, the importance of quality-of-life issues for young scholars) for deans and chairs.
- rewarding what is valued. As mentioned earlier in this chapter, all too often there is a disconnection between the espoused values of academic institutions and what is actually rewarded. For example, if excellence in teaching is truly expected, it should be rewarded in the promotion and tenure process. The same may be said of service, advising, mentoring, and outreach.

The following section with advice for deans draws on a piece I wrote for the fall 2008 *COACHE Update* newsletter (Trower 2008b, pp. 4–5).

For Deans

After recently addressing a group of academic deans about the barriers to interdisciplinary scholarship and changes needed to overcome them, a dean asked, "But what's a dean to do? We are seen as middle meddlers." He elaborated by saying that it's difficult to manage or affect change from the decanal vantage point because of the organizational hierarchy and power structure; there's a provost and president above him and senior, department chairs and tenured faculty in various departments around him.

Since that question was posed to me, I've met with several academic administrators, and here's what I've learned about what deans can do to affect change on any issue, whether it is promoting interdisciplinary scholarship and supporting such scholars for success, increasing the numbers, status, and success of women in STEM disciplines and of faculty of color, or creating a great place to work for pre-tenure faculty. I hope these suggestions will prove helpful for COACHE member institutions as they focus on the issues related to faculty recruitment, retention and development on their campuses as uncovered by the COACHE survey.

- Focus attention. Most issues have low salience for most people most of the time. In addition, there are always multiple concerns on college campuses and all too often the "crisis du jour" can distract us from persistent, systemic problems. Deans can help focus the attention of faculty and other administrators by spending time, over time, on the issues upon which s/he wishes to influence.

• Gather data. Deans are in a prime position to call attention to issues or problems by bringing data to bear on them. Research shows that what gets measured gets done. In some cases, the data are quantitative and in others help will come in the form of stories and anecdotes. In any case, marshal the evidence to make the case.

• Engage colleagues up, down, and across campus. Build alliances with other deans by discussing areas of mutual concern, defining the problems, and thinking of possible solutions. Involve the faculty in those conversations. One administrator with whom I spoke recently said that he plans to form an advisory task force of key senior faculty to figure out how to make progress recruiting and retaining scholars of color. Take the ideas to the provost; in other words, make your best case and make it known that you have support on multiple fronts. Offer solutions, not more problems.

• Don't accept the status quo; persist. Some decisions in academic institutions are made by accretion, and just because one's proposal is rejected today doesn't mean that it won't be accepted later. Deans can persist until progress, even incremental, is made. An effective strategy is not only to anticipate the costs of policy implementation (e.g., modified duties, flextime, stop-the-clock provisions, dual-career hires) but also to discuss the cost of maintaining the status quo.

• Ask questions. Instead of feeling the need to have all the answers all of the time, pose questions in a variety of forums where you already have people's attention. As one dean said to me, "I lead by asking relevant questions at a variety of tables with various constituencies. Most often, those questions have no easy answers but I am able to put the issue effectively into play. Raising issues as questions puts academics in a mindset of problem solving. This is, after all, how we all approach our own scholarship—with questions, not with answers."

• Clarify. One reason some problems persist is because the issues get fuzzy over time and as they come up in multiple venues. Deans can help ensure action on stubborn problems through clarity: determine a definition and stick with it (e.g., what we mean by interdisciplinarity); list barriers to change (e.g., the reward structure; the locus of tenure in a department rather than an institute, center, or program); and delineate specific ways to overcome each individual barrier.

• Use carrots and sticks. As an equestrian friend once said to me, "When I want to lead my horse, carrots work. When I want him to turn around, I need a stick." Most of us prefer carrots to sticks, but some deans also use sticks effectively by turning back search pools that lack diverse candidates or withholding funds from unproductive departments.

• Hold departments accountable. One way that corporations have made progress on diversifying the workforce is by holding managers accountable for setting and achieving goals. Rewards flow to successful departments and are withheld from those that are not making an effort.

• Involve department heads/chairs. Department heads and chairs sit in pivotal positions in academic departments and can do a great deal to preserve the status quo or produce change in departmental culture. Seek their buy-in and commitment. Provide opportunities for chairs/heads to meet and discuss pre-tenure faculty issues, challenges, and successes.

• Garner resources. The deans I spoke with were most effective when their solutions went from pooling resources across divisions and schools to becoming a part of the university budget—funded by the central administration.

For Chairs

While the chair plays a pivotal role in shaping the culture within a department for all faculty, there is reason to believe that the chair is especially important to junior faculty.

> Chairs need to carefully scrutinize current policies and practices with an eye to academic culture. What kind of workplace do we have? What kind of workplace will best serve the faculty and the students? What do junior and senior faculty need and want from work? The chair's job is to make sure that his or her faculty are as productive as possible. Productive faculty are satisfied faculty, and satisfied faculty require a few essential elements in the workplace including "life friendly" policies (not everyone wants a family, but everyone wants a life), transparency, consistency surrounding tenure, flexibility, equity, mentoring, and opportunities for collaboration. (Trower 2005)

Around major themes addressed in this book, here are a number of ideas for chairs who are interested in creating a workplace culture of support for pre-tenure faculty members.

Tenure Process Clarity

- Ensure that your department has clearly documented criteria, standards, and procedures for tenure and promotion review.
- Provide sample dossiers of successful tenure bids.
- Provide clearly articulated, written, and fully distributed departmental policy for tenuring faculty with joint appointments (e.g., memo of understanding).
- Establish three- and five-year work plans with each faculty member.
- Provide clear annual evaluations of pre-tenure faculty members that include areas of strength and weakness.
- Ensure that the midterm review is on target, clear, and is provided orally and in writing.
- Keep a copy of "Good Practice in Tenure Evaluation" (ACE, AAUP, and UE 2000) close at hand and suggest that all members of the department also have copies (www.acenet.edu/bookstore/pdf/tenure -evaluation.pdf).

Time Management

- Tell faculty when they should hold off on developing new courses to focus on research.
- Talk to new faculty about which committees are worthwhile; give them permission to "blame the chair" when declining.
- Allow new hires a year off before they start to teach.
- Schedule department meetings for Fridays at noon (and provide lunch), rather than early mornings or evenings.

Culture of Support

- Keep an open door; stop by and really talk; make sure pre-tenure faculty are okay.
- Invite all junior faculty to lunch together monthly; then meet each individually once per semester.
- Signal that it is okay to ask for resources or to ask questions.
- Raise even a small amount of money from an outside source to fund small projects that are important to junior faculty members (e.g., to bring in a senior faculty member from another institution for a speech or workshops).

Work-Family Support

- Do not schedule departmental meetings during the times when parents may need to drop off or pick up kids from school; better to have meetings during the lunch hour.
- Ensure that you're aware of all campus policies and practices.
- Strive to foster a supportive climate in your department for the work-life needs of all members.
- Beware of supporting faculty parents at the expense of burdening "child-free" faculty.
- Avoid creating supports that exclude caregiving beyond that of a biological parent.
- Encourage conversations between older and younger faculty about the challenges they face with dual careers, finding child care or elder care, and juggling the many demands on their time.
- Implement policies equitably, fairly, and consistently.

Teaching Expectations

- Hold discussions with all faculty in the department about how teaching assignments are made and ensure that assignments are transparent and equitable in terms of load and level.
- Share syllabi and course notes on core courses with new faculty.
- Pair senior with junior faculty to team-teach a course during the first year on campus.
- Review exams for appropriate level of difficulty.
- Offer to observe junior faculty members who would like you to do so in order to provide feedback.

Research Expectations

- Encourage new faculty to apply for awards, requests for proposals, and other grant opportunities that come to your attention.
- Offer to lend equipment and supplies; work with tenured faculty to assist in this.
- Read manuscripts and research proposals; provide constructive criticism.
- Petition publishers and academic presses on behalf of pre-tenure faculty.

- Sponsor substantive brown-bag sessions on such topics as writing an effective grant proposal, supervising graduate students, and managing a lab.

Mentorship and Networking

- Ensure that the senior faculty mentor the junior faculty.
- Invite a tenured faculty member from outside institution (in the same field as a pre-tenure faculty member) to campus to spend a day or two discussing her/his research and giving feedback.
- Urge junior faculty to attend conferences to meet people in the field outside the university and offer travel funds.
- Send junior faculty on a "road show" to talk to students about research.
- Develop chairs to succeed you, and teach them to nurture new faculty.

For Senior Faculty

As a collective, a university's associate and full professors, more than any single individual, set and calibrate departmental culture. Deans and chairs matter, yes, through nominal leadership roles, but the day-to-day atmosphere is perpetuated by the conduct and actions of the senior faculty whose entire careers may be spent in a single department watching various presidents, provosts, deans, and chairs come and go.

Pre-tenure faculty members look to associate and full professor colleagues for guidance, support, mentoring, feedback, collaboration, and friendship. Tenure-track faculty members understand that they are the relative newcomers with much to learn from those who have been around longer.

In her chapter called "Legacies of Leadership in Place" (Wergin 2007, pp. 21–36), Susanne Morgan wrote about various "imaginary" departments wherein senior faculty create various cultures and how they are viewed by newer faculty members including, among others:

• Department of Protection Studies, in which the senior faculty, ever aware of the power differential between themselves and tenure-track faculty, are overly protective, fail to treat newer faculty as authentic colleagues, project onto them anxieties about the current standards for tenure, and guide them into such narrow definitions of excellence that the new faculty do not fully develop their own professional identities.

• Department of Fiefdom Studies, which have strong individual faculty members with clear curricular and research agendas based on the models they saw as graduate students. Newer faculty are "bewildered by the competitiveness and possessiveness of the senior faculty"; they see the "departmental tasks and resources as something to be shared"; and they view the senior faculty as "obstructing their attempts to simply get on with the business at hand" (p. 33).

• Department of Us-and-Them Studies, which is populated by "proud progressives" who have hired new faculty members "who also have a critical perspective." The new faculty members, however, "do not seem to challenge the administration enough." The senior faculty in this department are "skeptical" and "suspect that the newer faculty are being used for the (perhaps evil) purposes of the administration" (p. 33).

• Department of Collegiality Studies, which is characterized for decades by bitter divisions among the long-term faculty members. Several cranky faculty members have retired and those who remain want peace and unanimity; thus, they "seem to attack newer faculty" who ask questions and challenge the status quo. Just as the junior faculty are establishing their voice, it seems that the senior faculty are trying to silence them.

• Department of Baby-Card Studies, which includes "bewildered young faculty members who don't understand why their activist senior colleagues seem to obstruct their efforts to create a balanced life. The senior faculty make it clear that they themselves had to deal with heavy workloads and young children, so young faculty should not "play the baby card."

Morgan's imaginary departments, while admittedly somewhat extreme, may nonetheless strike a chord with many of us, as there is more than a bit of truth in such characterizations.

What matters is that the senior faculty have a strong influence on their newer colleagues. Through their words and actions, they can make the socialization process a positive or negative experience. They can create a warm, engaging, supportive departmental culture, a chilly, hostile, or even toxic environment, or something in between.

Conclusion

Before ending the book with a look into the future, I would like to commend the seven public institutions featured for making important strides forward in creating great workplaces for tenure-track faculty by providing some combination of the following:

1. Clarity about the expectations for tenure, including making clear at the outset the weights, percentages, or allocation of effort for the relevant realms of faculty work.
2. Meaningful annual and midpoint reviews with written feedback about performance and progress toward tenure.
3. Policies that allow flexibility for tenure-track faculty including provisions for part-time tenure, modified duties, stopping the tenure clock, and tenure windows (whereby faculty can stand early or later, depending on life circumstances).
4. Sample dossiers of tenure-track faculty who were promoted.
5. Opportunities for networking, instrumental mentoring, and collaboration.
6. Workshops on getting tenure, running a lab, supervising students, getting grants, and the like.
7. Support (monetary and nonmonetary) for excellence in teaching and research, including accommodations for leave, travel support, access to teaching and research assistants, centers for teaching excellence, pre- and post-award grant support, course release time, and protection from heavy service loads in the early years.
8. A welcoming and supportive climate for all faculty, including those with families.
9. Dedicated offices with personnel focused on creating a great workplace.
10. Clear, fair, equitable, and transparent policies and practices on work-life matters, including family-friendly and dual-careers provisions.
11. Ongoing education and training for chairs, deans, and senior faculty about issues affecting tenure-track faculty and creating an inclusive, supportive environment where faculty can thrive.
12. Informative websites where faculty can easily find everything they really need to know in one place.
13. Sustained leadership from the top about the centrality of cultivating faculty talent.

CHAPTER EIGHT

The Future of the Tenure Track

What might be the future of the tenure track, and what core assumptions might we rethink? Like most of us, I suspect, I wish I had a crystal ball so that I knew what the future will hold in store for faculty. Since I don't, I am wary of making predictions. Therefore, this concluding chapter will highlight, first, a "likely" scenario based on the faculty employment trends presented in chapter 1 and some of the current realities discussed in the introductions to the chapters on tenure, work-family, support for teaching and research, and collegiality; and, second, a "hopeful" or "optimistic" scenario based on what could be if we asked ourselves, "How do we want this to turn out?" and "What might we do to ensure a better future?"

The Likely Scenario

The cynic in me doesn't hold out much hope that the academy will change much in the next 50 years in terms of rethinking traditional tenure. Why? Because the academy is notoriously slow to rethink its principles and practices and is prone to accept business as usual until it's absolutely too late. Let's look back just a couple of months (from the time of this writing) at some articles in the *Chronicle of Higher Education*.

Topic: Quality and Student Learning Outcomes

Mediocrity happens. At this very moment, at an institution of higher education near you, a mildly hung-over student is finishing a mildly plagiarized paper on travel-industry marketing, for which he'll receive a B-plus. Across campus, an assistant professor is drafting a tepid scholarly article that will eventually be read by 43 people and cited by one. In yet another building, administrators are holding a five-hour meeting about how to spruce up the campus golf course, which is four more hours than they'll devote this month to discussing their stagnant graduation rate. (Glenn, "The Quality Question," August 29, 2010)

The writer notes that there are two sets of questions concerning the pursuit of quality. The first: How should quality in higher education be measured? The second: Are higher education's ostensible quality-control mechanisms (e.g., boards, accreditors, regulators, consumers) functioning well? "At many institutions, the incentives seem to be perverse: Students don't feel pressure to put much sweat into their academic work. Faculty members are rewarded for publishing flaccid research, not for teaching effectively. And administrators often feel stronger incentives to build glossy facilities than to lower costs or to improve student learning."

Toward the end of the article, the author quotes Robert Zemsky, chief executive of the Learning Alliance for Higher Education, who said: "We are the most moribund field that I know of . . . even more moribund than county government." While few have embraced Zemsky's "favorite remedy—a new system of three-year undergraduate degrees," why aren't more having the conversation about what we want students to be able to do when they graduate from college?

Topic: Teaching as a Priority

With lavish recreation centers and sophisticated laboratories, life on college campuses is drastically different from what it was 100 years ago. But one thing has stayed virtually the same: classroom teaching. (Wilson, "Why Teaching Is Not Priority No. 1," September 5, 2010)

This writer points out that "a roadblock" to making progress on measuring whether students are actually learning, reforming classes that don't deliver, colleges' demonstrating to accreditors that they are teaching what students need to know, and providing evidence of educational quality may be "faculty culture." The article quotes Adrianna Kezar, an associate professor of higher education at the University of Southern California: "Faculty rewards have nothing to do with the ability to assess student learning. I get promoted for writing lots of articles, not for demonstrating learning outcomes."

A 2009 survey by the National Institute for Learning Outcomes Assessment "found that provosts at doctoral universities identified 'faculty engagement' as their No. 1 challenge in making greater efforts to assess student learning.

Faculty members have long enjoyed autonomy in the classroom, and persuading them to change the way they teach is more difficult than it might sound."

Topic: The Corporatization of Higher Education

Writes Marvin Lazerson, a professor of public policy at Central European University,

> At the end of the first decade of the 21st century, the automobile industry appeared to collapse, along with the housing market—two of the mainstays of success in America. The weight of their failure had simply become too great: greed, callous indifference to the environment, and a failure to take foreign competition seriously, combined with the disappearance of easy credit. The higher education industry has not collapsed, but it has faced complaints similar to those hurled at the automobile and housing industries: chastised for offering overpriced, poor-quality products and services; as inefficient and bureaucratic, unwilling to adapt to new markets, technologically backward, administratively bloated, uninterested in teaching, and more concerned with frills than the core product. The automobile industry, at least, may remake itself—Americans have a way of doing that. The jury will be out for some time. And higher education? (Lazerson, "The Making of Corporate U.," October 17, 2010)

Lazerson notes that higher education is trying to remake itself after the endowments of the richest universities dropped by 25 to 30 percent, gifts declined, states faced bankruptcy, and the "costs of business as usual became too great." Institutions are taking "all the obvious steps" of cutting staffs and programs, canceling capital investments and delaying maintenance, renegotiating debt, freezing salaries, changing financial aid packages, and hiring part-time faculty. Lazerson predicted that "the selling and buying of higher education is going to intensify . . . corporatization is here to stay . . . the discontents both within and outside the higher education industry are not going away."

Topic: Academic Science

Academic science is in a crisis. At a time when scientific innovation is desperately needed to solve some of the world's most pressing environmental, technological, and medical problems, how scientists get money for their research stifles, rather than spurs, creativity. The structural defect causing this major problem can be stated simply: The failure rate for proposals submitted by academic scientists has reached such high levels that many professors must spend virtually all their time writing proposals, leaving the creative thinking to graduate students and postdoctoral associates. The result is science by proxy. (Carlson, "Science by Proxy," October 17, 2010)

Toby N. Carlson, professor emeritus at Penn State, added that the "increased importance academic administrators place on grant money when they consider professors' salary, tenure, and promotion" only exacerbates the problem. As young faculty members suffer from "excessive mental and physical stress," they neglect teaching in their "frantic search for funds" and the "exponentially increasing numbers of proposals are of declining quality."

According to Carlson, many factors have contributed to this situation, including a decrease in federal funding, more Ph.D.s applying for grants, the unchecked growth of universities, and increased competition between university scientists and researchers at the agencies that award the grants—some of whom submit proposals to their own agencies. Carlson concluded the piece with the sobering statement: "Unless and until the problems of grant awards and top-down science are resolved, abuses will continue, probably with a mass exodus of Americans from science. Times have changed since the golden age of academic science, and if we continue on our current path, we risk a degradation in the creativity of our universities."

Whether the subject is quality and student learning outcomes, teaching as a priority, the corporatization of American higher education, or academic science, these articles (and many others) point out the academy's apparent refusal or inability to question long-standing assumptions, rethink its practices, and ultimately, possibly reinvent itself.

Therefore, given increasing demands on the part of the public for accountability and transparency surrounding the costs and benefits of higher education, the need to educate an increasing number of first-generation students, and continued expectations for high faculty productivity in the classroom, the laboratory, and beyond, I believe that the likely scenario for the future of the faculty will include

- a continued, steady erosion of the ranks of the tenured and tenure-track along with a corresponding increase in full-time non-tenure track and part-time faculty;

- fewer people with doctorates seeking professorships at research universities;[1]
- growing intensity of demand for better teachers able to work with students of various backgrounds, preparation, and learning needs;
- increased pressure on tenure-track faculty to excel in research even as traditional publication venues decline;
- increasing demands for 24/7 attention to academic work (e.g., in labs, virtual classrooms, email) because of international competition and technological advances; and
- decreasing workplace satisfaction with increasing demands for accountability, further state appropriation cuts, and as faculty are asked to do more with less.

It is possible that tenure will die a natural death. Despite the steady trends to an ever smaller proportion of tenured faculty, driven by seemingly inexorable market forces, tenure's advocates somehow believe the practice will persist and even revive. Proponents of tenure have battled relentlessly, and in some ways successfully, against policy changes. As they battled changes in policy, they overlooked erosion in practice. But let's imagine that, before the last tenured professor retires or dies, tenure is rethought and the assumptions supporting it are reconsidered. What would that entail?

The Hopeful Scenario

To introduce this scenario, I have borrowed portions of a piece I wrote for the *Chronicle of Higher Education,* called "Rethinking Tenure for the Next Generation" (September 7, 2009).

In a *Harvard Business Review* article published in 1996, Gary Hamel, a scholar and expert on business strategy, wrote that every industry has "rule makers" who built the industry (such as, at the time, Merrill Lynch and United Airlines); "rule takers" who follow established norms (Smith Barney, US Airways); and "rule breakers"—innovators and radicals "shackled neither by convention nor by respect for precedent" (Charles Schwab, Southwest Airlines). The rule breakers rewrite the rules and thereby gain competitive advantage.

Place this in the context of the academy: The rule makers met under the auspices of the American Association of University Professors in 1940 to write "rules" that govern promotion and tenure policies. Many of the rule takers are four-year colleges and universities—a vast majority of academe—that abide by the AAUP code. With the exception of some nontraditional institutions (such as Evergreen State and Hampshire Colleges), many community colleges, and the ever more popular and powerful for-profits like DeVry, ITT Educational Services, and the University of Phoenix, there are few rule breakers. Most conform to the rules for tenure-track faculty members established some 70 years ago.

To pursue strategy as revolution, Hamel suggested that organizations first identify the 10 to 20 core assumptions or beliefs that dominate one's industry or profession. For the academy, these might include professorial autonomy, employment security, shared governance, peer review, independent scholarship, a three-rung promotion ladder, and disciplinary departments. Hamel encouraged organizations to then ask what new opportunities might arise if those beliefs are relaxed. He cautions that people at the top of an organizational pyramid (in academe, full professors) have the "least diversity of experience, the largest investment in the past, and the greatest reverence for the industry's dogma." It is very difficult for those who rank lower in the organizational hierarchy to challenge the combined forces of precedence, position, and power precisely when changes are most needed. Among other ideas, Hamel recommended inviting Generation Xers (born 1964–1980) into the conversation.

A Caveat

The remainder of this book describes a number of academe's core assumptions supporting the tenure system as it currently operates in the United States at *most* four-year colleges and universities. My caveat is this: I understand that "context counts" and that "almost 1,300 four-year colleges and universities, from public research universities to liberal arts colleges, and over 665 two-year colleges award faculty tenure" (Chait 2002, p. 309). These institutions differ drastically in substantive ways with respect to "governance, mission, structure, programs, curricula, culture, wealth, admissions criteria, student life to name a few variables" (p. 309). And yet "we often speak about the tenure 'system' as if there were just one" (p. 309). No, there is not just one tenure "system" that is enacted precisely the same across all types of academic institutions, but I use here as my benchmark the language adopted by many, if not most, institutions with tenure, and the core assumptions that many, if not most, of us would agree hold true in much of academe at four-year institutions.

Core Assumptions That Might Be Reconsidered

Since I wrote the *Chronicle* article quoted above, I have spoken with several colleagues and pondered which underlying assumptions might be reconsidered. I offer the following list for consideration.

Core Assumption 1

A) Tenure is necessary to protect academic freedom.

The Association of American University Professors 1940 Statement of Principles on Academic Freedom and Tenure states that tenure "is a means to certain ends; specifically, (1) freedom of teaching and research and of extramural activities, and (2) a sufficient degree of economic security to make the profession attractive to men and women of ability. Freedom and economic security, hence, tenure, are indispensable to the success of an institution in fulfilling its obligations to its students and to society" (AAUP 2001, p. 3).

This statement makes big assumptions. First, is it possible to decouple tenure and academic freedom? It depends on who you ask—there is no shortage of defenders and detractors—and I am unlikely to resolve the debate to everyone's (anyone's?) satisfaction, since no one has so far done so since the debate began.

In any case, here is a short summary of thinking on this debate. Those who believe that tenure and academic freedom cannot and should not be decoupled include Chemerinsky (1998), who wrote that "no alternative [to tenure] yet described is likely to succeed in providing both the procedural and the substantive protections accorded by tenure" (pp. 640–41); Burgan (Burgan and Greenberg 1995), who feared that because politics and economics will increasingly dominate institutional decisions about faculty (for the sake of efficiency), tenure and academic freedom must be defended more than ever; Beazley and Lobuts Jr. (1996), who wrote that "without the freedom of thought that tenure guarantees, American higher education will slip into an academic Dark Ages in which two conditions are likely to flourish: ransomed teaching[2] and indentured research[3]" (p. 31); Hohm and Shore (1998), who argued that without the protection provided by tenure, consumers (students and society in general) "will be shortchanged because professors will not *profess* what is *really* on their minds and will avoid areas of research that, in any way, can be defined as controversial" (p. 289); Perley (1998), who stressed that relying on the First Amendment (rather than tenure to protect academic freedom) would result in lengthy and costly court cases that would favor boards of trustees over the faculty; and, similarly, Van Alstyne (1978), who wrote that "tenure systems avoid the mutual expense and institutional fratricide of prolonged litigation by building in institutional procedures for the fair determination of cause" (p. 47).

Those who say, yes, it is indeed possible to decouple tenure and academic freedom include Cadwallader (1983), who argued that tenure is not a necessary condition for exercising academic freedom defined as the freedom to inquire and teach critically; Greenberg (Burgan and Greenberg 1995), who viewed tenure as an obstacle to improving higher education and offered alternatives to tenure that could protect academic freedom while eliminating the negatives of tenure;[4] Byrne (1997), who argued that tenure and academic freedom may effectively be decoupled under certain conditions;[5] Park (1972), who argued that "tenure inhibits rather than preserves academic freedom" (p. 35) because faculty who do not have it are restricted by those who do have it;[6] and O'Toole (1978), who believed that conditions have so changed since the early 1900s that tenure is probably inimical to the rights and freedoms of scholars—political freedom and academic freedom—today, that the courts "vigorously provide due process for professionals who are threatened for any reason" (p. 29), that "academic freedom is guaranteed not by the tenure system but by a thousand years of Anglo-American tradition" (p. 30), and further, that tenure "takes away the freedom of the untenured" (p. 30).

I make no claims that either list of authors and arguments is complete. Further, it is clear that the debate will continue as long as there is tenure, so let's move on to the AAUP's other "certain end."

B) Tenure is required to attract men and women of ability.

Tenure is still the goal for most doctoral students. More than a decade ago, I wrote about data showing declining interest in academic careers among doctoral candidates:

> Thirty-seven percent of more than 4,000 doctoral candidates in a recent study sponsored by the Pew Charitable Trusts reported that their interests in becoming a university professor declined after they entered graduate school (the sharpest drop for any career category). Three fields with traditionally high proportions of students entering the academy showed the highest percentages of students with "no interest" in a faculty career: mathematics (27 percent);

English (24 percent); and history (23 percent). And, in 1998, according to another study, the percentage of doctorate recipients who said they planned to
work in academics dropped from 1997 levels in 9 out of 14 fields, including business, education, engineering, life sciences, chemistry, physics, economics (a
sharp decrease from 53 percent to 42 percent), history, and sociology. (Trower
2000, pp. 8–9)

I noted six reasons noted for such numbers: in certain fields the job market is dreadful; the academic lifestyle is no longer so attractive; the research/
teaching equation is a trap; the tenure process is broken; comparatively speaking, the pay stinks; and more attractive options exist outside the academy
(Trower 2000).

Research has shown that doctoral students are concerned about the academic workplace and faculty careers; they express concerns about the faculty
lifestyle and perceived lack of balance; mixed messages about the proper mix
of teaching and research; having space for their own passions (Wulff et al.
2004); and the stresses and pressures of conflicting personal and professional
commitments (Austin 2002). Doctoral students have also expressed, in qualitative and quantitative terms, their ambivalence about tenure as a condition
of employment[7] (Trower et al. 2001).

While doctoral candidates preferred tenure-track job offers to offers off
the tenure track *most* of the time, some will choose non-tenure-track appointment that is in a preferred geographic location with the preferred mix
of research and teaching (Trower 2002a). Among doctoral candidates who
would choose non-tenure-track appointments, there are at least three camps:
strategists, who say that quality of life is what most matters to them and that
"they are not interested in living like their professors—all work and no play,
all job and no family time"; *pragmatists,* for whom the decision to take a non-
tenure-track job is less about trade-offs than about accepting reality. "For this
group of scholars, their decision was based on pragmatic considerations. Bottom line—they needed a job and the odds of it being on the tenure track
seemed long . . . many pragmatists feel that tenure is no longer a guarantee
anyway"; and *nonconformists,* "who want greater flexibility in their careers.
They like the idea of working free of the tenure clock, and are simply less, or
not at all, concerned about their economic security and their academic freedom. Some dislike the very idea of tenure, or have concerns about the process" (Trower 2001a).

I have written elsewhere in this text about more recent and alarming results reported by Mason et al. (2009b) about why graduate students are rejecting the research university fast track, so I will not belabor the point. It is enough to say here that these researchers' results, and those of others, including mine, fly in the face of the AAUP's second "certain end" of tenure.

Finally, on this point, it should be noted that the Franklin W. Olin College of Engineering, an institution without tenure that opened ten years ago, attracts 140 applicants for every faculty position, and has been able to hire its top choice in all but three faculty searches (Riley 2010).

Core Assumption 2

All faculty must excel in research, teaching, and service—and, at some institutions, outreach.

Ramsey and Miller (2009), in the context of medical schools, describe the mission of "health for all" (the first "modern" mission statement at King's College, Cambridge) as the "ultimate raison d'être of all health professions." According to the authors, adherence to this mission on the part of academic medicine continues to be carried out using the tripartite mission model: teaching the next generation of physicians, performing research to advance the human understanding of human biology and the practice of medicine, and providing direct health care for individual patients and populations. The authors argued that while these activities are connected and interdependent in fundamental ways, they are "in danger of becoming ends in themselves rather than activities in support of a common purpose," and the expectation has developed that faculty members will excel in all three. "Whether it was ever possible for more than a small number of productive and highly efficient individuals to achieve excellence in all 3 activities, the triple threat has in recent years been seen as increasingly endangered and counterproductive . . . [a] more efficient model of specialization is required in which each faculty member specializes in one or two areas" (p. 1475).

Another risk of the tripartite model is that "pressures from an inefficient, stressed, and overly demanding health care delivery system are driving trainees from the academic medical setting." The authors advocate having some faculty members assume all three roles as teachers, researchers, and clinicians, and that others should specialize in one or two areas, and they "should be valued and supported for their contributions to the mission" (Ramsey and Miller 2009, p. 1476). By doing so, all will be able to give their best efforts toward achieving the common goal of health for all.

This issue was taken up recently by Associated Press writer Andrew Welsh-Huggins (February 4, 2010). who wrote that "tenure review, which took its current form in the 1940s, typically emphasizes publications over teaching and sometimes weighs whether a professor brings in research grants."

COLUMBUS, Ohio—The leader of the country's largest university thinks it's time to re-examine how professors are awarded tenure, a type of job-for-life protection virtually unknown outside academia.

Ohio State University President Gordon Gee says the traditional formula that rewards publishing in scholarly journals over excellence in teaching and other contributions is outdated and too often favors the quantity of a professor's output over quality.

"Someone should gain recognition at the university for writing the great American novel or for discovering the cure for cancer," he told The Associated Press. "In a very complex world, you can no longer expect everyone to be great at everything." Plenty of people have raised the issue over the years, but Gee is one of the few American college presidents with the reputation and political prowess—not to mention the golden touch at fundraising—who might be able to begin the transformation.

Still, some professors are already skeptical.

Skeptics abound, feeling that tenure should not be awarded strictly on the basis of excellent teaching—that faculty members must also have a solid record of research, scholarly publications (in most disciplines, obviously the performing arts are different), and grant awards. The article stated that it was unclear how Gee would make changes to the tenure system at OSU, but he believes that the time is right. The article continued:

Gee said a new approach to tenure is needed to ensure the university stays relevant to students and the outside world. The recession has helped highlight the importance of higher education to the economy, he said, so now is the right time to make big changes. "The universities of the 21st century are going to be the smokestacks of the century," Gee said, referring to the heavy industry that once dominated the American economy. "The notion of the large, massive public university that can exist in isolated splendor is dead." One challenge is the complexity of big universities, which have numerous divisions accustomed to doing things their own way. Ohio State has more than 100 academic units capable of granting tenure. "In effect, there are a hundred different sets of criteria for granting promotion or evaluating an individual faculty member's case," said Tim Gerber, a longtime music professor and chairman of the university's faculty council.

It will be interesting to see if Ohio State changes how and to whom tenure is granted, which could lead others to follow suit. No matter how this case turns out, this second assumption is being reconsidered.

Core Assumptions 3 and 4

The scholarship of discovery (rather than integration, application, or
   teaching) should count the most in promotion and tenure decisions.
Research in the discipline should count the most in promotion and
   tenure decisions (rather than interdisciplinary work).

The third and fourth core assumptions that might be reconsidered tie in with the second. Many faculty at all kinds of institutions feel pressure to discover new knowledge and publish those discoveries as original research, also known as traditional scholarship. In the seminal work *Scholarship Reconsidered* (1990), E. L. Boyer took issue with the assumptions we make about what constitutes "scholarship," noting that scholarly work does not flow in linear fashion from research to publication to teaching. He noted that "the arrow of causality can, and frequently does, point in both directions. Theory surely leads to practice. But practice also leads to theory. Teaching, at its best, shapes both research and practice" (p. 16). While asking such questions as "What is to be known? What is yet to be found?" (p. 19) is important and essential to academic life, faculty members go beyond to integrate, apply, and teach that which becomes known.

Integration, according to the Boyer model, is "making connections across the disciplines, placing the specialties in larger context, illuminating data in a revealing way." Integration "seeks to interpret, draw together, and bring new insight to bear on original research" (pp. 18–19). A scholar interprets one's research beyond one's own discipline so that it can be integrated into a larger body of knowledge. Boyer noted that the global economy, rapid societal and technological changes, converging disciplines, and blurring lines between disciplines have elevated this type of scholarship. Integration involves asking, "What do the findings *mean*? Is it possible to interpret what has been discovered in ways that provide a larger, more comprehensive understanding?" (p. 19).

Application "moves toward engagement as the scholar asks, 'How can knowledge be responsibly applied to consequential problems?' 'How can it be helpful to individuals as well as to institutions?'" (p. 21). Connecting theory to practice, service activities of faculty members would be included here; the beneficiaries of scholarly applications include commercial entities, other nonprofit organizations, and professional associations. Indeed, Boyer writes that "new intellectual understandings can arise out of the very act of application"; "theory and practice vitally interact, and one renews the other" (p. 23).

To be considered consequential, a scholar's work must be understood by others, which is where teaching comes in. "Teaching, at its best," writes Boyer, "means not only transmitting knowledge, but *transforming* and *extending* it as well," and by interacting with students, professors themselves are pushed in creative new directions (p. 24). The primary question is "How can knowledge best be transmitted to others and best learned?"

Despite the fact that Boyer's expanded definition of scholarship was well received and a lot of excitement was aroused, assessment of quality has been a stumbling block (Glassick 2000). While Boyer and Gene Rice, who was working with Boyer at the time, found that faculty interest lay in teaching, that most faculty felt that effective teaching should be the primary criteria for promotion, and that the majority of faculty felt teaching to be a central mission, other pressures exist. "Most faculty at four-year institutions also reported that the reward system was heavily weighted toward published teaching, not effective teaching, and more than one third of faculty supported the proposition that at their institutions, publications were 'just counted, not qualitatively measured.' Even at research universities, a surprising 42 percent agreed with this conclusion" (Glassick 2000, p. 878).

Glassick (2000) further noted that while several colleges and universities adapted or utilized Boyer's model, "the process of adoption has proved to be arduous" and that the two primary hurdles were the meaning of "the scholarship of teaching" and the question of how the quality of scholarship should be measured (p. 878). In *Scholarship Assessed* (Glassick et al. 1997), the authors recommended applying six principles to measuring quality,[8] and Lee Shulman, president of the Carnegie Foundation, suggested separating the scholarship of teaching from scholarly teaching,[9] but the precise definition of the scholarship of teaching has remained elusive (p. 880).

At academic medical centers, as elsewhere in the academy, "rank and tenure committees primarily have promoted and rewarded those faculty who have produced peer-review publications that resulted from basic or clinical science research; obtained competitively awarded grant monies for research projects; and obtained national recognition" (Nieman et al. 1997, p. 496). Little attention had been paid to "developing and rewarding faculty for teaching, clinical, or community service roles because of the elite status of American scientific research and the difficulty of documenting educational scholarship, clinical scholarship, or community service" (pp. 496–97). However, market conditions and economic forces have caused medical schools to reexamine faculty roles and rewards for competitive reasons, in order to hire and retain top faculty talent, and in order to ensure that even tenured faculty remain current and productive.

Nieman et al. describe how one academic health center developed a strategy with the following characteristics: "the establishment of formally defined performance expectations; the vertical alignment of the individual faculty member's objectives with the department's mission; and an increasing emphasis upon faculty interdependence, accountability, and use of sound business practices" (p. 496).

One final note on this topic, the National Academy of Science has stated that the tenure and promotion system, as presently configured, is a substantial barrier to interdisciplinary scholarship (NAP 2004, p. 88). The NAS has suggested numerous reforms including longer start-up times, more time overall, and more flexibility; being a Co-Principal Investigator should count; and interdisciplinary committees should be established to critically assess such work. The NAP report lists several methods to increase the porosity of academic institutions;[10] Curtin (2008) and Pfirman et al. (2005b) offer a myriad of ideas that foster, count, and reward interdisciplinary work.

Perhaps it's time all of the academy—not just certain segments—realized the need for expanded definitions of scholarship, and that interdisciplinary work (integration), applied research, and teaching should be rewarded in promotion and tenure decisions.

Core Assumptions 5 and 6

Tenure serves all faculty equally well regardless of faculty sex and race.
The university is a meritocracy in which the most meritorious are
    promoted and tenured.

A number of years ago, I wrote an article for the New England Resource
Center for Higher Education (NERCHE) entitled "Leveling the Field" (Trower
2003) that laid out the myriad of issues for women and scholars of color
on the tenure track. The issues for women have been well documented by
others, and many were discussed in chapter 4 of this volume.

It is no secret that the biological clock collides with the tenure clock, as
noted by molecular biologist, now Princeton president, Shirley Tilghman.

In a 1993 *New York Times* Op-Ed piece, Tilghman called for the abolition of tenure, labeling it a "dirty trick," and "no friend to women." Tilghman argued that,
coming as it does during a woman's peak child-bearing and child-rearing years,
tenure discriminates against women. Tilghman now supports tenure, but says
she favors a review of the tenure process. "Academic freedom is inviolate, inviolate," she said in a recent *New York Times* interview. "What I would challenge is
whether in fact the current process by which we go through tenure review is
inviolate, or whether, in fact, like all the things we do that are built on tradition, there are times when it is worthwhile to reflect on whether it is a perfect
system. I suspect that there is nothing that is perfect." (Austin 2001)

Just as the United States Constitution reflects the views and privileges of
those who wrote it, so does the AAUP's *Statement of Principles of Academic Freedom and Tenure* (Trower 2008a). Just as the U.S. Constitution has been amended
to reflect a more diverse populace, so should the AAUP's statement and provisions be adjusted to reflect today's world. As noted in the article just cited and
elsewhere, women and faculty of color have greater teaching and service loads
than white men. In addition, "Cultural taxation on faculty of color is common because (1) many campuses have few faculty of color, (2) junior faculty of
color feel they cannot say "no" to advising minority students and serving on
multiple committees, and (3) some faculty of color actually entered the professoriate so that they might serve in these ways" (Trower 2008a, p. 17).

Another issue for women and faculty of color is bias in peer review. A national study of more than 37,000 faculty members, including over 4,000 fac-

ulty of color, revealed that several issues affect the tenure and promotion of faculty of color including challenges to (1) the nature of their research when is focused on ethnicity/racial issues, (2) the use of alternative research methods that are more action-oriented or applied than traditional methods, and (3) the significance to the larger academic community of their research findings (Jayakumar et al. 2009). In addition, these researchers noted that faculty of color have higher teaching and service workloads, are intellectually isolated, and have no or few mentors or role models to tell them the unwritten rules of the tenure process and help guide them through difficult times.

How many more studies do we need on the subject of the challenges faced by faculty of color and white women before we do something about it?

Core Assumptions 7 and 8

Tenure should be "forever," even in the absence of early retirement and the presence of longer lives and careers.

Tenure (e.g., lifetime employment security) ensures that faculty will remain productive over an academic career.

The issue of the aging and staying professoriate, like those before and after in this list, is tricky and wrought with controversy. As with the other complex problems, there is no easy answer, but a look at a 2010 "Room for Debate" discussion in the *New York Times* presents interesting food for thought (see www .nytimes.com/roomfordebate/2010/08/15/aging-professors-who-wont-retire/).

Colleges should experiment with policies like phase-outs, financial incentives, post-tenure reviews, and creating new opportunities for older scholars. Such policies might help by creating more jobs for younger scholars and improve working life for faculty on the verge of retirement. (Associate Professor Fabio Rojas)

You heard it here first: I will retire as a tenured professor no later than the spring of 2025. I will be 67. Under federal law, my university cannot require retirement at any age, whether I am vigorous and productive, or a colleague with deteriorating skills and energy. Because of this, we need to imagine voluntary retirement as a foundation for the 21st century university. Why go at 67? I believe that if senior scholars offer experience, young Ph.D.'s challenge us with new knowledge. Furthermore, while a classroom presence does not necessarily deteriorate with age, we don't always notice, or want to admit it, when we become diminished. Setting a voluntary retirement date, well in advance of any decline, respects this reality. (Professor Claire Potter)

With lifetime contracts, universities become top-heavy with senior faculty. In many academic fields (granted, not in all), a professor's best research is usually completed by the time she reaches age 60; the final 15, 20 or 25 years of one's service in the classroom or lab is often marked with fewer contributions to the advancement of knowledge. Delaying retirement also provides less opportunity for younger and more robust teachers to come up the academic ranks. And, not inconsequentially, the salaries and benefits of most senior faculty are higher than those of more junior professors. These issues matter more in times of economic challenge than otherwise. Let's keep job security until about age 70, replacing life tenure with contracts lasting 20, 30 or even 40 years. Afterward, faculty would move to year-to-year contracts. This plan would bring three benefits: (1) restore flexibility in academic planning for necessary changes in curriculum and other needs; (2) provide room for younger scholars and teachers; (3) allow for humanely addressing problems that advanced age inevitably brings. (President Emeritus Stephen Joel Trachtenberg)

To remain competitive in the 21st century, we need to bring more young people into higher education as quickly as possible. Faculty members who infinitely defer retirement should stop complaining about the lack of jobs for their graduate students and have the wisdom and grace to step aside and let a new generation take over. The solution is clear but its implementation is difficult: abolish tenure and reinstate the policy of mandatory retirement at the age of 70, which was abolished as recently as 1994. (Department Chair Mark Taylor)

Just as there are a variety of opinions about appropriate retirement ages for faculty, the literature on research productivity is mixed. Holley (1977) showed that pre-tenure published output was substantially higher than post-tenure output among 97 sociologists studied. Fairweather (2002) demonstrated that, regardless of tenure status, "few faculty were able to achieve above average teaching and research levels at the same time" (p. 44) because spending more time with students necessarily takes time away from writing and publishing. Antony and Raveling's 1998 study showed that faculty with tenure are not less productive than their counterparts without tenure; and faculty with tenure teach less but perform more service and administrative activity.

In all fairness, the AAUP never stated that lifetime productivity through the granting of tenure was one of the "certain ends," but even a cursory examination of the literature on the topic of tenure and productivity shows that this assumption is another one we might question.

Core Assumption 9

To be an effective faculty member, one must spend one's entire career in academe.

What was once the normative faculty career—moving from doctoral work and a post-doctoral appointment in some disciplines to assistant professor on the tenure track to associate professor for some number of years to full professor at the same institution—is simply no longer neither the norm nor necessarily everyone's ideal. The selfless 24/7 total devotion to career and high rewards for such a commitment—the "ideal worker" norm (Drago 2007) framed around the traditional life patterns of men with stay-at-home wives (Williams 2000)—is no longer necessarily viewed as ideal for early career faculty and doctoral students considering faculty careers.

In fact, postdoctoral training in industry is being strongly recommended because of the benefits awarded to those who follow such a path, including a vibrant atmosphere of collaboration, not worrying about grant writing and funding, higher salaries, team productivity, development of valuable industry contacts, and symbiosis (Wong 2005).

Further, "the current emphasis on translational research is starting to blur differences between research environments in academic and industry" and has "opened up a two-way street for academic researchers to go to work in industry and . . . to then return to academia" (Wilan 2007, p. 211). Wilan pointed out that a number of trends have lowered the barriers to moving back and forth, including a squeeze in funding for academic laboratories, the creation of quasi-university-like research organizations, and Ph.D. and post-doctoral students educated in an environment where applied research is more common (p. 211).

Core Assumption 10

The soon-to-be minority (i.e., full-time, tenure/tenure-track faculty) must have lifetime employment and protection. The soon-to-be majority (part-time faculty and full-time researchers at interdisciplinary research centers) need not.

As the data presented in chapter 1 reveal, the numbers of part-time faculty and those working outside of the tenure system are increasing. The latest data from the National Center for Education Statistics (Knapp et al. 2010) show that, in 2009–10, excluding medical schools, there were 650,973 full-time and 709,247 part-time staff whose primary responsibility was instruction, research, and/or public service (p. 5, table 1). Of the 647,790 full-time staff with faculty status at Title IX degree-granting institutions, excluding medical schools, 291,594 (45 percent) had tenure, 121,406 (19 percent) were on the tenure track, 142,405 (22 percent) were not on the tenure track, and 92,385 (14 percent) were at institutions without a tenure system. This means that 36 percent of the full-time instructional faculty were working without tenure or at institutions without a tenure system.

Kezar and Sam's (2011) interviews with non-tenure-track faculty members showed that these faculty deal daily with a barrage of negative assumptions and biases that make it difficult for them to do quality work, and that at least three assumptions about non-tenure-track faculty should be questioned, including the notion that those who don't have tenure are in some way deficient; that they are not professionals; and that they are less committed, satisfied, and productive.

Finally, based on the voices of many pre-tenure faculty members reported on in this volume, and years of prior research, an additional six assumptions about tenure processes and criteria might be questioned, including that

1. a probationary period of six years, up or out, makes good sense (even allowing a one- or two-year stopping of the tenure clock);
2. the three-rung faculty ladder from assistant, to associate, to full professor is attractive;
3. excellence is best achieved through competition rather than through collaboration;
4. secrecy in promotion and tenure processes ensures that the best faculty members are tenured and promoted;
5. opacity in promotion and tenure decisions and processes is good business; and
6. solo-authored papers and books should count the most; or only solo-authored work should count toward promotion and tenure.

I'm sure that others could add to this list of underlying assumptions that might be reconsidered in the twenty-first century, and that would be a good thing. Perhaps more important, I wish there were actually a way to explicitly tackle all (or at least some) of these issues rather than just skirting them or pretending like they do not matter. In the end, I remain somewhat perplexed about the knee-jerk reactions in every discussion of tenure; the polemics on both sides are entrenched, and each side digs in still further when questioned. This attitude gets us nowhere. We make no progress and the world looks at us and scoffs. I find myself saying what I said fifteen years ago—why can't we mend, not end? What is so threatening about reconsidering old policies and practices from a bygone era to see what might be in our best interests going forward?

Said Dr. Paul Batalden, well known for his work on healthcare system quality improvement, "Every system is perfectly designed to get the results it gets," and "If we keep doing what we have been doing, we'll keep getting what we've always gotten." Another pretty smart guy—Albert Einstein—said, "We cannot solve our problems with the same thinking we used when we created them," and "Insanity: doing the same thing over and over again and expecting different results." All these years later, the academy is still full of great thinkers. Perhaps it's time to put them to work rethinking what we do and how we do it so that we can preserve the best of what was and make the most of what is yet to be.

Appendixes

Appendix A
In-Depth Interview Guide

General Questions
For Pre-Tenure Faculty

- What do you like best about working here?
- What do you like least about working here?
- What most affects your satisfaction with your department? Who could do what that would most improve your chances of earning tenure?
- What will most affect your decision to stay here, assuming you achieve tenure?

For Senior Faculty

- What do you think are the most important factors in the level of work satisfaction among junior faculty?
- What specifically do you do, or what do your tenured faculty colleagues routinely do, to improve the quality of work life and work satisfaction for junior faculty?

For Department Chairs

- What do you think are the most important factors in the level of work satisfaction among junior faculty?
- What, specifically, do you, as Chair, routinely do, to improve the quality of work life and work satisfaction for junior faculty?

For Senior Administrators

- What do you think are the most important factors in determining the level of work satisfaction among junior faculty?
- What, specifically, does the administration routinely do to improve the quality of work life and work satisfaction for junior faculty?
- What hypotheses explain these scores? (What's your hypothesis?)
- Can you tell us about any policy changes you have made?
- What changes in practice have resulted?
- Who are the people who play/have played a leadership role on these issues?
  - Administrators, senior faculty, Chairs, Deans, tenure committees, special committees (status of women, minorities), the Board

- What did they do?
  - ○ Were these largely symbolic behaviors?
  - ○ Major speeches?
  - ○ Series of appointments?
  - ○ Create a post? (e.g., VP for Faculty Development)
  - ○ Structural changes?
  - ○ Resource allocation?
- Was there ever a time money was put at the issue?
- How did you use COACHE data?
- Of all we've discussed, what's the most important reason for success?

Tenure Questions

As you may know, [institution] scored particularly well in terms of some of its tenure policies and practices, on the COACHE Survey. We are here to learn more about why [institution] received such high scores in this category.

For Pre-Tenure Faculty

- To what extent would you describe the tenure process at [institution] as clear or transparent? As reasonable?
- Can you provide any concrete examples (policies or practices) that support the clarity or reasonableness of the tenure process, standards, or criteria?
  - ○ What were you told about the requirements for tenure when you interviewed?
  - ○ Since you got here?
  - ○ Tell me about the nature of your annual reviews. Are the results written down? How specific is the feedback?
  - ○ Is there a still more extensive mid-point review?
  - ○ Do you have any suggestions about what would make all of this still more clear? Is there anything that concerns you?
  - ○ Do you feel that you have the support you need to achieve tenure? If yes, please describe. If no, what's lacking?

For Senior Faculty

- Why do you think your campus scored so well on tenure clarity? What are your hypotheses?
- Did you stand for tenure at [institution]?
  - ○ If yes, to what extent would you describe the tenure process at [institution] as clear or transparent? As reasonable?
  - ○ Can you provide any concrete examples (policies or practices) that support the clarity or reasonableness of the tenure process, standards, or criteria?

    ◦ If no, how familiar are you with the tenure policies? [Probe about the history of tenure clarity at the institution.]

    ◦ Do you provide feedback to tenure-track faculty about their progress toward tenure? Describe the nature of that feedback. What kinds of questions do they have about achieving tenure here?

    ◦ Do you mentor pre-tenure faculty?

    ◦ What, if any, are a tenured faculty member's responsibilities to pre-tenure faculty members?

For Department Chairs

- Why do you think your campus scored so well on tenure clarity? What are your hypotheses?
- What, if any, specific actions do you, as Chair, take to ensure a clear, reasonable and equitable tenure process?
- Have you participated in training programs about how to give constructive feedback regarding a pre-tenure faculty member's progress toward tenure?
- What do tenure-track faculty members most want to discuss concerning tenure?
- What do you tell them?
- What resources are available to them? (to help with teaching, research)
- Do you protect them from service? Too much advising? Too much teaching? How? What do you tell them?
- What do you do to ensure a culture of support for tenure-track faculty?
- How much transparency should there be in tenure policies and practices? Why?
- Is it possible to make it as clear as pre-tenure faculty would like? If so, how? If not, why not?

For Administrators

- Why do you think your campus scored so highly in tenure clarity? Why are your hypotheses?
- Are there specific actions taken to ensure a clear, reasonable and equitable tenure process? By whom?
- What is spelled out in the Faculty Handbook?
- Has it always been this way, or was there a time when there was less clarity?
- What changed? Who was responsible?
- Are chairs trained in how to give feedback to pre-tenure faculty members about their progress toward tenure?

Work-Life Quality and Balance Questions

As you may know, [institution] scored particularly well in terms of work and family on the COACHE Survey. We are here to learn more about why [institution] received such high scores in this category.

For Pre-Tenure Faculty

- Do you feel you are currently able to effectively strike a reasonable balance between your work life and your home life? What most accounts for that?
- Do you think your current work-life balance will change after getting tenure? If yes, how do you think it will change?
- To what extent would you describe the overall climate in which you work as family-friendly? [Probe if necessary—on a scale of 1 to 10 where 10 is most positive.]
  - Can you provide any concrete examples (policies or practices) that support the family-friendly environment?
  - What hinders family-work life balance?
- To what extent would you describe the overall climate in which you work as conducive to work-life balance? [Probe if necessary . . . scale of 1 to 10.]
  - Can you provide any concrete examples (policies or practices) that support a healthy or manageable work-life balance for faculty?

[If the interviewee says that the climate is not good, ask why—what hinders it?]

For Senior Faculty

- How do you feel about your current work-life balance?
- Was your work-life balance different before getting tenure? How so?
- To what extent would you describe the overall climate in which you work as family-friendly?
  - Can you provide any concrete examples (policies or practices) that support the family-friendly environment?
  - Overall, how do you think these efforts are going?
- To what extent would you describe the overall climate in which you work as conducive to work-life balance?
  - Can you provide any concrete examples (policies or practices) that support a healthy or manageable work-life balance for faculty?
  - Overall, how do you think these efforts are going?

For Department Chairs

- What, in your view, are the primary work-life issues of junior faculty?
- To what extent would you describe the climate for faculty at [institution] and in your department as family-friendly and conducive to work-life balance?

- Has your department undertaken any initiatives in an effort to become more family-friendly or related to promoting a healthy work-life balance?
  - If yes, please describe these efforts, including any specific policies and practices. How have the faculty responded? Do you think there are differences in how junior and senior faculty have responded? Overall, how do you think these efforts are going?
  - If no, are any such efforts being planned or under consideration?

For Administrators

- What, in your view, are the primary work-life issues of junior faculty?
- To what extent would you describe the climate for faculty at [institution] as family-friendly and conductive to work-life balance?
- Has [institution] undertaken any initiatives in an effort to become more family-friendly or related to promoting a healthy work-life balance?
  - If yes, please describe these efforts, including any specific policies and practices. How have the faculty responded? Do you think there are differences in how junior and senior faculty have responded? Overall, how do you think these efforts are going?
  - If no, are any such efforts being planned or under consideration?

Nature of Work: Teaching Questions

As you may know, [institution] scored particularly well in terms of the nature of work - teaching on the COACHE Survey. We are here to learn more about why [institution] received such high scores in this category.

For Pre-Tenure Faculty

- What specifically does your department do to support you as a teacher?
  - Your Chair?
  - Your senior colleagues?
  - Your institution (at the administrative level)?
- What kinds of teaching support do you find most valuable?
- Please identify activities or resources that would further contribute to your success (or your peers' success) as a teacher.
- Please identify impediments or barriers that detract from your success (or your peers' success) as a teacher.
- How satisfied or dissatisfied are you with your teaching experience here? What impact does your level of satisfaction with teaching have on your decision to remain at [institution]?

For Senior Faculty

- What specifically does your department do to support you as a teacher?
  ○ Your Chair?
  ○ Your senior colleagues?
  ○ Your institution (at the administrative level)?
- What specifically do you do support your junior colleagues as teachers?
- How satisfied or dissatisfied are you with your teaching experience here? What impact does your level of satisfaction with teaching have on your decision to remain at [institution]?

For Department Chairs

- What, specifically, do you or does your department do to support pre-tenure faculty as teachers?
  ○ To help make balancing teaching, research and service obligations on the tenure- track more manageable?

For Administrators

- What, specifically, does [institution] do to support pre-tenure faculty as teachers?
  ○ To help make balancing teaching, research and service obligations on the tenure- track more manageable?

Nature of Work: Research Questions

As you may know, [institution] scored particularly well in terms of the nature of work - research on the COACHE Survey. We are here to learn more about why [institution] received such high scores in this category.

For Pre-Tenure Faculty

- What, specifically, does your department do to support you as a researcher/scholar?
  ○ Your Chair?
  ○ Your senior colleagues?
  ○ Your institution (at the administrative level?
- What kinds of research support do you find most valuable?
- How satisfied or dissatisfied are you with your research experience here? What impact does your level of satisfaction with your institution's/department's support of your research have on your decision to remain at [institution]?
- Are you currently engaged in any interdisciplinary work?
  ○ If yes, how do you think this work is regarding by your colleagues?
  ○ If no, why not? Do you anticipate doing any interdisciplinary work in the future?

- Please identify activities or resources that would further contribute to your success (or your peers' success) as a researcher/scholar.
- Please identify impediments or barriers that detract from your success (or your peers' success) as a researcher/scholar.

For Senior Faculty

- What, specifically, do you do to support your junior departmental colleagues' in their research?
- How satisfied or dissatisfied are you with your research experience here? What impact does your level of satisfaction with your institution's/department's support of your research have on your decision to remain at [institution]?
- How common is it for faculty in your department to be engaged in interdisciplinary work? Do you think there are differences in terms of attitudes toward interdisciplinary work among junior and senior faculty?

For Department Chairs

- What, specifically, do you, as Chair, do to support your junior faculty in their research? What policies and practices are in place?
- How do you foster interaction and engagement of senior faculty and junior faculty within your department with regard to research?
- How common is it for faculty in your department to be engaged in interdisciplinary work?
  - Do you think there are differences in terms of attitudes toward interdisciplinary work among junior and senior faculty?
  - Does your department have any particular policies in place regarding interdisciplinary work, for example in the tenure code?

For Administrators

- What, specifically, does the institution do to support your junior faculty as researchers/scholars? What policies and practices are in place?
- How common is it for faculty at [institution] to be engaged in interdisciplinary work?
  - Do you think there are differences in terms of attitudes toward interdisciplinary work among junior and senior faculty?
  - Does your institution have any particular policies in place regarding interdisciplinary work, for example in the tenure code?

Climate, Culture, and Collegiality Questions

As you may know, [institution] scored particularly well in terms of climate, culture and collegiality on the COACHE Survey. We are here to learn more about why [institution] received such high scores in this category.

For Pre-Tenure Faculty

- How would you describe the overall climate at [institution]? [Probe if necessary on a scale of 1 to 10 where 10 is highly collegial.]
- How would you describe the climate in your department? [Same probe]
- How connected do you feel to your department? To your institution?
  - What specifically makes you feel connected to your department? To [institution]?
- Do you have a mentor or mentors—either formal or informal?
  - If yes, please describe your relationship with him/her.
  - If no, would you like to have a mentor?
- Have tenured faculty demonstrated what you feel is an appropriate level of interest in your success?
  - If yes, please explain, how so?
  - If no, what should they do, or do better?

For Senior Faculty

- How would you describe the overall climate at [institution]?
- How would you describe the climate in your department?
- How connected do you feel to your department? To your institution?
  - What specifically makes you feel connected to your department? To [institution]?
- Does your department have any formal mentoring programs for junior faculty?
  - If yes, in your opinion, how successful is this program? Do you serve as a mentor?
- What specifically does the senior faculty routinely do to improve the quality of work life and work satisfaction for junior faculty?

For Department Chairs

- How would you describe the overall climate at [institution]?
- How would you describe the climate in your department?
- Does your department have any formal mentoring programs for junior faculty? [If respondent mentions that it happens more informally, ask them to describe and probe about how they know if it's happening and happening effectively.]
  - If yes, in your opinion, how successful is this program?

- In your opinion, are tenured faculty members supportive of their junior colleagues?
  - How so?
  - As Chair, what specifically do you do to engage tenured faculty in junior faculty issues?
- As Chair, what specifically do you do to foster a supportive departmental culture for your early-career faculty?

For Senior Administrators

- How would you describe the overall climate at [institution]?
- How would you describe the climate in your department?
- Does [institution] have any formal mentoring programs for junior faculty?
  - If yes, in your opinion, how successful is this program?
  - As an administrator, what specifically do you do, or what specifically does the institution do, to foster a supportive institutional culture for your early-career faculty?

Appendix B
Master List of Interview Categories for Coding

Administrative support

Autonomy/academic freedom

Child and elder care

COACHE data use

Creating/sustaining a culture of support:
Deans

Creating/sustaining a culture of support:
Department Heads/Chairs

Creating/sustaining a culture of support:
Faculty governance

Creating/sustaining a culture of support:
President, Provost, Vice
Provosts/Presidents

Culture/climate

Diversity: Gender and racial/ethnic
equity

Dual-career hiring

Extra-institutional interactions

Facilities

Faculty recruitment/retention

Flexible academic career paths (e.g.,
windows, part-time tenure, modified
duties)

Geographic location/community

Grant support

Interaction among junior faculty

Interaction between senior and junior
faculty

Interdisciplinary research/collaboration
across disciplines

Joint appointments

Leadership development

Leadership/teams (general)

Mentoring, networks, and relationship-
building

Miscellaneous

Parental/personal leave

Peers reviews

Protection from teaching/service
overload

Quality of colleagues/students

Research leave

Research support

Research travel funds

Salary/benefits

Start-up package

Stop-the-clock/tenure extension

Support for families

Teaching support/Center for Teaching
and Learning

Tenure: Clarity of standards, process,
criteria

Tenure: Evaluation, feedback, reviews

Tenure: Reasonableness of expectations

Tenure: Transparency, consistency,
equity

Tenure: Window/flexibility

Work-life: Balance and flexibility/
family-friendly policies

Workshops, orientation, seminars

Appendix C
University of Iowa College of Liberal Arts and Sciences Faculty Appointments and Review

Annual Review of Probationary Faculty
Purpose of the Review

Each year the DEO or a departmental committee reviews every non-tenured, tenure-track faculty member in the department. The review provides the faculty member with an assessment of his or her performance in teaching, scholarly or creative work, and professional service. The review ensures that the faculty member receives the guidance necessary for meeting promotion and tenure standards, but it does not in any way prejudge the review for promotion and tenure.

For jointly appointed faculty, the review committee must have access to the original agreement between the DEOs of the jointly appointing units and the probationary faculty member concerning his/her teaching and service commitments to each unit. Since these agreements may be updated annually, the review committee must also have access to any revisions of the original agreement.

The DEO provides a copy of the assessment to the probationary faculty member, who may respond in writing. The response is transmitted to the Office of the Dean as part of the review file.

Deadlines for Transmission to the College

The DEO forwards probationary review materials to the Dean's Office in March, by dates established each year by the College. For third-year contract-renewal reviews, the Dean and Associate Deans discuss the review materials and make a recommendation to the Provost on renewal of the contract.

First Year of Initial Three-Year Contract. The faculty member receives an abbreviated review in the spring semester, including an evaluation of teaching.

Second-Year Review. The faculty member receives a review based on his or her record in teaching and scholarly or creative work since the appointment began. The primary purpose of the review is to advise the faculty member on how well he or she is progressing toward meeting departmental and collegiate expectations of a tenurable record. The review report should outline substantive suggestions and specific expectations for teaching, research, and service.

In rare cases, it may be clear during the second-year review that the department is extremely unlikely to make a positive recommendation for contract renewal in the third-year review. If the Office of the Dean and the Office of the Provost approve a departmental recommendation that the third year be the final year of appointment, the faculty member receives a notice of termination from the Dean. According to University policy, a faculty member who has been in a tenure-track position for two or more years must receive at least 12 months' notice of non-renewal (*Operations Manual*, III-12.2).

Third-Year Contract-Renewal Review. The faculty member receives a comprehensive review that covers the entire period since the initial appointment. University policy states that this review will "take into account the faculty member's proven teaching effectiveness and research productivity and potential. It also should include an evaluation of departmental, collegiate, and university educational goals and a determination of the likely role of the faculty member in achieving those goals" (*Operations Manual*, III-10.1a(4)(a)). The review addresses the question, "Is this individual making appropriate progress toward a tenure review that is likely to have positive results?"

The process used in this review parallels the process described in the CLAS/UI Procedures for Promotion and Tenure Decision-Making, with an important difference being that external evaluations of the candidate's creative or scholarly work are not sought. The DEO creates a timeline for the review that allows the process to be completed, including the submission of the candidate's response to the review report, by the College's deadline, which falls early in March each year.

With the advice of the DEO, the candidate for contract renewal compiles and submits a dossier containing:

- a current CV and summary of his/her teaching record, both following the Collegiate models;
- a statement of accomplishments and future plans in teaching, scholarly/creative work, and service (ordinarily not to exceed four pages);
- course materials;
- student evaluations of teaching;
- for joint appointees, the original agreement between the faculty member and the DEOs concerning teaching and service contributions to each unit, and any subsequent revisions of or additions to that agreement;
- completed scholarly/creative work;
- scholarly/creative work in progress (in cases where a book not yet in print will be part of the eventual promotion and tenure dossier, the dossier must include the current draft, with the College's Checklist on Progress toward Publication of a Book); and
- other materials allowed under the Collegiate/University Procedural Guidelines for Promotion and Tenure Decision-making.

The departmental review committee must have at least two members, and preferably three. (If the candidate holds a joint appointment in another department or college, the structure of the review committee and of the DCG discussion and vote will be determined according to the current memorandum of understanding between the college(s), the departments, and the faculty member and the principles expressed in the Collegiate/University procedures for promotion and tenure decision-making, appendix E, part A.)

The review committee's report (ordinarily not to exceed four pages) addresses the criteria of the department, the College, and the University for the rank of associate professor. It provides informative and useful evaluation of progress made to date and work that remains before the candidate reaches tenure review. The review report includes as appendices the written records of classroom observations conducted for this and earlier probationary reviews.

The candidate has the right to respond within five days of receiving the review report, and the response will be included in the record available to the departmental consulting group.

The departmental consulting group (DCG), consisting of all tenured faculty members in the department at or above the rank that will be sought in the eventual tenure decision, meets to discuss the report and the candidate's record, with the chair of the review committee chairing the DCG. The DCG votes by secret ballot on whether to renew the contract through the year of the tenure decision or to offer the candidate a one-year terminal contract. A 60% majority of those present for the discussion and vote defines a positive recommendation for contract renewal.

In a letter to the Dean (with a copy to the candidate), the DEO reports the vote of the DCG and makes his/her independent assessment and recommendation. (No separate summary of the DCG discussion is required.) The DEO's letter is forwarded to the Dean's Office early in March, with the materials specified in the "Checklist of Third-year Probationary Review Materials." If the DCG vote or the DEO recommendation is negative, the candidate has the right to respond, in a letter to the Dean (with a copy to the DEO), within five days of receiving the DEO's letter.

The Dean and Associate Deans of the College discuss these materials and then transmit them to the Office of the Provost with the College's recommendation on contract renewal. The Executive Associate Dean writes a response to the review, addressed to the DEO and copied to the faculty member, concerning issues raised in the review.

The Provost makes the final decision on contract renewal.

Fourth-Year Review. The faculty member receives a review that concentrates on the previous year's activities, assessing progress made since the third-year review and progress still to be made for the tenure review.

Fifth-Year Review. The fifth-year review advises the faculty member on progress still to be made for the tenure review. During this review, the department should begin planning for the tenure review, including consideration of potential external referees.

Sixth-Year Tenure Review. The faculty member undergoes a comprehensive review of teaching, scholarship or creative work, and service from the time of the initial appointment (*see* the CLAS/UI Procedures for Tenure and Promotion Decision-Making).

Appendix D
University of Kansas General Principles
for Developing Faculty Evaluation Plans

1. Faculty evaluation criteria, procedures and instruments shall be developed through faculty participation in each department, college or division and express the performance expectations of the faculty in the areas of teaching/advising, research or creative activity, service, and (as applicable) professional performance (Regents Guidelines 1992).
2. The criteria for and process of annual evaluation should be adopted by a vote of the faculty.
3. Faculty evaluation criteria should include clear standards for adequate performance of academic responsibilities that are consistent with expectations for faculty at a research university. "Tenure . . . does not accord freedom from accountability . . . Sustained failure of a faculty member to carry out his or her academic responsibilities, despite the opportunities for University faculty development or other appropriate interventions, is a ground for consideration of dismissal from the University of Kansas, by the procedures adopted by the Faculty Code of Conduct for such actions" (Faculty Council, Chancellor, and Board of Regents, 1996).
4. Annual evaluation procedures and instruments should call for multiple measures of performance in each area, be sufficiently flexible to meet the objectives of the unit, and be sensitive to multi-year faculty activities and outcomes.
5. The annual evaluation process should yield multiple outcomes including information for departmental planning, merit salary decisions, progress toward promotion and/or tenure, differential allocation of effort, and strategies for renewal or development.
6. The outcomes of the evaluation of faculty performance and expectations for the future shall be shared in writing with faculty members and a copy kept on file in the unit.
7. The evaluation plan shall provide a mechanism to assure due process for faculty, including the opportunity to discuss evaluations and a procedure by which faculty who disagree with their evaluation may request a review.

Required Format (with checklist) for Department/Center/ School Faculty Evaluation Plans: 2008–9

A single document should be generated that describes the expectations, processes and outcomes for faculty evaluation in each unit. All plans should be written using the following format to ensure that the Provost's and Dean's Offices have complete information to respond to requests for, or analyses of, our criteria and procedures. Promotion and tenure criteria should be included as an Appendix to support candidate review by the University Committee on Promotion and Tenure. Note that promotion and tenure criteria and procedures should be submitted also to the Faculty Senate Committee on Standards and Procedures for Promotion and Tenure after approval by the Dean or Vice Provost for Research.

Format:

Unit Name

Faculty Evaluation Plan

Approved by the Faculty on _____, 200__

Introduction

Statement of Performance Expectations

1. Unit expectations: Statement of expectations for faculty in teaching (including advising), scholarly or creative activity and service with the weights assigned to each area indicating the department expected distribution of effort. If applicable, expectations in professional performance should be addressed.
2. Standards for Acceptable Performance for Tenured Faculty: Statement of the acceptable level of performance that meets faculty academic responsibilities during the post tenure period. Should identify the level of performance that will trigger the process for failure to meet academic responsibilities.
3. Differential Allocation of Effort: Description of the process and guidelines for determining individualized goals and expectations (differential allocation of effort).

Annual Evaluation System

1. *Overview:* Description of the structure and timelines used in the annual evaluation process, including who is responsible for conducting the evaluation. NOTE: The faculty evaluation process must allow sufficient time for the written evaluation report to faculty and the opportunity for discussion of the report prior to the timelines established for merit salary decisions. Data for merit salary decisions is only one of multiple outcomes of the evaluation process.
2. *Portfolio or Annual Report Preparation:* Guidelines for preparation of the annual report should specify the required categories and multiple sources of data to be

provided to document teaching/advising, scholarly or creative activity, service, and, if applicable, professional performance. The period of time that should be documented should also be stated (e.g., current and previous year, three year period, etc.).

Note: the new Student Survey of Teaching and guidelines on peer evaluation of teaching may require some modification to existing requirements for annual reports. For example, departments should no longer need to collect original student evaluation forms when they have access to the official summary data report on each faculty member. Student comments on teaching evaluations should be requested only if the unit has voted to consider those in evaluation. Guidelines on peer evaluation can be found on the Center for Teaching Evaluation web site in the report of the Task Force on the Assessment of Teaching: www.cte.ku.edu/teachingInnovations/kuInitiatives/.

3. *Portfolio or Annual Report Review and Evaluation:* Unit procedures for portfolio review, including the variables (e.g., quality, quantity, significance, impact, etc.) considered in evaluating each area of responsibility over the specified evaluation period.

4. *Annual Evaluation Feedback Process:*
   - Specification that a written summary of the evaluation will be provided to the faculty member and description of the elements of the written summary, including performance in each area in relation to expectations, information on progress toward tenure and/or promotion, suggested strategies for improvement or renewal, etc.
   - Written summary must also inform faculty member of opportunity to discuss the evaluation.
   - A copy of the written summary should be retained in the unit.

5. *Conflict Resolution/Review Process (in the case of disagreement concerning the evaluation):*
   - Description of the administrative review process within the unit
   - Description of the department procedures and policies for input of additional information, as appropriate
   - Statement that faculty members not satisfied with the outcome of the administrative review within the unit may appeal the evaluation through the grievance procedure process at the next level (e.g., school or college, university).

6. *Outcomes of the Annual Performance Evaluation*
   - Description of the integration of the annual evaluation process and the following: achievement of department and individual professional goals, differential allocation of effort, personnel decisions (including promotion and tenure, non-reappointment, etc.), and merit salary decisions

- Description of outcomes for failing to meet performance expectations, ranging from performance intervention plans to a recommendation for dismissal following sustained failure to meet expectations.

Faculty Development Initiatives

Descriptions of department-initiated faculty development opportunities, including the mentoring program for new faculty and other programs designed to provide professional development for faculty.

Appendices

Appendix A—Instrument(s) used for the student evaluation of teaching

The common issues to be addressed on all instruments include student perspectives on (a) delivery of instruction, (b) assessment of learning, (c) the availability of the faculty member to students and (d) whether goals and objectives of the course were met (November 30, 1995 memo from the Provost).

Appendix B —Promotion and tenure criteria and procedures

Criteria and procedures, including committee membership, should be consistent with *Faculty Senate Rules and Regulations, Article VI* as approved by the Chancellor in September, 2007.

Note: Additional appendices such as the required annual report format may be included.

www.provost.ku.edu/areas/faculty/docs/faculty_eval_plans_checklist.pdf

Appendix E
Ohio State University Core Dossier Outline
(Criteria for Tenure)

Modified slightly from the original

Office of Academic Affairs Policies and Procedures Handbook Volume 3, rev. June 2009, oaa.osu.edu/OAAP_PHandbook.php

4.1.2.4 Core Dossier Outline

Revised: 06/01/09; Edited: 06/01/09

Teaching

1) Undergraduate, graduate, and professional courses taught. List each course taught and clinical instruction (see Courses/Clinical Instruction in Forms Section), including the following information:
   - courses taught by quarter (AU, WI, SP, SU) and year
   - course number, title, and number of credit hours
   - official final course enrollment
   - percentage of course taught by candidate based on proportion of total student contact hours in course
     o brief explanation (approximately 250 words) of candidate's role, if candidate was not solely responsible for course, including GTA supervision, course management, and team teaching
   - indicate whether formal course evaluations were completed by students and/or faculty peers by placing a check mark in the appropriate column

If the candidate has not obtained student evaluations in every regular classroom course, explain why this was not done. Such evaluation is required by Faculty Rule 3335-3-35 (C) (14).

Do not include in this list extension, continuing education, or other non-credit courses.

2) Involvement in graduate/professional exams, theses, and dissertations
   a) Graduate students: list completed and current and include:
      i) doctoral students (dissertation advisor): For advisees who have graduated, list name of student, year of graduation, and title of dissertation. Also provide the current position of the former student, if known.

    ii) master's students plan A (thesis advisor): For advisees who have graduated, list name of student, year of graduation, and title of thesis. Also provide the current position of the former student, if known.

    iii) master's students plan B (advisor)

    iv) doctoral students (dissertation committee member): Do not include service as a Graduate School representative.

    v) doctoral students (general examination committee chair)

    vi) doctoral students (general examination committee member): Do not include service as a Graduate School representative.

    vii) master's students (thesis committee member)

    viii) master's students (examination committee member)

  b) Describe any noteworthy accomplishments of graduate students for whom the candidate has been the advisor of record, for example, publications during or emanating from graduate program, awards for graduate work, prestigious post-docs or first post-graduate positions.

  c) Senior honor theses: give name of student, title of thesis, quarter of graduation, and noteworthy outcomes of this mentorship such as publications, presentations, honors or student awards.

  d) Describe any noteworthy accomplishments of undergraduate students, in particular related to research, for whom the candidate has been the advisor of record (publications, posters, honors or student awards).

3) Involvement with postdoctoral scholars and researchers. List completed and current postdoctoral scholars and/or researchers under the candidate's supervision.

4) Extension and continuing education instruction. Summarize briefly the major instructional activities (workshops, non-credit courses) which the candidate has conducted. Identify the candidate's role in the instruction and the number of participants.

5) Curriculum development. Give specific examples of the candidate's involvement in curriculum development (role in the design and implementation of new or revised courses); development of new teaching methods or materials (undergraduate, graduate, or professional); creation of new programs.

6) Brief description of the candidate's approach to and goals in teaching, major accomplishments, plans for the future in teaching.

7) Evaluation of teaching. Brief description of how the candidate has used the evaluation information to improve the quality of instruction.

8) Awards and formal recognition for teaching. List awards the candidate has received for excellence in teaching. Nominations for such awards should not be listed. These awards may include citations from academic or professional units (department/school, college, university, professional associations) which have

formal procedures and stated criteria for awards for outstanding teaching performance.

9) Academic advising. Brief description of academic advising not included in section 2 under teaching or section 7 under service.

Research

1) List of books, articles, and other published papers.

Only papers and other scholarly works that have been formally accepted without qualification for publication or presentation, or have actually been published or presented, should be listed in Items a-g below. Works under review must be listed separately in Item j.

Use the standard citation style for the candidate's discipline with authors listed exactly as they are listed on the publication. Candidates must list themselves even if they are the only author.

In cases of multiple authorship for Items 1a - 1e, a narrative description (approximately 50 words) of the candidate's intellectual contribution is required. Examples of appropriate formats for this information include:

• I designed the experiment (which was carried out by the graduate student co-authors), and wrote the article.

• I identified the patients for the study, administered the drug regimen, reported results to the consortium and reviewed the draft manuscript.

• I completed and wrote the literature review for the paper, shared equally with the co-author in the analysis and interpretation of the data, and reviewed the complete draft manuscript.

Statements such as the following are not acceptable: "All authors contributed equally"; "50% effort." Do not refer to past dossiers for models of how to write the required description, since they occasionally include unacceptable statements such as these.

Candidates may provide the approximate percentage of their contribution in relation to the total intellectual effort involved in the work if the unit or college requires this information. This information is not required by OAA and under no circumstances is it an acceptable substitute for the required narrative description.

For Items 1f - 1j: the above information is not needed unless the unit requires it.

Include as separate categories:

a) Books (other than edited volumes) and monographs; b) Edited books; c) Chapters in edited books; d) Bulletins and technical reports; e) Peer-reviewed journal articles; f) Editor-reviewed journal articles; g) Reviews (indicate whether peer reviewed); h) Abstracts and short entries (indicate whether peer reviewed); i) Papers in proceedings (indicate whether peer reviewed); j) Unpublished scholarly presentations (indicate whether peer reviewed); k) Potential publications under review (indicate authorship, date of submission, and to what journal or; l) publisher the work has been submitted)

2) List of creative works pertinent to the candidate's professional focus (If the candidate has no creative works to list, write "None" for number 2. Do not list each individual letter.)

   a) Artwork; b) Choreography; c) Collections; d) Compositions; e) Curated exhibits; f) Exhibited artwork; g) Inventions and patents; h) Moving image; i) Multimedia/databases/websites; j) Radio and television; k) Recitals and performances; l) Recordings; m) Other creative works).

3) Brief description of the focus of the candidate's research, scholarly or creative work, major accomplishments, and plans for the future

4) Description of quality indicators of the candidate's research, scholarly or creative work such as citations, publication outlet quality indicators such as acceptance rates, ranking or impact factors of journal or publisher. Individual units should determine what kinds of information could be described here, if any.

5) Research funding. In cases of multiple authorship for Items 5a - 5b, a narrative description (of the type described above for Item 1, approximately 50 words) of the candidate's intellectual contribution is required. List the author or authors in the order in which they appear on the grant proposal. The candidate may provide the approximate percentage of his/her contribution in relation to the total intellectual effort involved in the grant proposal if the unit or college requires this information. This information is not required by OAA and under no circumstances is it an acceptable substitute for the required narrative description.

   a) Funded research on which the candidate is or has been the principal investigator
   - period of funding
   - source and amount of funding
   - whether funding is in the form of a contract or grant

   b) Funded research on which the candidate is or has been a co-investigator
   - period of funding
   - source and amount of funding
   - whether funding is in the form of a contract or grant

   c) Proposals for research funding that are pending or were submitted but not funded
   - date of submission
   - title of project
   - authors in the order listed on the proposal

- agency to which proposal was submitted
- priority score received by proposal, if applicable

d) Funded training grants on which the candidate is or has been the equivalent of the principal investigator
- source and amount of funding
- whether funding is in the form of a contract or grant

e) Proposals for training grants that are pending or were submitted but not funded
- date of submission
- title of project
- authors in the order listed on the proposal
- agency to which proposal was submitted
- priority score received by proposal, if applicable

f) Any other funding received for the candidate's academic work
   Provide the type of information requested above as appropriate.

6) List of prizes and awards for research, scholarly or creative work. Nominations for such awards should not be listed.

Service

1) List of editorships or service as a reviewer for journals, university presses, or other learned publications.
2) List of offices held and other service to professional societies. List organization in which office was held or service performed. Describe nature of organization (open or elected membership, honorary).
3) List of consultation activity (industry, education, government). Give time period in which consultation was provided and other information as appropriate.
4) Clinical services. State specific clinical assignments.
5) Other professional/public service such as reviewer of grants or proposals or as external examiner, if not listed elsewhere.
6) Administrative service. Give dates and description of responsibility.
   a) Unit committees
   b) College or university committees
   c) Initiatives undertaken to enhance diversity in your unit, college or the university
   d) Administrative positions held, e.g. graduate studies chair
   e) Service as a graduate faculty representative on a dissertation in another unit or university
7) Advisor to student groups and organizations
8) List name of group or organization and specific responsibilities as advisor.
9) Office of Student Life committees

a) List Office of Student Life committees on which you have served.

b) Summarize participation in Student Life programs such as fireside discussions, lectures to student groups outside your unit, addresses or participation at student orientation.

10) List of prizes and awards for service to your profession, the university, or your unit. Nominations for such awards should not be listed.

Brief elaboration that provides additional information about service activities listed above.

Appendix F
University of Iowa Tenure Dossier

The Tenure Dossier

1) It is the candidate's responsibility, with the advice of the DEO (Departmental Executive Officer), to compile and submit substantive material for inclusion in the promotion dossier (the core of the Promotion Record) on or before the date specified in the college's written Procedures governing promotion decision making. In the absence of such a specified date in the college's written Procedures, the specified date will be September 1 of the academic year in which the promotion decision is to be made.

2) It is the responsibility of the DEO to advise the candidate in compiling material for the dossier, to complete the compilation of the dossier (and subsequently to complete compilation of the Promotion Record by adding materials to it throughout the departmental decision-making process), and to ensure to the greatest extent possible that the Promotion Record serves as a fair and accurate evaluation of the candidate's strengths and weaknesses, and is not purely a record of advocacy for the candidate. The responsibility to advise the candidate in compiling the dossier material is not limited to the immediate period of the tenure and promotion review, but rather is an ongoing responsibility that begins when the faculty member is appointed to the department.

3) The dossier will contain the following, in the order listed unless otherwise noted. A current CV in the college's standard format may be used in place of the individual items listed below, provided that either all the listed elements are contained in the CV or any missing elements are supplied separately:

   a) the "Recommendation for Faculty Promotion" cover sheet, with the section that is to be filled out by the candidate completed (see Appendix B);

   b) a record of the candidate's educational and professional history (C.V.), including at least the following sections, preferably in the order listed:

   (i) a list of *institutions of higher education attended*, preferably from most to least recent, indicating for each one the name of the institution, dates attended, field of study, degree obtained, and date the degree was awarded;

(ii) a list of *professional and academic positions held*, preferably from most to least recent, indicating for each one the title of the position, the dates of service, and the location or institution at which the position was held; and

(iii) a list of *honors, awards, recognitions, and outstanding achievements*, preferably from most to least recent.

c) a record of the candidate's teaching at The University of Iowa, including:

(i) the candidate's *personal statement on teaching*, consisting of a summary and explanation—normally not to exceed three pages—of the candidate's accomplishments and future plans concerning teaching, and comments on these accomplishments and plans and on other items included in the dossier related to teaching;

(ii) a list of the candidate's *teaching assignments* on a semester-by-semester basis, preferably from most to least recent;

(iii) a list of *graduate students, fellows, or other postdoctoral students supervised*, including each student's name, degree objective, and first post-graduate position;

(iv) a list of *residents for whom the faculty member has provided substantial and prolonged supervision* throughout all or most of their training program, including each student's name and first post-residency position;

(v) a list of *other contributions* to instructional programs;

(vi) copies of *course materials*, including syllabi, instructional Web pages, computer laboratory materials, and so forth (see I.(B)(4));

(vii) and, as an appendix to the dossier, copies of teaching evaluations by students for each course taught (the candidate will include all student teaching evaluations in her or his custody for each course taught) (see I.(B)(4));

d) a record of the candidate's scholarship, including:

(i) the candidate's *personal statement on scholarship*, consisting of a summary and explanation—normally not to exceed three pages—of the candidate's accomplishments and future plans concerning scholarship, and comments on these accomplishments and plans and on other items included in the dossier related to scholarship;

(ii) a list, preferably from most to least recent, of the candidate's *publications or creative works* with, for each multi-authored work or coherent series of multi-authored works, a brief statement of the candidate's contribution to the work or series of works;

(iii) a list of all *published reviews of scholarship* of which the candidate has knowledge;

(iv) a list of *attained support including grants and contracts* received by the candidate;

    (v) a list of *invited lectures* and *conference presentations*;

    (vi) a list of *pending decisions* regarding the candidate's scholarship *that might affect the promotion deliberations*, including, for example, grant proposals, book contracts, and other publishing decisions anticipated in the near future;

    (vii) a list of all *inventions and patents*;

    (viii) and, as an appendix to the dossier, copies of the candidate's published work (and work that is in print or has been accepted for publication), indicating where each work has been or will be published;

  e) a record of the candidate's service to the department, college, university, profession, community, and State of Iowa including:

    (i) the candidate's *personal statement on service*, consisting of a summary and explanation—normally not to exceed two pages—of the candidate's accomplishments and future plans concerning service, and comments on these accomplishments and plans and on other items included in the dossier related to service; and

    (ii) a categorized list, preferably from most to least recent, of *offices* held in professional organizations; *editorships* of journals or other scholarly publications; *service on review panels*; service on departmental, collegiate, or university *committees*; departmental, collegiate, or university *service positions*; relevant *community involvement* and *service to the State of Iowa*; and other contributions;

  f) within the appropriate section(s) of the dossier as listed above, other information relevant to the candidate's record in teaching, scholarship, or service that is deemed to be important in the candidate's judgment or required by the college's written Procedures governing promotion decision making.

4) Where the volume of material of a particular kind which is required to be included in the dossier is large and potentially unmanageable, a candidate, in consultation with the DEO, may select and identify representative portions of the required material for special attention. Only the material selected as representative will become part of the Promotion Record and will be transmitted to successive participants in the promotion decision-making process. Required materials segregated from the representative material will be available for review and will be located in a readily accessible location under the DEO's custody. If any participant in the promotion decision-making process relies upon initially segregated material in preparing a written evaluation of the candidate's qualifications, that material should be added to the Promotion Record, the fact of that addition should be noted in the written evaluation, and the candidate should be notified in writing of the addition at the time it is made.

5) The candidate's work in progress that is not completed by the specified date but that is anticipated to be completed in the fall—early enough for full and deliberate evaluation, as determined by the DEO—may be identified at the time the dossier is submitted and added to the dossier if and when it is completed.

6) Other materials (including updated CVs and personal statements) that could not have been available by the specified date but that are completed early enough for full and deliberate evaluation may be added to the promotion dossier by the candidate at any time through the DEO. Materials added to the original dossier or materials in the original dossier that are amended, should be labeled as such, including the date when added or amended and with any amendments clearly marked.

Appendix G
University of Illinois at Urbana-Champaign
Dual-Career Academic Couples Program

OFFICE OF THE PROVOST
COMMUNICATION NO. 8
AUGUST 2008; REVISED JULY 2008

Overview

The University of Illinois at Urbana-Champaign is committed to building and maintaining a faculty that is excellent in many dimensions. The Office of the Provost supports three programs in which partial or total central financial support for academic positions may be provided: the Faculty Excellence Program (see Communication No. 4); the Targets of Opportunity Program (see Communication No. 7) and the Dual Career Program, described here.

We require all appointees to faculty and academic staff positions to meet the highest standards in teaching, research and service. Normally, faculty and academic staff members meeting these criteria are best identified though the regular recruitment and search processes, funded through departmental and college procedures. In special circumstances, however, the Provost may provide funding (as described below) for a position and/or authorize a waiver of search when a special recruitment will contribute to the university's excellence through attraction of highly qualified individuals whose recruitment supports strategic objectives and institutional priorities.

Except in rare circumstances as noted below, financial support and waivers are not available through these programs when a candidate is identified through a search that has been approved, funded and initiated at the school or college level.

The overriding criterion for granting financial support and/or a waiver of search is whether the request contributes to academic excellence in the unit, as measured by usual standards for hiring and as outlined in the strategic goals of the unit, college, and campus.

Further criteria for different categories of requests are described below. Decisions on requests for financial support and/or waivers of search under this policy are made by the Provost in the best interests of the University. Decisions of the Provost are final.

Dual-Career Academic Couples Program

Waivers of search in the case of academic couples enhance the ability of the campus to recruit and retain faculty members when the appointment or retention of one person is contingent upon employment of another. The Champaign-Urbana labor market, compared with those where many peer universities are located, has limited employment opportunities for a faculty member's partner. The result is that the University of Illinois at Urbana-Champaign is at a competitive disadvantage in the recruitment and retention of faculty. Requests for waivers of search are designed to address this problem and, where necessary, provide resources to the unit that hires the accompanying partner.

Guidelines

1. Dual-career academic couple nominations are accepted for partners who are entry-level, highly tenurable, and tenured faculty prospects. The term "highly tenurable" applies to individuals who are currently holding assistant professorships elsewhere and have begun to establish a substantial record, but who are deemed not quite ready for a tenured appointment.
2. The requested waiver must support the excellence of both the unit in which the faculty member is being recruited or retained and the unit to which the partner would be appointed.
3. The executive officer of the first unit (i.e., the unit that is either recruiting a faculty member through a regular search process or trying to retain a current faculty member) is responsible for contacting the appropriate unit for possible employment of the partner and for negotiating an appropriate position.
4. The executive officer of the first unit must provide justification to appoint the partner in order to successfully recruit or retain the faculty member and must be willing to furnish at least 1/3 of the salary of the partner on an on-going basis.
5. The executive officer of the second unit (i.e., the prospective employer of the partner) must be able to justify the appointment on the basis of legitimate unit needs and the candidate's qualifications, and must be willing to support 1/3 of the partner's proposed salary on an on-going basis.
6. The units should forward the proposal through the appropriate channels (i.e., the deans of both the first and second units). Upon approval of a proposal from the two units, the Provost will provide a waiver of search and up to 1/3 of the partner's salary.

Nominations are accepted for tenure-track and tenured faculty prospects. Although this policy is geared to appointments to the faculty, requests for partner appointments to academic professional positions will be entertained when a suitable case is made. Visiting appointments are not generally eligible for support from the Provost, except in special circumstances.

Approval Process

Upon agreement between the executive officers of the two units, the executive officer of the employing unit of the partner should transmit, through appropriate channels, a request to the Office of the Provost to appoint the individual. The checklist in Attachment 1 specifies the documentation required for such appointments. Please note that a separate waiver of search request is not necessary.

Review Process

Unless tenure is involved in the proposed appointment, the Provost acts without consultation. This process normally takes 2 to 4 workdays after the papers are received in the Office of the Provost.

If tenure is involved, the decision at the campus level is made by the Provost after consultation with the Chancellor, the Associate Chancellor, the Vice Chancellor for Research, the Dean of the Graduate College, and the Chair of the Campus Committee on Promotion and Tenure. This process normally takes 5 to 10 workdays after the papers are received in the Office of the Provost.

Funding Limits and Appropriation Guidelines

Subject to the availability of funds, the campus administration will provide up to 1/3 of the required recurring funding for the salary of an approved candidate. Upon the resignation, termination, or retirement of the faculty member, the funds allocated by the campus to the unit and by the requesting unit to the hiring unit, plus any salary increments that have accrued against the line, will revert to the initial funding units.

Research funds may also be requested from the Vice Chancellor for Research. Questions about these funds should be directed to that office (333-0034).

Appointments Other Than Faculty Appointments

As indicated above, this policy is geared toward appointments of partners to faculty positions.

However, requests for partner appointments to academic professional positions will be entertained when a compelling case is made. If an academic professional appointment is being sought, it is important that the executive officer involved contact the Office of Academic Human

Resources to consult about the establishment of an appropriate title for such a position. Visiting appointments are not generally eligible for support from the Provost.

Appendix H
Mentoring at the University of Iowa

Tippie College of Business

The College supports a formal but voluntary mentoring program for probationary tenure-track faculty members with fewer than three years of full-time experience. Participants in the program (mentors and protégés) will move through the program as a cohort. The mentor's role is to provide career functions such as sponsorship, coaching, etc., and psychosocial functions such as role modeling and counseling. The exact functions appropriate to an academic setting need to be specified.

The identification of mentors and protégés is a critical issue for program success. Because "the chemistry" of the mentor-protégé relationship is so important, the matching process should carefully consider personality characteristics of the prospective participants. Protégé candidates may nominate up to three faculty members, any of whom could serve as a mentor.

Exact benefits to the mentor of program participation need to be specified in advance. Possible benefits include reduced collegiate committee assignments, partial summer support, release time, etc. Program participation should require explicitly stated responsibilities for both the mentor and the protégé. These include established criteria for frequency and duration of contract. Withdrawal from the program by either mentor or protégé is permitted at any time without penalty.

Orientation, training, and support should be provided to program participants. The mentoring program should be evaluated frequently to monitor goal achievement for mentors, protégés, and the College.

College of Education

The College of Education holds a New Faculty Orientation at the beginning of fall semester for new hires. New faculty meet as a group with the Deans and DEOs to discuss key policies and procedures and to learn about the different programs in the College. A tour of the College introduces faculty to staff in the main departments. New faculty are introduced to the College as a whole at the Faculty and Staff Meeting and picnic lunch the following day.

The College provides mentoring to the New Faculty Group, which includes faculty in their first three years. The College arranges informational sessions several times each semester on topics such as services available in the Office of Teacher Education and Student Services, library orientation, grant services and funding opportunities, grant management, promotion and tenure, annual reviews, Old Gold Summer Fellowships, handling difficult students, managing graduate assistants and advising, understanding faculty benefits, working with staff, etc. There is a social gathering each semester for this group to strengthen cross-departmental connections.

With some variation by department, mentoring relationships are established for new faculty by matching them with senior faculty members with similar research interests, and/or by identifying individuals in the College who match the personal characteristics and type of support the new faculty member seeks. Mentoring on policies and procedures is provided by DEOs and the Associate Dean for Academic Affairs and Graduate Programs.

College of Engineering Faculty Mentor Program

The main purpose of the mentor program is to provide unofficial, informal, and confidential assistance and suggestions to tenure-track faculty members. The program can include, but is not limited to, matters concerning students such as advising, grading policies, office hours, and use of TAs and RAs; providing information on publishing and funding environments; reading and critiquing grant proposals and journal articles; and College and Department dynamics.

Faculty Mentor Program

Policy Statement. Each Department in the College of Engineering shall establish a mentor program for tenure-track faculty members. The program shall be informal and unofficial with voluntary participation.

Mentor Program. The main purpose of the mentor program is to provide unofficial, informal, and confidential assistance and suggestions to tenure-track faculty members. The program could include, but not be limited to, matters concerning students such as advising, grading policies, office hours, and use of TAs and RAs; providing information on publishing and funding environments, reading and critiquing grant proposals and journal articles, and College and Department dynamics.

The DEO of each Department shall explain the mentor program and introduce potential volunteer mentor or mentors from the senior faculty, with their prior consent, to each tenure-track faculty member. A tenure-track faculty member who decides to participate may then choose a mentor, or a group of mentors. Suggestions made by a mentor are informal and unofficial. All participants are free to terminate their participation in the program at any time.

The program is not a replacement for existing procedures such as annual reviews and guidance from the DEO. Questions and inquiries of an official nature should be directed to appropriate administrators rather than to a mentor.

College of Law

The College of Law provides both formal and informal mentoring. In consultation with the Dean, the pre-tenure faculty member formally chooses a tenured person as a mentor, and that person must be agreeable to accepting the responsibility throughout the pre-tenure period. The mentor provides advice in a non-evaluative fashion concerning various aspects of the teaching, scholarship and service missions. Informally, many colleagues may provide additional assistance.

College of Liberal Arts and Sciences—Overview of Mentoring Programs

The primary responsibility for mentoring faculty rests with departments. Because of the great breadth and variety of programs within the College of Liberal Arts & Sciences, each department has flexibility in developing mentoring programs that will work for its faculty, given its size and discipline. Several large departments have very structured programs that are formally linked to the promotion and tenure process; others have simpler formal programs that may or may not play a role in reviewing faculty.

Carver College of Medicine Faculty Mentoring Program

For optimum effectiveness, faculty mentoring must be instituted at the departmental level. Each department is encouraged to structure a faculty mentoring system that fits the particular needs of the faculty and department. The Office of Faculty Affairs can assist departments in this effort by providing guidance on the development of a successful mentoring program, resources on successful mentoring, and other assistance as needed. The website includes several resources, including the CCOM's "A Practical Guide to Mentoring."

www.medicine.uiowa.edu/faculty/facultyaffairs/pdfs/Guide%20to%20Mentoring.pdf

Appendix I
Ohio State University Academic Plan Scorecard, Update 2006

Strategic Indicator	Ohio State	Benchmark Universities	OSU Change from Previous Reported Year
Strategy 1: Build a World Class Faculty		Benchmark Average	
1. Academic Honors and Awards (2005)	61.0	85.9	6.0
2. Market Share of Publications (2002–4)	0.4	0.5	NC
3. Market Share of Citations (2002–4)	0.6	0.8	NC
4. Market Share of Federal Research Dollars (2004)	1.04	1.42	0.23
5. Average Faculty Compensation (FY2006)	$86,460	$86.905	$988
Strategy 2: Define Ohio State as Leading Public Land Grant			
1. *U.S. News* Academic Reputation Score (2006)	3.7	4.0	0.1
2. *U.S. News* Arts & Sciences Ph.D. programs among the Top 25 (2006)*	4.0	8.4	NC
3. *U.S. News* Professional Colleges among the Top 25 (2006)*	7.0	6.9	–1
4. *U.S. News* Professional College Ph.D. Programs/Subdisciplines among the Top 25 (2006)*	17.0	18.4	NC
5. NRC Academic Ph.D. programs among the Top 25% (1992)	9.0	20.0	NC

Strategic Indicator	Ohio State	Benchmark Universities	OSU Change from Previous Reported Year
Strategy 3: Enhance the Quality of the Teaching & Learning Environment		National Average	
1. % of Faculty Satisfied Overall (2005)	79.3	77.1	5.7
2. % of Seniors Satisfied with Quality of Educational Experience	80.0	86.0	NC
3. % of Seniors Satisfied with Class Size	75.0	79.0	NC
4. % of Seniors Satisfied with Quality of Instruction	81.0	88.0	NC
5. % of Seniors Satisfied with Relationships with Faculty	70.0	78.0	NC
Strategy 4: Enhance and Better Serve the Student Body		Benchmark Average	
1. % of Freshmen in the Top 10% of H.S. Class (2005 cohort)	39.0	60.9	5
2. Freshmen Retention Rate (2005 data; 2004 cohort)	90.0	91.7	2
3. Six-year Graduation Rate (2005 data; 1999 cohort)	68.0	76.4	6
4. Four-year Graduation Rate (2005 data; 2001 cohort)	40.0	52.0	1
5. Average GMAT Score for MBA students (2005)	662	665	–2
6. Average LSAT Range for Law students (2005)	158–164	160–165	2
7. Average GRE Verbal Score for Graduate Students (2005)[†]	520	493[‡]	–2
8. Average GRE Quantitative Score for Graduate Students (2005)[†]	644	642[‡]	–4
9. % of Seniors Satisfied with Quality of Academic Advising	63.0	64.0[‡]	NC

Notes

CHAPTER ONE: Introduction

1. Clark and Corcoran (1986); Collins et al. (1998); Finkelstein (1984); Philipsen (2008); Valian (2000); West (1995).
2. Antonio (2002); de la Luz Reyes and Halcon (1988); Johnsrud and Sadao (1998); Smith et al. (2002); Trower (2009); Turner and Myers (2000).
3. Aguirre (2000); Cooper and Stevens (2002); Johnsrud and DesJarlais (1994); Menges and Exum (1983); Rai and Critzer (2000); Tack and Patitu (1992); Tierney and Bensimon (1996); Trower and Chait (2002); Trower (2003, 2008a); Turner (2002).
4. Ceci and Williams (2007); Etzkowitz et al. (2000); Fox (1995b); National Academy of Sciences (2007); Preston (1994); Selby (1999); Sonnert and Holton (1995); Thom (2001); Trower (2001b, 2002b, c, d); Zuckerman (2001).
5. AAU (2001); Curtis and Jacobe (2006); AFT Higher Education (2003); Baldwin and Chronister (2001, 2002); Ehrenberg (2006); Gappa and Leslie (1993); Lederman (2007), Schuster and Finkelstein (2006).
6. U.S. Department of Education, National Center for Education Statistics, IPEDS Data Center; four-year public and private not-for-profit U.S. universities.
7. U.S. Department of Education, National Center for Education Statistics, IPEDS Data Center. Data for four-year public and private not-for-profit U.S. institutions; full-time instruction/research/public service staff, by tenure status and academic rank. Numbers vary from previous data because not all institutions report all data every year.
8. National Survey of Postsecondary Faculty (NSOPF 04), U.S. Department of Education's National Center for Education Statistics.
9. The generations have been split differently by those who have written on the topic, and in the case of the oldest generation still alive, different names have been used. See Strauss and Howe (1997): Silent (1925–42), Baby Boomer (1943–60), Gen X (1961–81), Millennial (1982–2001); and Marston (2007): Matures (prior to 1945), Baby Boomer (1946–64), Gen X (1965–79), Millennial (1980–2000). The demarcations I use are from Lancaster and Stillman (2002): Traditionalists (1900–1945), Baby Boomer (1946–64), Gen X (1965–80), Millennial (1981–2000).

CHAPTER TWO: Study Background and Methodology

1. Sources for institutional data include The Carnegie Foundation for the Advancement of Teaching, the IPEDS (Integrated Postsecondary Education Data Statistics from the National Center for Education Statistics, U.S. Department of Education), and institutional websites/fact-books.

CHAPTER THREE: Tenure

1. A special thanks to Gregory Esposito for his research and written synopsis of the current tenure debate. The introduction to this chapter contains edited excerpts from his excellent summary and bibliographic essay.

2. Policy Excerpt: The faculty member and department head are encouraged to consider the following in development of the SME:

2.1. Initially the SME should reflect the responsibilities and expectations of both the faculty member and the department agreed to in the letter of offer.

2.2. The faculty member should have adequate flexibility and intellectual freedom to pursue promising leads and special opportunities for creative scholarship in all of his or her mutually agreed-upon realms of responsibility.

2.3. A close and well-recognized linkage should exist between each individual faculty member's SME and the mission and goals developed by that faculty member's department(s), college(s) and university.

2.4. The faculty member's SME might include a brief description of the following items as appropriate and consistent with the Academic Tenure Policy and college and departmental reappointment, promotion and tenure standards and procedures rules.

2.4.1. List of appropriate mix of realms of responsibility agreed to by the faculty member, the department head representing the department and others as appropriate to the appointment, and the dean of the college, including approximate percentage distribution of effort expected in those realms listed.

3. Policy Excerpt: Faculty Goals and Realms of Responsibility. Creative scholarship in all of the following six realms of faculty responsibility is valued and rewarded by NC State University. Scholarly contributions in an appropriate mix of these six realms must be—both in fact and in faculty perceptions—the principal criteria for decisions about faculty reappointment, promotion, and tenure. The nature of the "appropriate" mix is defined by each academic unit's Reappointment, Promotion and Tenure rule and agreed upon in each faculty member's Statement of Mutual Expectations.

5.2.1 Teaching and Mentoring of Undergraduate and Graduate Students. Transmission of knowledge to students and the development of wisdom are two primary reasons universities exist. The goal is to develop students who can play effective and socially constructive roles in a wide variety of institutions and endeavors and who can understand their service in a global and societal context. Knowledge, insights, and understanding are transmitted through disciplinary, interdisciplinary, and multidisciplinary learning.

5.2.2 Discovery of Knowledge through Discipline-Guided Inquiry. Such inquiry involves inductive and deductive reasoning; qualitative and quantitative methodologies; hypotheses and propositions; measurements; accumulation of evidence; analysis and argument; interpretation and evaluation; and communication/publication of findings, concepts, and conclusions. Basic research is inquiry aimed at understanding the world around us. Applied research is inquiry aimed at enhancing the arts of teaching and learning, management of nature and human institutions, and developing practices and technologies useful to society. Discovery of knowledge can be achieved by working either as an individual or as part of a collaborative team.

5.2.3 Creative Artistry and Literature. Creative artistry involves the creation, production, interpretation, and evaluation of cultural artifacts that generate new insights and interpretations with the potential to inspire and advance the quality of life in society. Creative artistry can be expressed through literary, performing, fine, and applied arts.

5.2.4 Technological and Managerial Innovation. Technological innovation provides the means by which knowledge and imagination in the sciences, humanities, and creative arts can be harnessed to drive the economic and social systems of the state, nation, and world, and ultimately, provide new products, processes, and services.

5.2.5 Extension and Engagement with Constituencies outside the University. Engagement with people and organizational constituencies outside the university are the principal means by which NC State University and other land-grant universities fulfill their unique mission. Accomplishments in extension and engagement represent an ongoing two-way interchange of knowledge, information, understanding, and services between the university and the state, nation, and world.

5.2.6 Service in Professional Societies and Service and Engagement within the University Itself. Complex research-extensive universities and discipline-focused scientific and professional societies simply do not work effectively, efficiently, or for long, without the dedicated and continuing investment of university faculty time and creative energy in the programs and governance of these organizations. Thus, service to and engagement within all parts of the university and its affiliated organizations, including professional scientific and literary associations is valued, appreciated, and rewarded by NC State University.

4. See the UI Chemistry Department's specific tenure criteria at www.clas.uiowa .edu/_includes/documents/faculty/criteria_chemistry.pdf.

5. Policy Excerpt

6.3.2.1. As used in this article, the term criteria refers to the unit level articulation of disciplinary expectations for meeting university promotion and tenure standards for teaching (or professional performance), scholarship, and service, including their relative weights.

6.3.2.2. The criteria shall provide for the evaluation of teaching (or professional performance), scholarship, and service as "excellent," "very good," "good," "marginal," or "poor," defined as follows:

(a) "Excellent" means that the candidate substantially exceeds disciplinary and department/unit expectations for tenure and/or promotion to this rank.

(b) "Very Good" means the candidate exceeds disciplinary and department/unit expectations for tenure and/or promotion to this rank.

(c) "Good" means the candidate meets disciplinary and department/unit expectations for tenure and/or promotion to this rank.

(d) "Marginal" means the candidate falls below disciplinary and department/unit expectations for tenure and/or promotion to this rank.

(e) "Poor" means the candidate falls significantly below disciplinary and department/unit expectations for tenure and/or promotion to this rank.

6.3.2.3. Absent exceptional circumstances, successful candidates for promotion and tenure will meet disciplinary expectations in all categories, and strong candidates are likely to exceed normal expectations in one or more categories. https://documents.ku.edu/policies/governance/FSRR.htm#art6sect3

CHAPTER FOUR: Work-Life Integration

1. A special thanks to Megan Mitrovich for her research and written synopsis of the current work-life integration literature and policy landscape. The introduction to this chapter contains edited excerpts from her excellent summary and bibliographic essay.

2. The revised COACHE survey now also asks about eldercare, modified duties (e.g., course release) for parental or other family reasons, and part-time tenure.

3. See Sylvia Ann Hewlett's book, *Off-ramps and On-ramps: Keeping Talented Women on the Road to Success* Boston: Harvard Business School, 2007.

4. Policy Excerpt: 3.0 Dual Career Hiring Program.

The successful recruitment of well-qualified faculty often requires that the university must accommodate a dual career couple. In these instances, OAA (Office of Academic Affairs) expects deans and department chairs to cooperate willingly, constructively and in good faith with the hiring unit for the target candidate to accommodate the other half of the academic couple. In some cases, OAA is able to assist units making such hires through its Dual Career Hiring Program. OAA provides cash to cover one third of the salary of the partner following the targeted hire for the first three years of the appointment. The other two thirds of the salary and all of the benefits are split between the units of the targeted hire and the partner hire respectively. Dual career requests for additional cost-sharing will be evaluated on a case by case basis. The university does not expect any department/college to hire candidates that do not meet the same quality standards as candidates hired in the receiving department. The process will be conducted with all deliberate speed to reach a final agreement in time to allow a successful recruitment of the target candidate.

CHAPTER FIVE: Support for Research and Teaching

1. A special thanks to Brendan Russell for his research and written synopsis of the current literature on support for teaching and research. The introduction to this chapter contains edited excerpts from his excellent summary and bibliographic essay.

2. A statement that begins, "I believe that this is a practical world and that I can count only on what I earn. Therefore, I believe in work, hard work."

CHAPTER SIX: Culture, Climate, and Collegiality

1. A special thanks to Brendan Russell and Megan Mitrovich for their research and written synopses of the current literature on climate, culture, and collegiality. The in-

troduction to this chapter contains edited excerpts from their summaries and bibliographic essays.

2. The full text of the Auburn University Creed, by George Petrie (1945), is as follows:

I believe that this is a practical world and that I can count only on what I earn. Therefore, I believe in work, hard work. I believe in education, which gives me the knowledge to work wisely and trains my mind and my hands to work skillfully. I believe in honesty and truthfulness, without which I cannot win the respect and confidence of my fellow men. I believe in a sound mind, in a sound body and a spirit that is not afraid, and in clean sports that develop these qualities. I believe in obedience to law because it protects the rights of all. I believe in the human touch, which cultivates sympathy with my fellow men and mutual helpfulness and brings happiness for all. I believe in my Country, because it is a land of freedom and because it is my own home, and that I can best serve that country by "doing justly, loving mercy, and walking humbly with my God." And because Auburn men and women believe in these things, I believe in Auburn and love it.

CHAPTER SEVEN: Engaging Leaders across the Campus

1. A garbage can in this context is a metaphorical dumping ground for an organization's accumulated problems and solutions, usually unrelated to one another.

CHAPTER EIGHT: The Future of the Tenure Track

1. A recent study of over 8,000 doctoral students in the University of California system showed that upon beginning their studies, 45 percent of men and 39 percent of women wanted to pursue careers as professors with an emphasis on research, but those percentages dropped to 36 percent and 27 percent respectively as time progressed. In the sciences, the shift was more dramatic. Why? For both men and women, a major factor was the perceived inflexibility of an academic career at a research university; and for women specifically, concerns about being unable to reconcile family life with career pressures in this environment were a key factor (Mason et al. 2009b).

2. Ransomed teaching occurs when a professor's continued employment depends in the degree of compatibility of his or her views with those of the university president, board of trustees, or large corporate donors (Beazley and Lobuts Jr. 1996, p. 31).

3. Indentured research occurs when the likelihood of a professor's continued employment rests on the degree of compatibility of his or her research findings with the views of the university president, board of trustees, or the sponsoring party (Beazley and Lobuts Jr. 1996, p. 32).

4. These included elevating the status of non-tenure-track appointments, creating a national commission to defend academic freedom, easing "financial exigency" requirements, setting a faculty code of conduct, varying tenure standards by institutional mission, and avoiding specific timetables for faculty to achieve tenure.

5. Institutions should define academic freedom; establish fair and rigorous evaluation procedures; offer contracts of longer duration for faculty who do not have tenure;

institute fair internal appeals processes that assure due process; have critical peer re-view systems; and offer enhanced job security to the faculty who decide on employ-ment decisions to promote their independence (Byrne 1997).

6. "Tenure promotes and fosters [a] kind of intellectually restricted reward system in a particularly pernicious way, because it adds a period of at least five years of narrow channeling to the necessary specialization of graduate school, keeping the groove straight and narrow through strong economic, social and psychological pressures for conformity" (Park Jr. 1972, p. 35).

7. On one hand, tenure is the one symbol the academy has of legitimacy and vali-dation of peers; it is synonymous with security, status, and prestige. On the other hand, doctoral students expressed deep reservations about the tenure process and be-lieved that faculty members stagnate after receiving it. Others were concerned about trying to "be all things to all people," juggling teaching, research and service and try-ing to have a balanced home life (Trower et al. 2001, pp. 4–5).

8. These included clear goals, adequate preparation, appropriate methods, signifi-cant results, effective presentation, and reflective critique (Glassick et al. 1997).

9. To be scholarship, the work must meet these criteria—it must be: public; avail-able for peer review and critique according to accepted standards; and able to be repro-duced and built upon by other scholars (Glassick 2000, p. 879).

10. Some methods include centralized funding; internal leave for study in a new discipline; hiring faculty with interdisciplinary research background; portable fellow-ships within institutions; and locating people and departments together rather than separating them by space and buildings/floors (NAP 2004).

References

Aagaard, E., and K. Hauer. 2003. A cross-sectional descriptive study of mentoring relationships formed by medical students. *Journal of General Internal Medicine* 18(4):
298–302.

Aguirre Jr. A. 2000. *Women and minority faculty in the academic workplace: Recruitment
retention, and academic culture.* ASHE-ERIC higher education report. 27(6). San Francisco: Jossey-Bass.

Aisenberg, N., and M. Harrington. 1988. *Women of academe: Outsiders in the sacred
grove.* Amherst: University of Massachusetts Press.

American Association of University Professors (AAUP). 2001a. *Policy documents and reports,* 9th ed. Baltimore: Johns Hopkins University Press.

———. *Statement of Principles on Family Responsibilities and Academic Work.* 2001b. Retrieved January 15, 2010, from www.aaup.org/AAUP/pubsres/policydocs/contents
/workfam-stmt.htm.

American Federation of Teachers (AFT). 2003. *The growth of full-time nontenure-track
faculty.* Washington, DC.

———. 2009. *American academic: The state of the higher education workforce 1997–2007.*
Washington, DC.

Amy, L., and A. Crow. 2000. Shaping the imaginary domain: Strategies for tenure and
promotion at one institution. *Computers and Composition* 17(1): 57–68.

Anderson, E. 2002. *The new professoriate.* American Council on Education, Center for
Policy Analysis. Retrieved November 2, 2009, from www.acenet.edu/bookstore/pdf
/2002_new_professoriate.pdf.

Antonio, A. L. 2002. Faculty of color reconsidered: Reassessing contributions to scholarship. *Journal of Higher Education* 73(5): 582–602.

Antony, J. S., and J. S. Raveling. 1998. A comparative analysis of tenure and faculty
productivity: Moving beyond traditional approaches. Paper presented at the 1998
annual meeting of the Association for the Study of Higher Education (ASHE), Mi-
ami, FL. Downloaded November 19, 2010.

Argyris, C. 1976. *Increasing leadership effectiveness.* New York: Wiley-Interscience.

———. 1993. *Knowledge for action: A guide to overcoming barriers to organizational change.*
San Francisco: Jossey-Bass.

Armenti, C. 2004a. May babies and posttenure babies: Maternal decisions of women
professors. *Review of Higher Education* 27(2): 211–31.

———. 2004b. Women faculty seeking tenure and parenthood: Lessons from previous
generations. *Cambridge Journal of Education* 34(1): 65–83.

Association of American Universities (AAU). 2001. *Non-tenure-track faculty report.* Retrieved September 30, 2009, from www.aau.edu/publications/reports.aspx?id=6900.

Auburn University *Faculty Personnel Policies and Procedures.* Downloaded December 2, 2009, from www.auburn.edu/academic/provost/handbook/policies.html.

Austin, A. E. 1994. Understanding and assessing faculty cultures and climates. *New Directions for Institutional Research* 84 (1994): 47–63.

———. 2002. Preparing the next generation of faculty: Graduate school as socialization to the academic career. *Journal of Higher Education (Columbus, Ohio)* 73(1): 94–122.

Austin, J. 2001. Tenure: Under fire, but hunkered down. *Science Careers – online Science Magazine.* Downloaded November 3, 2010, from sciencecareers.sciencemag.org/career_magazine/previous_issues/articles/2001_06_22/noDOI.8698163634114799815.

Bailey, L., A. Harbaugh, K. Hartman, T. Heafner, C. Hutchinson, T. Petty, and L. Quach. 2007. Dealing with shifting expectations in a college of education. *Curriculum & Teaching Dialogue* 9(1): 247–266.

Balancing teaching, scholarship, and service. 2005. *Academic Leader,* 21(6): 3–8. Retrieved January 25, 2010, from www.magnapubs.com/newsletter/issue/509/.

Baldwin, R., and J. Chronister. 2001. *Teaching without tenure: Policies and practices for a new era.* Baltimore: Johns Hopkins University Press.

———. 2002. *What happened to the tenure track?* In *The Questions of Tenure,* edited by R. Chait. Cambridge, MA: Harvard University Press.

Bauer, T. N., T. Bodner, B. Erdogan, D.M . Truxillo, and J. S. Tucker. 2007. Newcomer adjustment during organizational socialization: A meta-analytic review of antecedents, outcomes, and methods. *Journal of Applied Psychology* 92(3): 707–21.

Beazley, H., and J. Lobuts Jr. 1996. Ransomed teaching, indentured research, and the loss of reason. *Academe* 82(1): 30–32.

Belcher, W. L. 2009. *Writing your journal article in twelve weeks: A guide to academic publishing success.* Thousand Oaks, CA: Sage Publications.

Bellas, M. L. 1997. The scholarly productivity of academic couples. In *Academic couples: Problems and promises,* ed. M. A. Ferber and J. W. Loeb, 156–81. Urbana: University of Illinois Press.

Bensimon, E. M., K. Ward, and K. Sanders. 2000. *The department chair's role in developing new faculty into teachers and scholars.* Bolton, MA: Anker Publishing Company, Inc.

Bickel, J., and A. Brown. 2005. Generation X: Implications for faculty recruitment and development in academic health centers. *Academic Medicine* 80(3): 205–10.

Biggs, J. 2008. Allocating the credit in collaborative research. *Political Science & Politics* 41(1): 246–47.

Birnbaum, R. 1988. *How colleges work: The cybernetics of academic organization and leadership* (1st ed.). San Francisco: Jossey-Bass.

Blackburn, R. T., and J. H. Lawrence. 1995. *Faculty at work: Motivation, expectation, satisfaction.* Baltimore: Johns Hopkins University Press.

Boardman, C., and B. Bozeman. 2007. Role strain in university research centers. *Journal of Higher Education* 78(4): 430–63.

Boardman, C., and B. L. Ponomariov. 2007. Reward systems and NSF university research centers: The impact of tenure on university scientists' valuation of applied and commercially relevant research. *Journal of Higher Education* 78(1): 51–70.

Bond, M. A., and Others. 1993. *Campus sexual harassment and departmental climate.* Paper presented at the Annual Meeting of the American Psychological Association. Toronto.

Boyer, E. L. 1990. *Scholarship reconsidered: Priorities of the professoriate.* Princeton, NJ: Carnegie Foundation for the Advancement of Teaching.

Boyle, P., and B. Boice. 1998. *Best practices for enculturation: Collegiality, mentoring, and structure.* Thousand Oaks, CA: Jossey-Bass Publishers.

Brooks, H. 1978. Problem of research priorities. *Daedalus* 107(2): 171–90.

Burgan, M., and M. Greenberg. 1995. Considering tenure. *Educational Record* 76(4): 34–37.

Byrne, P. 1997. *Academic freedom without tenure?* New Pathways: Faculty Career and Employment for the 21st Century Working Paper Series, Inquiry #5.

Cadwallader, M. L. 1983. Reflections on academic freedom and tenure. *Liberal Education* 69(1): 1–17.

Caplan, P. J. 1993. *Lifting a ton of feathers: A woman's guide for surviving in the academic world.* Toronto: University of Toronto Press.

Carr, P., J. Bickel, and T. Inui. 2004. Taking root in a forest clearing: A resource guide for medical faculty. Boston: Boston University School of Medicine.

Carroll, V. S. 2003. The teacher, the scholar, the self: Fitting thinking and writing into a four-four load. *College Teaching* 51(1): 22–26.

Cawyer, C., and G. Friedrich. 1998. Organizational socialization: processes for new communication faculty. *Communication Education* 47(3): 234–45. Retrieved from Education Abstracts (H. W. Wilson) database.

Cawyer, C., C. Simonds, and S. Davis. 2002. Mentoring to facilitate socialization: The case of the new faculty member. *International Journal of Qualitative Studies in Education (QSE)* 15(2): 225–42. doi:10.1080/09518390110111938.

Ceci, S. J., and W. M. Williams. 2007. *Why aren't there more women in science: Top researchers debate the evidence.* Washington: American Psychological Association.

Chaffee, E. E., W. G. Tierney, P. Ewell, and J. Y. Krakower. 1988. *Collegiate culture and leadership strategies.* New York: American Council on Education: Macmillan.

Chait, R. P. (ed.) 2002. *The questions of tenure.* Cambridge, MA: Harvard University Press.

Chapman, A., and L. GuayWoodford. 2008. Nurturing passion in a time of academic climate change: The modern-day challenge of junior faculty development. *Clinical Journal of the American Society of Nephrology* 3: 1878–83.

Chemerinsky, E. 1998. Is tenure necessary to protect academic freedom? *American Behavioral Scientist* 41(5): 638–51.

Chew, L. D., J. M. Watanabe, D. Buchwald, and D. S. Lessler. 2003. Junior faculty's perspectives on mentoring. *Academic Medicine* 78(6): 652.

Civian, J. 2009. *Work/Life programs: Lifesavers in a scary economy.* Women in Higher Education 18(8): 1–3.

Clark, S. M., and M. Corcoran. 1986. Perspectives on the professional socialization of women faculty: A case of accumulative disadvantage. *Journal of Higher Education* 57(1): 20–43.

Clayton, J. 2007. Make way for the next generation: Junior faculty are moving in. *Science* 317(5844): 1569–73.

Colbeck, C. L., and R. Drago. 2005. Accept, avoid, resist: How faculty members respond to bias against caregiving . . . and how departments can help. *Change* 37(6): 10–17.

Collins, L. H., J. C. Chrisler, and K. Quina (eds.). 1998. *Arming Athena: Career strategies for women in academe.* London: Sage Publications.

Cooke, T. J. 2001. "Trailing wife" or "trailing mother"? The effect of parental status on the relationship between family migration and the labor-market participation of married women. *Environment and Planning A* 33(3):419–30.

Cooper, J. E., and D. D. Stevens (eds.). 2002. *Tenure in the sacred grove: Issues and strategies for women and minority faculty.* Albany: SUNY Press.

Cooper-Thomas, H., and N. Anderson. 2002. Newcomer adjustment: The relationship between organizational socialization tactics, information acquisition and attitudes. *Journal of Occupational & Organizational Psychology* 75(4): 423–37.

Curtin, C. 2008. Works well with others. *Genome Technology.* Downloaded November 2, 2010, from www.genomeweb.com/works-well-others.

Curtis, J. W., and M. F. Jacobe. 2006. *AAUP contingent faculty index.* Washington: American Association of University Professors.

Davidson, C. N. 2004. The futures of scholarly publishing. *Journal of Scholarly Publishing* 35(3): 129–42.

Davis, D. E., and Astin, H. S. 1990. Life cycle, career patterns and gender stratification in academe: Breaking myths and exposing truths. In *Storming the tower: Women in the academic world,* edited by S. S. Lie and V. E. O'Leary, 89–107. East Brunswick, NJ: Nichols/GP Publishing.

de Janasz, S. C., and S. E. Sullivan. 2004. Multiple mentoring in academe: Developing the professorial network. *Journal of Vocational Behavior* 64(2) (4): 263–83.

de la Luz Reyes, M., and J. J. Halcon. 1988. Racism in academia: The old wolf revisited. *Harvard Educational Review* 58(3): 299–314.

Delta Cost Project. 2009. *Trends in college spending: Where does the money come from? Where does it go? What does it buy?* Supported by Making Opportunity Affordable, an initiative of Lumina Foundation for Education. Retrieved on December 14, 2009, from: www.deltacostproject.org/resources/pdf/trends_in_spending-report.pdf.

Donoghue, F. 2008. *The last professors: The corporate university and the fate of the humanities.* New York: Fordham University Press.

Drago, R. 2002. "Consultant report on gender equity and work/family issues." For North Carolina State University, March 30, 2002. Downloaded February 22, 2010, from www.ncsu.edu/awf/Drago_report.pdf.

———. 2007. Striking a balance: Work, family, life. Boston, MA: Economic Affairs Bureau, Inc.

Drago, R., C. Colbeck, K. D. Stauffer, A. Pirretti, K. Burkum, J. Fazioli, G. Lazzaro, and T. Habasevich. 2006. The avoidance of bias against caregiving: The case of academic faculty. *The American Behavioral Scientist* 49(9): 1222–47.

Drago, R., and J. Williams. 2000. A half-time tenure track proposal. *Change* 32(6): 46–51.

Edmonson, S., A. Fisher, G. Brown, B. Irby, and F. Lunenburg. 2002. Creating a collaborative culture. *Catalyst for Change* 31(3): 9–12.

Ehrenberg, R. 2006. *What's happening to public higher education?* Santa Barbara: Greenwood Press.

Emans, S. J., C. T. Goldberg, M. E. Milstein, and J. Dobriner. 2008. Creating a faculty development office in an academic pediatric hospital: Challenges and successes. *Pediatrics* 121(2): 390–401. doi:10.1542/peds.2007-1176.

Etzkowitz, H., C. Kemelgor, and B. Uzzi. 2000. *Athena unbound: The advancement of women in science and technology.* Cambridge: Cambridge University Press.

Fairweather, J. S. (2002). The mythologies of faculty productivity: Implications for institutional policy and decision making. *Journal of Higher Education.* 73(1): 26–48.

Feldman, M. S., and J. G. March. 1981. Information in organizations as signal and symbol. *Administrative Science Quarterly* 26: 171–86.

Ferber, M. A. and J. W. Loeb (eds.) 1997. *Academic couples: Problems and promises.* Urbana: University of Illinois Press.

Finder, A. 2007. Decline of the tenure track raises concerns. *New York Times,* November 20. Retrieved September 15, 2009, from www.nytimes.com/2007/11/20/education /20adjunct.html?_r=1&pagewanted=print.

Finkel, S. K., and S. G. Olswang. 1996. Child rearing as a career impediment to women assistant professors. *Review of Higher Education* 19(2): 129–39.

Finkel, S. K., S. G. Olswang, and N. She. 1994. The implications of childbirth on tenure and promotion for women faculty. *Review of Higher Education* 17(3): 259–70.

Finkelstein, M. J. 1984. The status of academic women: An assessment of five competing explanations. *Review of Higher Education* 7(3): 223–46.

Finkelstein, M. J., R. K. Seal, and J. H. Schuster. 1998. *The new academic generation: A profession in transformation.* Baltimore: Johns Hopkins University Press.

Fleig-Palmer, M., J. Murrin, D. K. Palmer, and C. Rathert. 2003. Meeting the needs of dual career couples in academia. *CUPA-HR Journal* 54(3): 12–15.

Fox, M. F. 1995a. Women and higher education: Gender differences in the status of students and scholars. In *Women: A feminist perspective,* 5th ed., edited by Jo Freeman. Mountain View, CA: Mayfield Publishing Company.

———. 1995b. Women in scientific careers. In *Handbook of Science and Technology Studies,* edited by S. Jasanoff, G. E. Markel, J. C. Peterson, and T. J. Pinch, 205–24. Thousand Oaks, CA: Sage Publications.

———. 2005. Gender, family characteristics, and publication productivity among scientists. *Social Studies of Science* 35(1): 131–50.

Fritschler, A. L., and B. L. R. Smith. 2009. The new climate of timidity on campuses. *Chronicle of Higher Education* 55(23): A80.

Frost, S. H., and P. M. Jean. 2003. Bridging the disciplines: Interdisciplinary discourse and faculty scholarship. *Journal of Higher Education (Columbus, Ohio)* 74(2): 119–49.

Fuller, K., M. Maniscalco-Feichtl, and M. Droege. 2008. *The Role of the Mentor in Retaining Junior Pharmacy Faculty Members.* Retrieved July 14, 2010, from www.ncbi.nlm.nih .gov/pmc/articles/PMC2384216/.

Gaff, J. G. 2002. Preparing future faculty and doctoral education. *Change* 34(6): 63.

Gappa, J., and D. Leslie (1993). *The invisible faculty: Improving the status of part-timers in higher education.* San Francisco: Jossey-Bass.

Gaugler, J. E. 2004. On the tenure track in gerontology: I wish I had known then what I know now. *Educational Gerontology* 30(6): 517–36.

Gibson, S. K. 2004. Mentoring in business and industry: The need for a phenomenological perspective. *Mentoring and Tutoring* 12(2): 259–75.

Gillespie, D., N. Dolsak, and B. Kochis. 2005. Research circles: Supporting the scholarship of junior faculty. *Innovative Higher Education* 30(3): 149–62.

Glassick, C. E. 2000. Boyer's expanded definition of scholarship, the standards for assessing scholarship, and the elusiveness of the scholarship of teaching. *Academic Medicine* 75(9): 877–80.

Glassick, C. E., M. T. Huber, and G. I. Maeroff. 1997. *Scholarship assessed: Evaluation of the Professoriate*. San Francisco: Jossey Bass.

Good practice in tenure evaluation: Advice for tenured faculty, department chairs, and academic administrators. 2000. Report of American Council on Education, The American Association of University Professors, and United Educators Insurance. Washington, DC: ACE.

Grant, L., I. Kennelly, and K. B. Ward. 2000. Revisiting the gender, marriage, and parenthood puzzle in scientific careers. *Women's Studies Quarterly* 28(1/2): 62–85.

Gunn, E. 1995. Mentoring: The democratic version. *Training* 32(8): 64.

Hamilton, K. 2000. Johnson c. smith faculty release policy praised and questioned. *Black Issues in Higher Education* 17(17): 36–37.

Harper, E. P., R. G. Baldwin, B. G. Gansneder, and J. L. Chronister. 2001. Full-time women faculty off the tenure track: Profile and practice. *Review of Higher Education* 24(3): 237–57.

Hermanowicz, J. C. 2009. Stars are not enough. *Lives in science: How institutions affect academic careers*. Chicago: University of Chicago Press.

Hewlett, S., A. 2007. *On-ramps and off-ramps: Keeping talented women on the road to success*. Boston: Harvard Business School.

Hill, L., and N. Kamprath. 2008. *Beyond the myth of the perfect mentor: Building a network of developmental relationships*. Retrieved July 14, 2010, from csma.aas.org/spectrum_files/spectrum_Jun08.pdf.

Hitchcock, M. A., C. J. Bland, F. P. Hekelman, and M. G. Blumenthal. 1995. Professional networks: The influence of colleagues on the academic success of faculty. *Academic Medicine* 70(12):1108–16.

Hochschild, A. 1997. *The time bind: When work becomes home and home becomes work*. New York: Metropolitan Books.

Hohm, C. F., and H. B. Shore. 1998. The academy under siege: Informing the public about the merits of academic tenure. *Sociological Perspectives* 41(4): 827–32.

Holley, J. W. 1977. Tenure and research productivity. *Research in Higher Education*. 6: 181–92.

Hornosty, J. M. 1998. Balancing childcare and work. In *The illusion of inclusion: women in post-secondary education,* edited by J. Stalker and S. Prentice, 180–193. Halifax: Fernwood Publishing.

Jaschik, S. June 11, 2008. The last professors. *Inside Higher Education*. Retrieved January 12, 2010, from www.insidehighereducation.com/news/2008/06/11/lastprofs.

———. February 9, 2009a. Ignorance about stop-the-clock policies. *Inside Higher Education*. Retrieved January 20, 2010, from www.insidehighered.com/news/2009/01/06/stc.

———. March 23, 2009b. Farewell to the printed monograph. *Inside Higher Education*. Retrieved January 6, 2010, from www.insidehighereducation.com/news/2009/03/23/michigan.

———. May 12, 2009c. The disappearing tenure-track job. *Inside Higher Education*. Retrieved September 15, 2009, fromwww.insidehighered.com/news/2009/05/12/workforce.

Jayakumar, U. M., T. C. Howard, W .R. Allen, and J. C. Han. 2009. Racial privilege in the professoriate: An exploration of campus climate, retention, and satisfaction. *The Journal of Higher Education* 80(5): 538–63.

Johnson, W. B. 2007. *On being a mentor: A guide for higher education faculty.* Mahwah, N.J.: Lawrence Erlbaum Associates.

Johnson-Bailey, J., and R. M. Cervero. 2004. Mentoring in black and white: The intricacies of cross-cultural mentoring. *Mentoring and Tutoring* 12(1): 7–21.

Johnsrud, L. K., and C. D. DesJarlais. 1994. Barriers to tenure for women and minorities. *Review of Higher Education* 17(4): 335–53.

Johnsrud, L. K., and K. C. Sadao. 1998. The common experience of "otherness": Ethnic and racial minority faculty. *Review of Higher Education* 21(4): 315–42.

Jossi. F. 1997. Mentoring in changing times. *Training & Development* 51(8): 50–54.

June, A. 2009. Who's teaching at American colleges? Increasingly, instructors off the tenure track. *Chronicle of Higher Education*, May 12. Retrieved September 15, 2009, from www.chronicle.com/article/Teaching-Is-Increasingly-Off/47247.

Kanter, R. M. 1983. *The change masters. Innovation & entrepreneurship in the American corporation.* New York: Simon & Schuster, Inc.

Katz, S. J. 2008. WEBS: Practicing faculty mentorship. *Bioscience* 58(1): 15.

Kezar, A., and C. Sam. 2011. *Understanding the new majority: Contingent faculty in higher education.* ASHE Higher Education Report Series. San Francisco: Jossey Bass.

King, J. 2008. *Too many rungs on the ladder? Faculty demographics and the future leadership of higher education.* Washington, DC: American Council on Education Center for Policy Analysis.

Knapp, Laura G., J. E. Kelly-Reid, and S. A. Ginder. 2010. *Employees in postsecondary institutions, fall 2009, and salaries of full-time instructional staff, 2009–2010* (NCES 2011-150). U.S. Department of Education. Washington, DC: National Center for Education Statistics. Retrieved November 29, 2010, from nces.ed.gov/pubsearch.

Kolodny, A. 1998. Creating the family-friendly campus. In *The family track: Keeping your faculties while you mentor, nurture, teach, and serve,* edited by C. Coiner and D. H. George, 131–58. Urbana: University of Illinois Press.

Kosoko-Lasaki, O., R. E. Sonnino, and M. L. Voytko. 2006. Mentoring for women and underrepresented minority faculty and students: Experience at two institutions of higher education. *Journal of the National Medical Association* 98 (9): 1449–59.

Kyvik, S. 1990. Motherhood and scientific productivity. *Social Studies of Science* 20(1): 149–60.

Lancaster, L. C., and D. Stillman. 2002. *When generations collide.* New York: HarperBusiness.

Lattuca, L. R. 2001. *Creating interdisciplinarity: Interdisciplinary research and teaching among college and university faculty.* Nashville: Vanderbilt University Press.

Lederman, D. 2007. Inexorable march to a part-time faculty. *Inside Higher Education*, March 28. Retrieved September 30, 2009, from www.insidehighered.com/news /2007/03/28/faculty.

Lewin, K. 2009. Quasi-stationary social equilibria and the problem of permanent change. In *Organization change: A comprehensive reader,* edited by W. W. Burke, D. G. Lake, and J. W. Paine. San Francisco: John Wiley & Sons.

Long, J. S, P. D. Allison, and R. McGinnis. 1993. Rank advancement in academic careers: Sex differences and the effects of productivity. *American Sociological Review* 58(5):703–22.

Luecke, R. 2004. Coaching and mentoring: How to develop top talent and achieve stronger performance. Boston: Harvard Business School Press.

Marcus, J. 2007. Helping academics have families and tenure too: Universities discover their self-interest. *Change* 39(2): 27–32.

Marsh, H. W., and J. Hattie. 2002. The relation between research productivity and teaching effectiveness. *Journal of Higher Education* 73(5): 603–41.

Marston, C. 2007. *Motivating the "what's in it for me?" workforce.* Hoboken: John Wiley & Sons, Inc.

Mason, M. A., and M. Goulden. 2002. Do babies matter? The effect of family formation on the lifelong careers of academic men and women. *Academe* 88(6): 21–27.

———. 2004a. Do babies matter (part ii)? Closing the baby gap. *Academe* 90(6): 21–27.

———. 2004b. Marriage and baby blues: Redefining gender equity in the academy. *The Annals of the American Academy of Political and Social Science* 596(1): 86–103.

Mason, M. A., M. Goulden, and K. Frasch. 2009a. *Staying competitive: Patching the leaky pipeline in the sciences.* November 10. www.americanprogress.org/issues/2009/11/women_and_sciences.html.

———. 2009b. Why graduate students reject the fast track. *Academe* 95(1): 11–16.

Mason, M.A., M. Goulden, and N. H. Wolfinger. 2006. Babies matter: Pushing the gender equity revolution forward. In *The balancing act: Gendered perspectives in faculty roles and work lives,* edited by S. J. Bracken, J. K. Allen, and D. R. Dean, 9–29. Sterling, VA: Stylus Publishing.

Mather, J. 1998. Fostering women's full membership in the academy. In Status of Women Committee ed. *Status of Women Supplement. CAUT Bulletin Insert* 45(4): 2.

McElrath, K. 1992. Gender, career disruption and academic rewards. *Journal of Higher Education* 63(3): 269–81.

McGuire L. K., R. B. Merlynn, and M. L. Polan. 2004. Career advancement for women faculty in a U.S. school of medicine: Perceived needs. *Academic Medicine* 79: 319–25.

McMillin, L. A., and W. G. Berberet. 2002. *A new academic compact: Revisioning the relationship between faculty and their institutions.* Boston, MA: Anker Publications.

Menges, R. J., and W. H. Exum. 1983. Barriers to the progress of women and minority faculty. *Journal of Higher Education* 54(2): 123–44.

Menges, R. J., and Associates. 1999. *Faculty in new jobs: Guide to settling in, becoming established, and building institutional support* (1st edition). San Francisco: Jossey-Bass.

Mervis, J. 1999. Efforts to boost diversity face persistent problems. *Science* 284: 1757–59.

Miller, D. C., and A. Skeen. 1997. POSSLQs and PSSSLQs: Unmarried academic couples. In *Academic couples: Problems and promises,* edited by M. A. Ferber and J. W. Loeb, 106–27. Urbana: University of Illinois Press.

Miner, L. E., J. T. Miner, and J. Griffith. 2003. Best—and worst—practices in research administration. *Research Management Review* 13(1): 11–20.

Modern Language Association (MLA). 2006. *Report of the MLA Task Force on Evaluating Scholarship for Tenure and Promotion.* MLA Task Force on Evaluating Scholarship for Tenure and Promotion. Downloaded January 6, 2010, from www.mla.org/pdf/task_force_tenure_promo.pdf.

Moody, J. 2004. "Supporting Women and Minority Faculty." *Academe* 90(1): 47–52.

Murray, M. 2001. Beyond the myths and magic of mentoring: How to facilitate an effective mentoring process. San Francisco, CA: Jossey-Bass.

National Academies Press (NAP). 2004. *Facilitating interdisciplinary research.* Washington, CD: The National Academies Press. Downloaded November 2, 2010, from books.nap.edu/openbook.php?record_id=11153&page=R1.

National Academy of Sciences. 2007. *Beyond bias and barriers: Fulfilling the potential of women in academic science and engineering.* Washington: The National Academies Press.

National Science Foundation, Division of Science Resources Statistics. 2009. *Doctorate Recipients from U.S. Universities: Summary Report 2007–08.* Special Report NSF 10-309. Arlington, VA. Available at www.nsf.gov/statistics/nsf10309/.

Nieman, L. Z., G. D. Donoghue, L. L. Ross, and P. S. Morahan. 1997. Implementing a comprehensive approach to managing faculty roles, rewards, and development in an era of change. *Academic Medicine* 72(6): 496–504.

North Carolina State University *Guidelines on Tenure and Teaching at The University of North Carolina.* Downloaded December 8, 2009, from www.northcarolina.edu/pol icy/index.php.

The Ohio State University *OAA Policies and Procedures Handbook.* Downloaded December 10, 2009, from oaa.osu.edu/OAAP_PHandbook.php.

The Ohio State University Office of Human Resources. July 2005. *Parental Care Guidebook.* Downloaded February 2, 2010, from hr.osu.edu/hrpubs/Parentalcareguide book.pdf.

O'Laughlin, E. M., and L. G. Bischoff. 2005. Balancing parenthood and academia: Work/family stress as influenced by gender and tenure status. *Journal of Family Issues* 26(1): 79–106.

O'Meara, K., A. L. Terosky, and A. Neumann. 2008. *Faculty careers and work lives: A professional growth perspective.* San Francisco: Jossey-Bass.

O'Toole, J. 1978. Tenure: A conscientious objection. *Change* 10(6): 24–31.

Park Jr., D. 1972. A loyal AAUP member says "down with tenure!" *Change* 4(2): 32–37.

Patton, M. Q. 2002. *Qualitative research & evaluation methods.* Thousand Oaks, CA: Sage Publications.

Perley, J. E. 1998. Reflections on tenure. *Sociological Perspective.* 41(4): 723–28.

Perna, L. W. 2001. The relationship between family responsibilities and employment status. *Journal of Higher Education* 72(5): 584–611.

Pfirman, S. L., J. P. Collins, S. Lowes, and A. F. Michaels. 2005a. Collaborative efforts: Promoting interdisciplinary scholars. *Chronicle of Higher Education* 51(23): B15–16.

———. 2005b. To thrive and prosper: Hiring, supporting, and tenuring interdisciplinary scholars. *What Works: A Resource.* Project Kaleidoscope. Downloaded November 2, 2010, from www.pkal.org/documents/Pfirman_et-al_To-thrive-and-prosper .pdf.

Philipsen, M. I. 2008. *Challenges of the faculty career for women: Success & sacrifice.* San Francisco: Jossey-Bass.

Piercy, F., V. Giddings, and K. Allen. 2005. Improving campus climate to support faculty diversity and retention: A pilot program for new faculty. *Innovative Higher Education* 30(1), 53–66.

Pololi, L. H., S. M. Knight, K. Dennis, and R. M. Frankel. 2002. Helping medical school faculty realize their dreams: An innovative, collaborative mentoring program. *Academic Medicine* 77(5): 377–84.

Porter, R. 2004. Off the launching pad: Stimulating proposal development by junior faculty. *Journal of Research Administration* 35(1): 6–11.

Preston, A. 1994. Why have all the women gone? A study of the exit of women from the science and engineering professions. *American Economic Review* 84(5): 1446–62.

Price, J., and S. R. Cotten. 2006. Teaching, research, and service: Expectations of assistant professors. *American Sociologist* 37(1): 5–21.

Quinlan, K. M., and G. S. Akerlind. 2000. Factors affecting departmental peer collaboration for faculty development: Two cases in context. *Higher Education* 40(1): 23–52.

Quinn, K., and C. Trower. 2009. *Tips for recruiting and retaining faculty: What different generations want.* Orlando, FL: 26th Annual Academic Chairpersons Conference Proceedings.

Raabe, P. H. 1997. Work-family policies for faculty: How "career-and-family-friendly" is academe? In *Academic couples: Problems and promises,* edited by M. A. Ferber and J. W. Loeb, 208–25. Urbana: University of Illinois Press.

Ragins, B., and K. Kram. 2007. *The Handbook of mentoring: Theory, research, and practice.* Thousand Oaks, CA: Sage Publications, Inc.

Rai, K. B., and J. W. Critzer. 2000. *Affirmative action and the university: Race, ethnicity, and gender in higher education employment.* Lincoln: University of Nebraska Press.

Ramsey, P. G., and E. D. Miller. 2009. A single mission for academic medicine: Improving health. *JAMA* 301(14): 1475–76.

Riemenschnieder, A., and K.V. Harper. 1990. Women in academia: Guilty or not guilty? Conflict between caregiving and employment. *Initiatives* 53(2): 27–35.

Riley, N. S. 2010. How to succeed in teaching without lifetime tenure. *The Wall Street Journal.* November 20, 2010. Downloaded November 22, 2010, from online.wsj.com /article/SB10001424052748703440004575548320163094444.html.

Rosenthal, J., M. Cogan, R. Marshall, J. Meiland, P. Wion, and I. Molotsky. 1994. The work of faculty: Expectations, priorities, and rewards. *Academe* 80: 35–48.

Rosser, V. J. 2004. Faculty members' intentions to leave: A national study on their worklife and satisfaction. *Research in Higher Education* 45(3): 285–309.

Sands, R. G., L. A. Parson, and J. Duane. 1991. Faculty mentoring faculty at a public university. *Journal of Higher Education* 62: 174–93.

Santucci, A., J. Lingler, K. Schmidt, B. Nolan, D. Thatcher, and D. Polk. 2008. Peer-mentored research development meeting: A model for successful peer mentoring among junior level researchers. *Academic Psychiatry* 32(6): 493–97.

Sax, L. J., L. S. Hagedorn, A. Marisol, and F. A. Dicrisi III. 2002. Faculty research productivity: Exploring the role of gender and family-related factors. *Research in Higher Education* 43(4), 423–46.

Schein, E. H. 1990. Organizational culture. *American Psychologist* 45(2): 109–19. doi:10.1037/0003-066X.45.2.109.

———. 1992. *Organizational culture and leadership,* 2nd ed. San Francisco: Jossey-Bass.

———. 1993. How can organizations learn faster? The challenge of entering the green room. *Sloan Management Review* 34(2): 85–92.

Schrodt, P., C. S. Cawyer, and R. Sanders. 2003. An examination of academic mentoring behaviors and new faculty members' satisfaction with socialization and tenure and promotion processes. *Communication Education* 52(1): 17–29.

Schuster, J. H., and M. J. Finkelstein. 2006. *The American faculty: The restructuring of academic work and careers.* Baltimore: Johns Hopkins University Press.

Selby, C. C. 1999. ed. *Women in science and engineering: Choices for success.* Annals of the New York Academy of Sciences 869. New York: New York Academy of Science.

Shoben, E. W. 1997. From anti-nepotism rules to programs for partners: Legal issues. In *Academic couples: Problems and promises,* edited by M. A. Ferber and J. W. Loeb, 226–47. Urbana: University of Illinois Press.

Siegel, D. E., D. A. Waldman, L. E. Atwater, and A. N. Link. 2003. Commercial knowledge transfers from universities to firms: Improving the effectiveness of university-industry collaboration. *Journal of High Technology Management Research* 14(1): 111–33.

Smith, J. W., W. J. Smith, and S. E. Markham. 2000. Diversity issues in mentoring academic faculty. *Journal of Career Development* 26(4): 251–62.

Smith, W. A., P. G. Altbach, and K. Lomotey (eds.). 2002. *The racial crisis in American higher education.* Albany: SUNY Press.

Snyder, T. D., S. A. Dillow, C. M. Hoffman. 2009. *Digest of Education Statistics 2008* (NCES 2009-020). National Center for Education Statistics, Institute of Education Sciences, U.S. Department of Education. Washington, DC.

Somers, P., J. Cofer, J. L. Austin, D. Inman, T. Martin, S. Rook, T. Stokes, and L. Wilkinson. 1998. Faculty and staff: The weather radar of campus climate. *New Directions for Institutional Research* 98: 35.

Sonnert, G., and G. Holton. 1995. *Gender differences in science careers: The project access study.* New Brunswick, NJ: Rutgers University Press.

———. 1996. Career patterns of women and men in the sciences. *American Scientist* 84:63–71.

Sorcinelli, M. D., and D. A. Billings. 1993. *Career development of pre-tenure faculty: An institutional study.* University of Massachusetts, Amherst. Paper presented at the annual meeting of AERA, April 12–16, Atlanta, Georgia.

Sorcinelli, M. D., and J. Yun. 2007. From mentor to mentoring networks: Mentoring in the new academy. *Change* 39(6) (Nov.): 58–61.

Stack, S. 2004. Gender, children and research productivity. *Research in Higher Education* 45(8): 891–920.

Stanley, C., and Y. Lincoln. 2005. Cross-race faculty mentoring. *Change: The Magazine of Higher Learning* 37(2): 44–50.

Strauss, W., and N. Howe. 1997. *The fourth turning.* New York: Broadway Books.

Sweet, S., and P. Moen. 2004. Intimate academics: Coworking couples in two universities. *Innovative Higher Education* 28:252–74.

Tack, M. W., and C. L. Patitu. 1992. *Faculty job satisfaction: Women and minorities in peril.* ASHE-ERIC higher education report no. 4. Washington, DC: The George Washington University.

Thom, M. 2001. *Balancing the equation: Where are the girls in science, engineering and technology?* National Conference for Research on Women, New York.

Thornton, A., and L. Young-DeMarco. 2001. Four decades of trends in attitudes toward family issues in the United States: The 1960s through the 1990s. *Journal of Marriage and Family* 63(4): 1009–37.

Tierney, W. G. 1997. Organizational socialization in higher education. *Journal of Higher Education (Columbus, Ohio)* 68:1–16.

Tierney, W. G., and E. M. Bensimon. 1996. *Promotion and tenure: Community and socialization in academe.* Albany: SUNY Press.

Tierney, W. G., and R. A. Rhoads. 1993. Faculty socialization as cultural process: A mirror of institutional commitment. *ASHE-ERIC Higher Education Reports* (6): 1–96.

Toews, M. and A. Yazedjian. 2007. The three-ring circus of academia: How to become the ringmaster. *Innovative Higher Education* 32(2):113–22. doi:10.1007/s10755-007-9046-8.

Trower, C. A. 2000. Your faculty, reluctantly. *Trusteeship* 8(4): 8–12. Washington, DC: Association of Governing Boards.

———. 2001a. Negotiating the non-tenure track. Career Network Spotlight, online *Chronicle of Higher Education*, July 6. Retrieved December 29, 2009, from chronicle .com/article/Negotiating-the-Non-Tenure-/45495.

———. 2001b. Women without tenure, part 1. *Next Wave*, online *Science Magazine* www .nextwave.sciencemag.org/cgi/content/full/2001/09/12/3. Retrieved December 29, 2009, from sciencecareers.sciencemag.org/career_magazine/previous_issues/articles /2001_09_14/noDOI.10565480637185635938.

———. 2002a. Can colleges competitively recruit faculty without the prospect of tenure? In *The Questions of Tenure,* edited by R. P. Chait. Cambridge, MA: Harvard University Press.

———. 2002b. Women without tenure, part 2: The gender sieve. *Next Wave*, online *Science Magazine* www.nextwave.sciencemag.org/cgi/content/full/2002/01/24/7. Retrieved December 29, 2009, from sciencecareers.sciencemag.org/career_magazine /previous_issues/articles/2002_01_25/noDOI.7900867231599505905.

———. 2002c. Women without tenure, part 3: Why they leave. *Next Wave*, online *Science Magazine* www.nextwave.sciencemag.org/cgi/content/full/2002/03/18/3. Retrieved December 29, 2009, from sciencecareers.sciencemag.org/career_magazine /previous_issues/articles/2002_03_22/noDOI.8430223210060551899.

———. 2002d. Women without tenure, part 4: Why it matters; what to do. *Next Wave*, online *Science Magazine* www.nextwave.sciencemag.org/cgi/content/full/2002/04 /11/2. Retrieved December 29, 2009, from sciencecareers.sciencemag.org/career _magazine/previous_issues/articles/2002_04_12/noDOI.11088636106803699971.

———. 2003. Leveling the field. *The Academic Workplace* 14(2). Boston: New England Resource Center for Higher Education.

———. 2005. Gen x meets theory x: What new scholars want. *The Department Chair* 16(2). Bolton, MA: Anker Publishing Company, Inc.

———. 2006. Socrates, Thoreau, and the status quo. In *The New Balancing Act in the Business of Higher Education* (TIAA-CREF Institute Series on Higher Education), edited by R. L. Clark and M.B. d'Ambrosio. Northampton, MA: Elgar Publishing.

———. 2008a. Amending higher education's constitution. *Academe* 95(5): 16–18.

———. 2008b. What's a dean to do? *COACHE Update* 2(1): 4–5. Cambridge, MA: COACHE.

———. 2009. Towards a greater understanding of the tenure track for minorities. *Change* 41(5): 38–46.

Trower, C. A., A. E. Austin, and M. D. Sorcinelli. 2001, May. Paradise lost: How the academy converts enthusiastic recruits into early-career doubters. *AAHE Bulletin* 53(9). Washington, DC.

Trower, C. A., and R. Chait. 2002. Faculty diversity: Too little for too long. *Harvard Magazine* 104(4): 33–37, 98.

Trower, C. A., and A. S. Gallagher. 2008a. A call for clarity. *Chronicle of Higher Education* 55(4): A37 and A40.

———. 2008b. *Perspectives on what pre-tenure faculty want and what six research universities provide.* Cambridge, MA: COACHE.

———. 2008c. Why collegiality matters. *Chronicle of Higher Education* 55(11): A50–51.

Trower, C. A., and J. P. Honan. 2002. How might data be used? In *The Questions of Tenure,* edited by R. P. Chait. Cambridge, MA: Harvard University Press.

Trower, C. A., and K. Quinn. 2009. Generation matters: What chairs need to know about gen x and boomer pre-tenure faculty. *The Department Chair* 20(1): 10–12.

Turner, C. S. V. 2002. Women of color in academe: Living with multiple marginality. *Journal of Higher Education* 73(1): 74–93.

Turner, C. S. V., and S. L. Myers Jr. 2000. *Faculty of color in academe: Bittersweet success.* Needham Heights, MA: Allyn and Bacon.

University of Iowa *Operations Manual.* Downloaded December 14, 2009, from www .uiowa.edu/~our/opmanual/iii/10.htm#102, and *Faculty Handbook.* Downloaded December 14, 2009, from provost.uiowa.edu/faculty/fachandbk/policies/ptproce dures.pdf.

University of Kansas *Faculty Senate Rules and Regulations* downloaded December 21, 2009, from documents.ku.edu/policies/governance/FSRR.htm#ArticleVI.

University of North Carolina at Pembroke *Faculty Handbook.* Downloaded December 22, 2009, from www.uncp.edu/aa/handbook/97-98/4a-4a10.htm.

Valian, V. 2000. *Why so slow? The advancement of women.* Cambridge, MA: The MIT Press.

Van Alstyne, W. W. 1978. Tenure: A conscientious objective. *Change* 10(9): 44–47.

Van Maanen, J. 1984. Doing new things in old ways: The chains of socialization. In *College and university organization: Insights from the behavioral sciences,* edited by J. L. Bess, 211–247). New York: New York University Press.

Van Maanen, J., and E. H. Schein. 1979. *Toward a theory of organizational socialization.* Retrieved July 8, 2010, from dspace.mit.edu/bitstream/handle/1721.1/1934/SWP 0960-03581864.pdf?sequence=1.

Wasburn, M. 2007. Mentoring women faculty: an instrumental case study of strategic collaboration. *Mentoring & Tutoring: Partnership in Learning* 15(1): 57–72.

Weick, K. E. 1976. Educational organizations as loosely coupled systems. *Administrative Science Quarterly* 21:1–19.

Wergin, J. F. (ed.). 2007. *Leadership in place: How academic professionals can find their leadership voice.* Bolton, MA: Anker Publishing Company, Inc.

West, M.S. 1995. Women faculty: Frozen in time. *Academe* 81(4): 26–29.

Wilan, K. 2007. From bench to business and back again. *Cell* 131:211–13.

Williams, J. 2000. *Unbending gender: Why family and work conflict and what to do about it.* Oxford: Oxford University Press.

———. 2003. The subtle side of discrimination. *Chronicle of Higher Education* 49(32): C5.

Williams, J., T. Alon, and S. Bornstein. 2006. Beyond the "chilly climate": Eliminating bias against women and fathers in academe. *Thought & Action* 22:79–96.

Williams, J., and D. L. Norton. 2008. Building academic excellence through gender equity. *American Academic* 4(1): 185–208.

Wilson, P., D. Valentine, and P. Angela. 2002. Perceptions of new social work faculty about mentoring experiences. *Journal of Social Work Education* 38(2): 317–33.

Winkler, J. 2000. Faculty reappointment, tenure and promotion: Barriers for women. *Professional Geographer* 54(4): 737–50.

Wolf-Wendel, L., S. B. Twombly, and S. Rice. 2003. *The two-body problem: Dual career couples in higher education.* Baltimore: Johns Hopkins University Press.

Wolfinger, N. H, M. A. Mason, and M. Goulden. 2008. Problems in the pipeline: Gender, marriage, and fertility in the ivory tower. *Journal of Higher Education* 79(4): 388–405.

———. 2009. Stay in the game: Gender, family formation and alternative trajectories in the academic life course. *Social Forces* 87(3): 1591–1621.

Wong, G. 2005. Consider post-doctoral training in industry. *Nature Biotechnology* 23: 151–52.

Wright, M. 2005. Always at odds?: Congruence in faculty beliefs about teaching at a research university. *Journal of Higher Education (Columbus, Ohio)* 76(3): 331–53.

Wulff, D. H., A. E. Austin, J. D. Nyquist, and J. Sprague. 2004. The development of graduate students as teaching scholars: A four-year longitudinal study. In *Paths to the Professoriate: Strategies for Enriching the Preparation of Future Faculty,* edited by D. H. Wulff and A. E. Austin and Associates, 46–73. San Francisco: Jossey Bass.

Yoest, C., and S. E. Rhoads. 2004. "What if . . . parenthood wasn't a professional peril on the tenure track? Must academics parent and perish?" Paper presented at the Annual Meeting of the American Association of Public Policy Analysis and Management, November 7–9, 2002, Dallas, TX.

Zellers, D., V. Howard, and M. Barcic. 2008. Faculty mentoring programs: Reenvisioning rather than reinventing the wheel. *Review of Educational Research* 78(3): 552–88.

Zuckerman, H. 2001. The careers of men and women scientists: Gender differences in career attainments. In *Women, science, and technology: A reader in feminist studies,* edited by M. M. Wyer, D. Barbercheck, H. O. Ozturk, and M. Wayne. New York: Routledge.

Index

Italic page numbers refer to tables.